'G' MEN

JAMES CAGNEY
DVORAK
LINDSAY
ARMSTRONG
Ann Keighley
NATIONAL PICTURE

CAGNEY · SHE

STORY WITH ALL THE
FIRE AND FURY OF ITS
TWO GREAT STARS!

WHAT'S CAGNEY GOT THAT DAILEY WANTS?

Charmaine !!!

File

JAMES CAGNEY
CORINNE CALVET
DAN DAILEY

As rousing as bustin' up a wine
cellar in Gay Paree...as rollicking as
the songs they sang about the French
mam'selle...as immortal as Capt. Flagg
and Sgt. Quirt...who fought their way
from the coast of France to the toast
of France—Charmaine!

CITY FOR
CONQUEST

CRAVEN
CRISP
Jerome Cowan

FRANK McHUGH
ARTHUR KENNEDY
An Anatole Litvak Production

Presented by
WARNER BROS.

The New
WHAT PRICE
COLOUR BY Technicolor

with WILLIAM DEMAREST · CRAIG HILL · ROBERT WAGNER · MARISA PAVA

Produced by SOL C. SIEGEL   Directed by JOHN FORD   Screen Play

Presented by
WARNER BROS.

JAMES CAGNEY · BETTE DAVIS

"THE BRIDE CAME C.O.D."

DANDY

GEORGE M. COHAN

James Cagney

JAMES CAGNEY

a celebration by Richard Schickel

Little, Brown and Company
Boston   Toronto

For My Mother,
who, long ago, insisted on taking
me to see Yankee Doodle Dandy

Library of Congress Catalog Card no. 85–81004

First American Edition

Picture research by The Kobal Collection

Published simultaneously in Canada
by Little, Brown & Company (Canada) Limited

Printed in Great Britain

CONTENTS

ACKNOWLEDGEMENTS

The following illustrations appear by the kind
permission of: Museum of Modern Art/Film stills:
10, 21, 34, 50 (B), 64/5, 66, 81 (T), 88, 95 (Tr),
120 (Tl); Winconsin Center for Film & Theatre
Research: 15 (Tl), 29 (Bl), 30, 36, 89 (Tl, Tc, Tr), 100,
158; UPI/Bettmann: 24, 57, 81 (L), 94 (Tl), 112,
162 (C), 164 (L), 169, 172/3; Culver Pictures Inc.:
35 (Tl), 42, 81 (Br), 95 (Cl), 97 (T), 114, 118 (L),
137 (T); National Film Archive (London): 46 (B), 47,
154 (B); The Bettmann Archive: 132/3; CBS: 178.

The publishers acknowledge with thanks the
cooperation of the following:
Warner Brothers, Vitaphone, Cosmopolitan
Productions, First National, Grand National, United
Artists, 20th Century Fox, Paramount, M.G.M.,
Universal, C.B.S.

INTRODUCTION

IT SEEMS NECESSARY TO STATE THAT THIS BOOK, though it inevitably contains some biographical information, is not in any sense a biography. It is rather an essay that intends to analyze a screen character. Therefore, if it must be formally characterized I would prefer that it be thought of as criticism of a sort, an attempt to discern certain persistent themes in the way its subject presented himself, and found himself being presented, in over sixty movies made over the course of a half century in public life. I have come to believe that the images a handful of great and greatly beloved stars have presented over their long careers are in themselves works of art that far transcend in importance any of the individual movies in which they have appeared, and that the proper study of these images probably tells us as much about us, and about our changing interests and values, as individuals and as a society, as it does about the stars themselves. I have also come to believe, as a matter of principle, that the desire to penetrate their private lives, to discover what they are 'really like', is both feckless and socially undesirable. If we spent half the time we do trying to get behind the screen and devoted it instead to a thoughtful, nuanced contemplation of what is right there before our eyes on the screen, we would be the richer for it – and perhaps the better for it. At any rate that is what I have tried to do in this book – show the curve of a career against the social and historical context in which it played itself out and which, obviously, influenced its course.

Since I was fortunate enough to have conducted a lengthy interview with James Cagney, and to have spent some more, less formal, time with him, I have preferred to rely on the text of that interview wherever possible in preparing this text. I know that he has said many of the things he said to me to other interviewers, but the sound of his voice, its rhythms and inflections, still rings in my ears and I hope that by quoting him precisely as I heard him I can help the reader to catch its singular tone. And I hope my observations of him will grant the reader some insights into the man as I met him, at the age of eighty-one, and that these will illuminate some aspects of his art without violating his privacy.

R.S.

FRESH MUTT

ONE DAY IN 1929 JAMES CAGNEY, THEN THIRTY years old, up out of vaudeville and beginning to make a modest mark for himself in musical and straight plays, both on and off Broadway, found himself with twenty or thirty other players of roughly his age and station in life in the outer office of a Broadway producer awaiting a chance to audition for a role in a new play. It was called *Maggie the Magnificent*, and it was by George Kelly, who was also going to direct. Glancing through the open door, Kelly's shrewd eye fell upon Cagney. '"Send that boy in," he said to an assistant. And I went in and I got the job. It was easy.'

Recounting the tale over a half century later, James Cagney laughs and adds, 'He said I looked like a fresh mutt. I said, "Is that the reason?" He said, "Yes, everything that you are is in your face." I didn't know what he was talking about, but it didn't matter to me. It was a job.'

'It was a job.' The phrase is almost liturgical with him. It occurs and recurs in every interview with him, the principal bulwark in the defense of his creative privacy. Or perhaps he fancies it as the best explanation he can offer of that which is to anyone inexplicable, his or her own gift. Or perhaps, now that he is over eighty, he is just tired of the whole subject, this essentially modest man, and wishes to turn it aside as politely as he can.

Still, in the anecdote there appears to be an opening. And the canny interviewer attempts to squirm through it. 'Do you know now what he was talking about?'

Pause. Reflection. 'Yeah. I guess I do. Yeah . . . fresh mutt.' He laughs. 'Sure.'

Sure. In the beginning, before he developed his screen character, before he permitted people to know him – or it – a little better, that explanation would have done. But later . . .? When a certain vulnerability, even an air of victimization, was allowed to show? And still later, when he took his character into realms of psychopathy where no major screen star dared to linger as long as he did? No, it won't do. Though, of course, in recent years everyone has stopped thinking about him critically at all, permitting him to make the transition from mere celebrity status (where, as the celebrated phrase goes, one is known for one's well-knowness) to the status of legend (where, naturally, one is known for one's legendariness). This is an impermeable state, impenetrable by conventional journalistic means, because neither the journalists nor their audience are interested in returning him to the land of the living. It is so much easier, so much more comfortable, to love, honor, obey and, above all, cherish the image, the impossible (or anyway improbable) image.

But yet . . . Here he is. And here I am. And if decent impulse, common politeness, wishes to leave the man to his silences, the mystery of what he created, the force with which it worked on, continues to work on, our collective consciousness, abides. And tantalizes. May as well go ahead and ask the questions, create some kind of objective text to supplement the subjective one, that compound of imperfectly remembered movies and publicity that has accreted around him these many years.

It is November 1980. James Cagney and I are seated at a table in the center of the largest stage at the Shepperton Studios outside London. Workmen are putting the finishing touches on the set for what will be the most lavish interior sequence of *Ragtime*, the film adaptation of E. L. Doctorow's novel. The set is a reconstruction of the rooftop restaurant of the first Madison Square Garden in New York. In it, in a few days, director Milos Forman will stage a re-enactment of the first (but by no means last) 'crime of the century', the shooting there, in 1904, of Stanford White, famous architect and notorious sexual decadent, by Harry K. Thaw, the millionaire madman who conceived that White had 'ruined' his wife, the showgirl Evelyn Nesbitt.

For the moment my documentary crew and I are borrowing light and atmosphere as well as the star of the picture to conduct the inter-

view that will form the basis of a television film about Cagney that will be broadcast in the United States a year later, coincident with *Ragtime*'s theatrical release. It has been two decades since Cagney appeared in a film, and Forman's success in luring him out of retirement has been a publicity coup for his project, though the actor seems at most distantly bemused to find himself at the center of attention again. But his doctor had advised him that it would be good for his health to busy himself again professionally. Forman was a trusted friend (the director lives near the actor's Dutchess County farm, a little more than an hour out of New York City) and the part, though showy, was not large – it was something he could comfortably handle.

Equally important, aside from one brief, silent cutaway to him in a distant window, all of his work could be accomplished in England, within the security of the Shepperton lot or on a couple of easily policed locations around London. There would be no problems controlling crowds or press access. This was no small matter. Cagney looked well, but in fact he was physically very frail, so unsteady on his feet that Forman had to use a double in the few shots where Cagney's character, Police Commissioner Rhinelander Waldo (a man who was

supposed to be about twenty years younger than Cagney), had to walk a few steps.

There was something fragile about him psychologically as well. He appeared nowhere without a woman named Marge Zimmermann at his side. Also neighbors of Cagney's, she and her husband had obliged him by helping him and his wife out with various chores and errands, and as the years passed and his health weakened, Marge became a full-time aide. She was then a large, blunt, ferociously loyal woman in her late fifties, notable for a particularly short fuse on her temper, yet in her way quite likable. She and Cagney had a rather nice, humorously bantering relationship. Still, one could not help but notice that in their partnership she seemed to make all the decisions, both large and small, and that he was clearly the passive partner, constantly deferring to her. Considering the image we have all carried away from his movies, the force and energy of his public personality, this relationship, and his manner in it, excited a certain amount of speculation that would later spill over into the press in a highly unpleasant fashion.

Be that as it may, I felt Marge's influence was benign and essential, assuming (as I do) that the decision to return to the screen was not imposed on Cagney. The *Ragtime* cast and crew were ever solicitous, ever respectful (whenever he appeared on the set he was greeted with applause). But of course Forman, directing a complex and expensive production, could not guard and guide Cagney full-time, and the rest of his people had their own professional imperatives as well. In this situation he required someone like Marge, whose only interest was his interest.

This was particularly true when Cagney ventured away from studio or hotel. Crowds of unruly autograph seekers and *paparazzi* stalked him whenever he made an announced appearance in public. Beyond that, even the more respectable press was clamoring for time with him and those requests required constant sorting, constant diplomacy, balancing the

11

star's need for privacy against the production's desire for publicity. Finally there was a need to occupy Cagney's time pleasantly, since his scenes were scheduled intermittently over several weeks and the periods between them hung heavily upon him – a stranger virtually immobilized in a strange land.

It is perhaps fair to say that I and my television crew were given access to Cagney because, in some measure, we were perceived to be part of the solution to the problems both of guarding his privacy and giving him something safely entertaining to do with some of his free time. We could conduct our business in Shepperton's safe confines and it could be put about that he had granted exclusive right to a television interview to us and that could be used to limit access to him.

He was not, and never had been, an easy man to interview. Colleagues who had encountered him the last time he had made himself generally available to the press, when he was presented with the American Film Institute's Life Achievement Award in 1974, had told me that though Cagney was polite, pleasant and obviously trying to be as helpful as he could, his memory was strangely selective. And so it proved to be. He was capable of great warmth of feeling and much anecdotal detail about his early life, which he recounted in a wry and very winning style. Of his mother, of his three brothers and his sister (two other children died in infancy) and of the loving, decent life they shared as they strove to stay above the poverty line in turn-of-the-century Manhattan, of the children's struggle for the educations they had been firmly taught would provide them with a route out of the ghetto, he drew a vivid portrait, although his father, a bartender with a taste for the product he retailed, remained a rather shadowy figure. He was also good about his friends, the boys with whom he grew up on the streets of New York, and about his first forays into show business – about everything, in short, in which he could be cast in a humorous light, as an innocent making foolish

mistakes or tripping over himself in his eagerness for experience and a modest paycheck that would help out at home. It was only when he had to come to grips with his first minor successes in the theater that one began to sense a diminution of Cagney's interest in autobiography. When he arrived at the movies the sense of alienation from his own professional past that he imparted was almost total.

Oh, he could manage something agreeable but unrevealing about his movie friends and colleagues, and he would allow that especially in the early Thirties the hours were long, the work physically demanding and even, on occasion, risky. He would permit himself the mild observation that he and his co-workers, particularly the leading players and the director, frequently had to improve their scripts as they went along, improvising dialogue and business to plug the holes they discovered in them as they attempted to give them some sensible life on film. He seemed particularly pleased with himself that, socially, he had always refused to tread the Hollywood fast track. Once he had established himself it became his habit to leave town immediately after he finished work on a picture in flight to one of his farms.

But of the texture of his life during the three decades he worked in the movies he had almost nothing to say. That he has a perfect right to guard his personal life closely, no one can dispute. But there are purely professional matters one would like to know more about, something that would give a sense of the quality of his working days. What ambitions did he harbor that were frustrated? Which ones did he exert himself heavily to attain? What projects did he care about passionately? Which ones surprised him by turning out better, or worse, than he had imagined? If he didn't want to talk about the directors he came to dislike, could he at least try to recall those he came to trust and admire? What happened on the stage that made him laugh, at least for a moment? What gave him a sleepless night? Or sent him into rage or sulk or rebellion? More than that, since

12

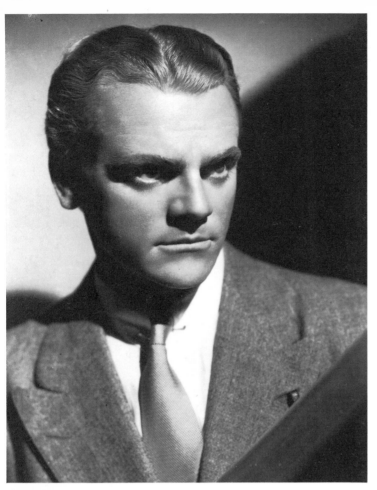

he had another two decades to contemplate in comfortable tranquillity those years of great and greatly beloved stardom, it did not seem unreasonable to seek from him some summarizing sense of what the experience meant to him, looking back on it. Nothing elaborate. Nothing pretentious. But something suggesting some continuing engagement with his own history even if he cannot bring himself to an engagement with the history of the medium with which he was so formatively involved.

But no, that was not to be. When it came to his movies there were only a handful of them he could recall at all, and those were the ones about which he is most often queried, so that he has worked up a little response – *The Public Enemy, Yankee Doodle Dandy*, of course, *White Heat*, and perhaps one or two others. The rest seem to have run together in his mind, and he repeated over and over his litany: 'It was just a job.' I haven't counted how often the phrase occurs in the transcript of our interview, but it must be there well over a dozen times. The impression he created was that he approached his work as any man might, as a means of putting food on his family's table and a roof over their heads. The implication was that there was nothing more singular about his activities than there might be about an insurance salesman's, perhaps, or even of someone still humbler in the social order, a truck driver, maybe, or a factory foreman. There was an implication throughout that acting, even when one is extraordinarily successful at it, certainly cannot and should not be compared to the professions, especially to medicine, which his two older brothers took up and to which Cagney himself at one time briefly aspired.

There are, or there could be, many explanations for this reticence. The most obvious is that, as an octogenarian, the victim of at least one minor stroke and heir to several other ills of the ageing, his memory simply is not all it might be. His insistence that what he was doing all those years was no more memorable or generally interesting than anyone's daily anonymous doings could be seen as a means of covering his embarrassment at being unable to bring to mind the material that most interests his interlocutors. But the clippings reveal he was dim on this material, and indifferent to it, long before illness was visited upon him. And, besides, his ability to recall events more distant and not necessarily more remarkable than his motion picture experiences must have been seems to belie this theory.

His admirable and (so far as one can tell) thoroughly ingrained habit of modesty perhaps offered a better explanation for his puzzled, puzzling silences. His reminiscences of his early family life indicated, if nothing else, that displays of selfishness, of egocentricity, would not have been tolerated. His mother, one thinks, would have belted any such nonsense out of a kid. And the Cagney siblings would have hooted at it. Life was too hard, the economic problems pressing in on them too real, too permanent, to tolerate any such waste of time and energy. And that view of life was surely reinforced by his early years in the lower levels of show biz, where every act, every performer, was instantly replaceable by members of the hungry multitude always in need of work. There has never been anything like the hard, precarious grind of cheap vaudeville to teach a young performer the virtues not merely of hard work, but of teamwork, of not advancing oneself at the expense of one's colleagues. That ethic obviously continued to sustain him in Hollywood, where Cagney was famous for his disciplined professionalism, which by all accounts included a genuine concern for the feelings and the welfare of everyone who worked with him on his sets. (He had a temper, of course, but as we shall see, it was reserved for people who did not fit his definition of working stiffs, that is for the executives and hangers on, people who lacked both the honest craftsmanship and the bred-in-the-bones instincts out of which shows are created, and fixed up.) The fact that he came to the movies during the depths of the Depression, and at the height of class consciousness in America, naturally reinforced this attitude. Cagney was, in those days, of the liberal persuasion politically, and he was active in the organization of the Screen Actors' Guild, serving for a time as its president. No matter what his salary was, or the level of his popularity with the public, no one was going to accuse him of what would nowadays be called star-tripping, throwing the weight of his ego around. That was a point of pride with him.

There was another such point, closely related to the first. It was that he wanted to make his work look easy. This was not just a matter of creating an aura of believable naturalism around his characters, though, of course, that was the effect his work had on audiences. No, this too was a question of privacy, of not wanting the people who worked with him to catch a glimpse of possibly disheartening creative insecurity, of self-doubt. A thing like that could infect an entire set with panic. It was irresponsible. And, anyway, those matters were his own business and no one else's. Even many years after the fact, when an old man could indulge his past follies, and enlist everyone else's indulgence of them, he refused to do so. To hear him tell it he never had any problems with any of his roles, unless, perhaps, it was getting into top physical shape for some of the more athletic ones. 'No strain, no stress' – that phrase, or some close variation on it, was almost as liturgical with him as 'just a job' was.

At one point in our interview, when the talk has turned to one of the several pictures in which he played a boxer, he rather shyly mentioned a compliment paid to his footwork by a professional boxer engaged to do one of the scenes in the ring with him. He dismissed his skill as the natural by-product of his training as a dancer ('It was easy,' he said, of course). And then his mind strayed to a boyhood hero. 'Packy McFarlane. You don't remember him? No [No. But my father used to mention him respectfully.] He was a helluva boxer, and he

was my idol. A real fighter, because he did it all and never even got a black eye. Which was great.' He paused and smiled at the sweet follies of youth. 'But the hero worship that was . . . there.' And he held his hand up, parallel to his forehead, indicating the height of his admiration. To do your work and not get wounded, or even mussed in the process, to betray nothing of what it cost you in hours and pain of preparation, that was once an ideal, surely, and not just among American males, either. It was an almost universal masculine goal in the days before psychology made the agonizing plunge into subjectivity an heroic act, something to trade upon in interviews, on the talk shows.

'I never understood these fellas who have to psych themselves up to get going. You know, very, very laboriously figure things out about the kind of character they are. In the first five minutes you can tell by reading the part what kind of so and so you are . . .' a distant smile flickered across his face, and he added: 'But mine was comparatively easy because I was generally the hoodlum and I understood that type perfectly well. No strain.'

I object. Out of politeness. And out of respect for critical nuance. 'But you did a lot of parts where you weren't a hoodlum.'

'There was a hunk of it in each one. There really was.' A chuckle, an acknowledgement of deviltries past, of irrepressible boyish high spirits, escaped him. 'Oh, sure.'

He was clearly content with that image. It was easy to hide behind, because it was so simple to understand, so entirely plausible. It required no tedious and possibly self-revealing explanations. And, admittedly, it was the first impression he created. We all know, have always known, since our mothers first advised us on the matter, that first impressions are the ones that last, the ones it takes a life-time to undo. So why bother to try? Especially since the public is as content with this one as its author appears to be.

Perhaps he long ago wearied of the struggle

against it. Consider that almost from the beginning, that is from the time his fifth picture, *The Public Enemy*, made him a star, he had been automatically identified in the press as 'tough guy' James Cagney or, perhaps, if there was a little more space, 'movie tough guy'. It was always a misnomer. Nowadays we would perhaps call his character 'street smart', which is a little closer to the truth of the figure as he generally appeared in the first decade of its existence. But that phrase was unavailable in those days, and so the more vulgar description was put forth. And continued to cling to him, despite his advanced years, despite the obvious gentleness of manner he displayed on his occasional public appearances – the tabloid deskman's hasty emblem as he bashes out caption, lead or headline under the pressure of his always onrushing deadline.

All right then: 'hoodlum', 'tough guy'. Implicitly agreed-upon descriptive conventions. But acceptant as Cagney appeared to be about them, acceptant as his public still appears to be with them, they leave at least one observer dissatisfied, edgy. The fit of these phrases is too loose. Norman Mailer was part of the *Ragtime* company, cast as Stanford White and one day, after he had finished a scene, he delivered himself of this thought about Cagney's screen character:

'Cagney was a gut fighter who was as tough as they come, and yet in nearly all the movies he made you always had the feeling, this is a very decent guy. That's one of the sweetest and most sentimental thoughts there is in all the world, that tough guys are very decent. That's what we all want. There's nothing more depressing than finding a guy as tough as nails and as mean as dirt.'

This insight is utterly basic. *The Public Enemy*, vivid as it was, and dirt-mean as Cagney was in two or three of its sequences – most notably, of course, the one involving him with Mae Clark and a grapefruit – was actually an anomaly in his career. In the vast majority of his Thirties movies, the movement was invariably from toughness to tenderness. Cagney was usually discovered in what amounted to a state of nature, urban nature that is: no safety valve corking his temper, his fists leading a life of their own, furiously letting fly at the slightest provocation. Also, he was frequently seen in the early reels as a bundle of mildly anti-social nerves, particularly resistant to submerging his singular self in the spirit of group enterprise even when the cause was good. What turned him around generally was the love of a good – although usually rather bland – woman. His female co-stars were, as a rule, drawn from the more forgettable ranks of the Warner Brothers contract players; it was as if the smarter and more spirited actresses understood that there was no standing up to his energy and chose not to try. Later Pat O'Brien, cast as priest, older brother or senior officer, succeeded to the role of surrogate super ego and that pairing worked better dramatically; Cagney could punch at him, or threaten to, without the loss of gallantry (and sympathy) that those scenes engendered when he shared them with a woman. But no matter. Whatever the situation, the point of the exercise was to civilize Jimmy, to let his best instincts, which the audience no less than his girl friend or Pat always knew were there, get the better of him.

That was in the comedies, of course. In the melodramas of the first decade a similar progress was made, but in these his final deliverance, his discovery of his best self, did not occur until after a capital crime had been committed, or until his carelessness or self-centeredness had caused him to be culpable in an innocent party's death. In either case, Cagney's character had to Pay the Price – offer his life to balance the moral books.

'Now a peculiar thing – you could kill a Cagney or a Bogart and still have a very successful picture. But you could never kill a Gable or a Cooper . . . the audience wouldn't stand for it.' This observation, which Raoul Walsh, who directed four of Cagney's films, once made to me, recurred to me on that stage at Shepperton. I mention it to Cagney, who is mildly interested but noncommittal. One must, perhaps, stipulate the obvious: he was the most instinctive, the least intellectual of actors. He went where his energy carried him, where his kinetic sense of his character took him. And that was, so often, to these spectacular death scenes. Walsh said that people were always asking him why it had taken Cagney so long to die in *The Roaring Twenties*, when Cagney, wounded in a gunfight with Bogart's mob, comes stumbling out of their lair (at top speed, of course), ricochets down a snow-covered street, bouncing off this and that impediment, then staggers up the steps of a church before finally expiring. 'It takes a long time to kill an actor,' Walsh would reply.

Especially this actor. There were, of course, factors other than personality working on his audience's sympathies. In the comedies the implicit understanding was that poverty, a lack of conventional opportunities, educational and otherwise, were responsible for the rough edges that needed to be polished off this diamond. You couldn't blame him for his lack of the social graces. Indeed, an instant identification was made, for most of us lack what he lacked in the way of smoothness and fine airs and could blame our failures on the cruel trick fate played on us by denying us access to a silver spoon for teething purposes. The fun was to see Cagney triumph over this flaw, and to do so without loss of his essential spirit. Something of the same thing, but much darker in tone, was going on in the melodramas.

Take the breakthrough film, *The Public Enemy*, for instance. Most people forget now that it came equipped with a cautionary post-script, explicitly blaming a bungled and corrupt social order for the amorality of Tom Powers (the petty killer, played by Cagney, whose rise to criminal power the film traces). The picture asks, in effect, what a bright nervy boy is to do if legitimate avenues for his energy are foreclosed. Beyond that, Cagney played

Tom as if, perhaps, he had a genetic screw loose – again something he could not be blamed for. In other words, he was a criminal operating under a no-fault insurance policy. His death may or may not have a dimension that takes us into the realms of Greek tragedy, but it certainly has elements of the gloomier aspects of predestination about it. Dwight MacDonald once noted that Cagney played Tom as a 'human wolf, with the heartlessness and grace and innocence of an animal, as incapable of hypocrisy as of feeling'. Animals, of course, are incapable of right reason, and are denied the Kingdom of Heaven on that basis. Closer to home they escape moral opprobrium on the same basis, while gathering to them sentimental sympathy when they are *in extremis*.

What was true of *The Public Enemy* was true of Cagney's other great explorations of doomed gangsterism later in the decade, *Angels With Dirty Faces* and *The Roaring Twenties*. In the former he and Pat O'Brien play childhood chums whose paths radically diverge, the former being twisted toward a life of crime, the latter being guided towards the priesthood. But, as O'Brien explains over a flashback, that was all a matter of chance. Again, poverty was a factor. As boys they were down at the railroad yards, stealing coal, when they were discovered by the police. In the ensuing chase the boy who would grow up to be a priest outruns the cops, and scrambles over a fence to freedom. The soon-to-be criminal is caught and hustled off to reform school. Where, of course, as one of the most persistent clichés of penology would have it, he is schooled not in the way of righteousness but of more sophisticated crime. From there the downward path to the electric chair is clear and straight (though, famously, Cagney is given a last-minute opportunity to find redemption in death). After which O'Brien, who runs a settlement house for wayward slum youths, invites them to the chapel to say a prayer for 'a boy who couldn't run as fast as I could'. Again, the fault is not within Cagney, but within the society that forms him, a society that, for example, tolerates a prison system that hardens rather than softens criminals, a society that hypocritically uses their services when it requires them, then hypocritically destroys them when they become inconvenient, embarrassing. In this picture, as in *The Public Enemy*, we understand Cagney to be a victim, but more than in the earlier picture we come to admire him for the way he stands up to his preordained fate, accepting it without complaint or whimper. He is almost an existential hero, a figure we might find in a novel by Camus, or at any rate in a *policier* influenced by him.

The last of this Thirties crime trilogy, *The Roaring Twenties*, is similar. It is structured in the semi-documentary manner, complete with a voice-over narration stressing the evils of prohibition and presenting the Cagney figure as a kind of Everyman, innocently betrayed by the world he never made. As a veteran returning from heroic service in World War One he cannot find legitimate work that fully utilizes his talents for organizing a business, since as a poor lad he lacks the capital and connections he needs. He turns to bootlegging, a victimless crime. Indeed, it was a crime which, if gracefully enough handled, earned the approval of some of society's most respectable members. Couldn't blame Cagney for any of this. Or for the fact that his career begins to decline when he is distracted by his love for a nice girl who does not return his affections, ends when repeal, something he certainly would not have voted for, puts him out of action for good – shunned by the very people who could not do enough for him when a certain glamour attached to his criminality. Through it all, he is destiny's plaything, a man who accepts the system into which he was born, plays by its rules – as he understands them – and finally, gallantly, accepts its disposition of his case, even, indeed, rushes almost suicidally to meet its judgment.

It is curious how often, even in somewhat lighter films, like *Strawberry Blonde* and *Cap-* *tains of the Clouds*, he touched on this theme of victimization – and how uncomfortable, uprooted, his character sometimes seems when that theme was not present in the script, when, for example (and always excepting his demonic impersonation of George M. Cohan in *Yankee Doodle Dandy*) he had to try to play rather conventional heroes. It could be argued, in fact, that once intellectual fashion changed and it was no longer convenient to shift the blame for anti-social behavior to impersonal and implacable social forces, Cagney's career was in crisis, a crisis that was not resolved until 1949 and *White Heat*, when he discovered psychosis. If a man is visibly and totally daft, and apparently has been so from birth, he could not be held responsible for his behavior, either. As we shall see, from that point onward, most of Cagney's roles were as more or less crazy people. We are not talking temporary insanity here, or curable neurosis. We are talking irredeemable lunacy of the sort that transcends conventional moral judgment, traditional definitions of good and evil. We are also talking art of quite a high order, since somehow, playing a succession of thoroughly unappetizing figures, he retained the affection of his public.

As our interview proceeded, I began to be nagged by the feeling that there was a correlation between the man and the roles he played which, perhaps, no one had been in a position to observe before. His intimates are not critics, after all, and few people with any detailed critical knowledge of the body of his work have ever talked to him at length. What I was sensing was that all the evasions he resorted to when the subject of his movie work was raised, that strange and discomfitting sense he imparted of being totally alienated from what was – how can he deny it? – his life's work, was analogous to the sense his characters so frequently imparted of being the helpless products of social and psychological determinism, creatures whose only option was to accept their fates more or less cheerfully and, perhaps, to go down swinging. Who knows, maybe the

ferocious energy of his youth, the often manic quality he brought to his work, especially when physical action was required of him, was rooted in a sort of panic. Perhaps it represented the desperate desire of his body to deny the gloomy signals it was receiving from his mind.

That, perhaps, is a bridge too far for us to tread. But this much is obvious: all his talk about movie acting being just a job, nothing very exciting or interesting about it, and something he undertook not because he especially wanted to, but because it offered him the best available paycheck, represents a denial of responsibility for his actions that was, in its way, analogous to the denials of responsibility for their actions that was written into his characters. In effect, he was saying that he signed on as a sort of corporate soldier, albeit a highly visible one, then did what he was told to do. Yes, of course, as a responsible professional he tried as best he could to improve upon his assignments but there were limits on that activity. And, yes, of course, there were some lovely, lucky accidents, a handful of pictures that even he has to admit weren't bad. But overall, no, he was not proud of what he had done and was not going to take all the blame for that record.

This position does not jibe with the public record of his movie work, or with the memories of his colleagues or, for that matter, with such unguarded memories as he sometimes lets slip. The portrait of Cagney 'on the job' is of a man ferociously fussing over the work, asserting himself tirelessly to improve his films. And to improve not only his lot but that of everyone connected with making movies. His angry contract disputes with Warner Brothers are legendary and were publicly reported at the time. His political and union activities in the Thirties were immediately directed at improving the lot of his fellow performers – and not just the stars, either. As soon as he was able, and rather in advance of other stars of his stature, he embraced independent production, which means that some of the pictures that pro-

vided him with 'jobs' were, in fact, movies that he instigated, movies that would not have been made if he had not insisted on making them.

It was all very odd, very disconcerting, this radical alienation from his past, therefore from his completely honorable and extraordinarily gifted self. It is the more so, of course, since his own judgment of his accomplishments is so wildly at odds with everyone else's. His fellow actors, for instance, continue to revere him for his attack, for the purity of his instincts, for his uncanny ability to physicalize emotion. The younger ones, in particular, appear awed by his ability to do thoughtlessly, and with heedless abandon, what it requires so many years of exercise and instruction to learn to do – express (or anyway imply) a character's inner life simply and directly, without any visible cerebration. The critics and the film historians are similarly respectful from their perspective. There is a common agreement that he was one of the truly singular presences in the history of the movies, an actor utterly *sui generis*, someone who has spawned no imitative type, who has no heirs. He was also a performer whose historical significance cannot be overestimated, the first definitely and defiantly urban character in the history of a medium that had, before him, preferred heroes of either a more rustic type (if they were Americans) or a more sinuously romantic type (if they were foreign born). Finally, and perhaps most important of all, ordinary moviegoers took him to heart almost instantly, remained astonishingly loyal to 'Jimmy' even though many of his later pictures were distinctly lacking in comfortable appeal. They have, as well, and despite his long retirement, remained loving and loyal through all the long years .

After all this he would have been logically entitled to many poses – great man, sage, egomaniac, even plutocrat. What he was not entitled to was the role he had chosen, which is that of a successful man who talks and acts like a failure. But that, finally, becomes the only way to sum up his private presence. If you didn't know who you were talking to you would think you were in the presence of a man who had suffered some terrible accident early in life, or endured some historical calamity, emerging from it physically intact but emotionally in a permanent state of shock, still connected with the promising and halcyon days before the disaster, but unable to contemplate the central horror and its aftermath.

So he affected me at any rate. In the years that have passed since I talked with him I have often wondered if, in the century of the victim, his hold on us did not derive, finally, from the implication – sometimes subtle, sometimes not so subtle – of victimization that arose from so many of his most memorable characterizations. Surely it was that aspect of his basic creation that balanced its sometimes brutal drive, its roughshod way with jokes and women. Surely it was that aspect of his screen character that permitted him to transcend in his appeal mere 'decency' (which, like mere toughness, is not uncommon in the movies), permitted entry into the deeper reaches of consciousness, establishing on us an imaginative hold that only a very few actors ever achieve. Surely that tragic sense of what destiny must hold for the over-reaching individual arose from something authentic in him, some congeries of genes and experience that in youth, when his preternatural energy ruled him, he could simply overwhelm, but which now, in age, appeared to have overwhelmed him. As we grow older, after all, we abandon our pretences, our self-distractions – and the illusions with which we entertain others. We no longer have the time or the energy for all that. We are reduced to our essences. And the essence of James Cagney, as I encountered him and who moved me in ways that were both powerful and unexpected, was a sadness as deep as it was logically inexplicable.

2 THE SIDEWALKS OF NEW YORK

'WHAT DID YOU BRING OFF THE STREETS OF New York?' I ask Cagney, as if I didn't know the answer. 'Everything,' he laughs. 'That's what it amounts to really.'

It is true. The join between the screen character he created and his personal history is seamless – more so than that of any actor one can readily recall. Especially in the formative years of that character its occupations and preoccupations were those that Cagney knew first hand, either from personal experience or from the experiences of the young men with whom he had grown up: their family lives; their struggles to establish themselves in a world where they lacked social and economic credentials, where their only weapons were energy, wit and a certain rough charm; the struggle against the tempting short-cut involving immorality if not outright legality, a struggle which, in the movies, they sometimes won, sometimes lost. All of this has analogies in his life. Indeed, as we shall see, Cagney would be at pains to insert into his scripts bits of dialogue that he recalled from his youth, into his character bits of behavior that he had observed in those days.

Finally, when he recalled for inquiring reporters, or for his autobiographies, his beginnings, the story of his early years would somehow come to read like the backstory for one of his more heartwarming comedies, something along the lines of *The Irish In Us*, or *The Strawberry Blonde*, something with plenty of raucous ruckus in it, but touched as well by simple sentiments and a certain romantic rue for the hard times that were also good times and are now lost beyond recall. In the mental movie he made of his boyhood, the young Cagney is poor, bright and brash, fast with his fists. And a hard worker. Above all, that – a hard worker.

Had to be. He was born on the lower East Side on July 17, 1899, the third child of James Francis Cagney Sr. who traced his ancestry to the O'Caignes of County Leitrim, and Carolyn Nelson, whose father was a Norwegian sea captain, but whose mother was Irish. The family soon moved to the upper East Side, first to East 79th Street, then to East 96th Street, those broad thoroughfares marking, respectively, the lower and upper boundaries of the section then known as Yorkville, predominently a neighborhood of German immigrants, many of whom were also Jews (Cagney may have passed one of the Marx Brothers in his boyhood streets, or Bert Lahr). Aside from one brief period when the family's fortunes improved and they moved to Long Island, Cagney would stay here until he began touring in shows. At this point, the senior Cagney begins to fade from the chronicle. In his son's accounts, he was a man of gentle and irresponsible charm, perhaps something of a womanizer as well as a drinker, and not a man to let the routines of a job interfere with more pleasurable pursuits. 'Very nice man, very gentle,' is how Cagney described him to me. 'He was always there when the chips were down. But when he drank, he drank. Oh, boy, really a man who knew how. But when he was sober, he was fine.' The impression one receives is of a capacity to disarm and distract covering the profound passivity that not infrequently accompanies alcoholism. One also gets the impression that if the ambitionless father offered his sons a powerful negative model as far as work was concerned, something of his ability to ingratiate even as he infuriated also obviously informed his namesake's character.

Something more was inherited as well, something harder to describe. There was, perhaps, some of the blackness that the father either found at the bottom of the bottle, or hoped to drown there. And, one thinks, the most salient quality of the son's, his ability to be absent though present. Pat O'Brien, who became Cagney's friend long before they began co-starring in movies (they met in 1927, in the theater), always referred to his friend as 'the far-away fella'. By which he meant simply that Cagney spent much of his time, even when he was with people, in a withdrawn state. There was never anything hostile about it, it was just

25

that he was otherwise, and mysteriously, engaged, mentally and emotionally, just as his father used to be so much of the time. The difference between them being, of course, that the younger Cagney required no help from the booze bottle to achieve this dreamy detachment.

His mother's character could not have been more at odds with her husband's. She was a pretty, red-haired woman, whom Cagney would revere for the rest of his life. If she was wilful, and that she surely was, there was nothing dour about her either. The Cagney home resounded with songs and a loudly thumped piano. A family anecdote has her being present on the night the song that later inspired the picture *The Strawberry Blonde* was premièred. Not only was she a strawberry blonde, but her date that night was named Casey, and people would remember them cutting a fine figure on the floor as 'the band played on'. The story may be apocryphal, but Cagney treasured the tale, and recounting it to me, his voice choked up and his eyes misted over. His attitude toward his mother can actually be summarized in songs of a slightly different quality. It can be found in those sentimental bar-room ballads about a mother's love being the only true love a man ever knows. 'M is for the million things you gaaave mee . . .'

Not that Carolyn Nelson Cagney indulged her children. Her affection was expressed in hard terms, because it was a hard world. 'My mother was – quite a character,' Cagney said to me. 'She would call her shots with her right hand – bang. No nonsense. Just get into line, boy.' She adored her wayward husband, and she seemed to forgive him – outwardly at least – all his transgressions. But her tolerance stopped there. She would see to it that her children did not take after their father in any of the ways she disapproved of. That meant that they would be taught the value of hard work and discipline, of immediate gratification denied in favor of larger, long-term rewards. She taught, above all, a special and old-fashioned kind of

ambition, perhaps best summed up in the phrase, 'make something of yourself', which can also be read, 'make anything of yourself' – as long as it is not criminal and as long as it seems to offer the possibility of prosperity and respectability in the long run. In the short run, of course, one learned the necessity for work at an early age, because without the children's contributions the family could not survive.

Carolyn Cagney was not singular in this respect. If, as Cagney was to put it, 'she decided what we'd be up to, the neighborhood decided that, too. Oh, sure. Poverty on all sides, people scrambling to make a living . . .' Naturally. No question about it. 'I almost can't remember a time when I wasn't working,' he wrote in *Cagney by Cagney*. He was doing odd jobs from the time he was allowed out on the streets alone. At fourteen he took his first formal employment, as an office boy at the New York *Sun*, rising at 5.30 a.m. to report for work at the newspaper's office far downtown on Park Row, where he picked up early editions of the paper and proofs of advertisements and began making the rounds of the large retail establishments so their advertising departments could check the placement of that day's ads, the contents of future ads. For this, he received five dollars a week. The load he set forth with every morning weighed almost as much as he did.

Within a year he and his two older brothers, Harry and Eddie, were working at the public library twenty-two and a half hours a week, for $12\frac{1}{2}$ cents an hour, picking up books where the readers had abandoned them on the tables and restoring them to the shelves. At the same time, he was working some nights at a settlement house (these were community centers for immigrants, financed and managed by charities) and weekends as a ticket taker at the Hudson River Day Line, whose boats plied the great river, offering excursionists brief relief from the city's heat and grime. He has also mentioned at various times wrapping packages at Wannemaker's department store, being a bellhop at

the Friar's Club, a theatrical club in those days consisting mainly of vaudevillians, and working as a draughtsman for the water department (he had a natural gift for drawing, and continued to paint avocationally the rest of his life). All the while he continued with his schooling.

It doesn't matter if the sequence of his jobs was muddled in various recollections. The impression he always wished to convey was of a blur of work, and that there is no reason to doubt. Not that Cagney ever sought to elicit sympathy for himself in these memories. Quite the contrary. He once told an interviewer, 'I feel sorry for a kid who has too cushy a time of it.' Hard work taught self-reliance. Better than that, it taught a young man not to be excessively choosy about his jobs. 'It's just a question of grabbing at something, to be something,' is how he put it to me. And suddenly

there was ferocity in his expression, all vagueness suddenly banished. 'That was all of it. You had to grab and hang on tight. That's all. Hope that it worked.'

Elsewhere he once explained how that attitude had abided with him all his working years. 'My philosophy has always been to do anything that comes my way seeking to be done. This willingness astonishes producers. When they ask tentatively, "How about doing so-and-so?" and I say "Why not?" they look at me funny. "What do you prefer to do?" they ask. "I don't prefer to do anything," I tell them. "If a good musical comes along, I'll do a musical. If a good comedy comes along, I'll do a comedy. If a good heavy drama comes my way, I'll do heavy drama." Back where I came from, if there was a buck to be made, you didn't ask questions. You just went ahead and made it.'

So that which would eventually take over his mind entirely was inculcated from the start, before he could conceive any sensible arguments against it. A job would always be, to borrow a phrase, 'just a job'. It would be foolish, an act of selfishness bordering on the egomaniacal, to expect from any employment any satisfactions beyond those contained in the pay packet at the end of the week. It might even be immoral. In the end it came to this: he would work as his mother had taught him to work, without thought of psychic compensation; but he would live as his father had taught him to live, as the far-away fella, in the country, as far as he could get from the job, his mind as far away from it as it could get, too, focused on farming, on sailing, on painting and reading.

The far-away fella. Any comment on that? What does he think Pat meant by the oft-repeated description? 'Well, not one of the crowd, I was always off there somewhere. You know, my wife's complained about that for years.' He laughed – affectionately and rue-fully. 'And I can understand that. But whenever I was alone I was off there somewhere.' He made a vague gesture, suggesting not a place but a state of mind.

27

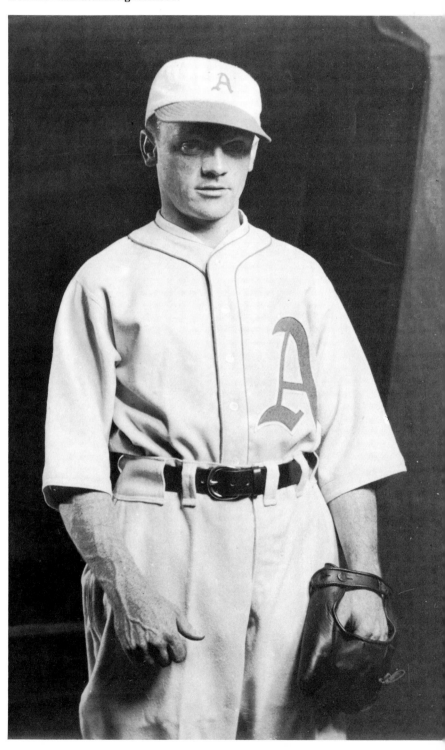

Schematically, all this makes sense. Like most of us, Cagney grew up an imperfect homogenization of his parents' strengths and weaknesses. What bound these elements together for him, for all the young Cagneys, was sheer energy – bounding and irrepressible. 'Such energy you never saw,' said James, describing his older brother, Harry. 'When the feet were on the ground he was unhappy. He used to exercise by hanging by his knees over a basement, and then he'd let go and land on his feet. If he had slipped, he'd have cracked his skull. Didn't bother him, though.' Harry would become an excellent ballplayer and 'champion fancy diver – could turn in the air without any trouble at all'. Eddie, the next in line, would become an all-city soccer player, and James would also play ball semi-professionally. And harbor ambitions as a boxer.

That was natural. The Irish boxers, hammering their way out of the slums, and very often graceful stylists in the ring, were heroes to boys of Cagney's age. And, besides, he had been scrapping in the streets almost from the time he could walk. The early chapters of the auto-biographies contain the records of brawl after brawl. You fought to avenge a beating administered to a friend. You fought because someone challenged you or your turf. You fought because that's what kids did in that place in that time. 'Were you the toughest kid on the block?' 'No, I wasn't what you'd call a tough kid. But the guy who was tough was really, really tough. And I liked him and he liked me, and I broke my hand on him...' That fight was called a draw by mutual consent, and by the time Cagney's hand had healed their friendship was sealed in mutual respect.

Mostly, though, it seemed that 'Red' Cagney won. And there came a time in mid-adolescence when it occurred to him that he might as well be paid for his trouble and his cuts and bruises. There was a small boxing club in the neighborhood, as there were all over New York in those days, and Cagney began frequenting it, getting into shape, learning

28

The mature athlete. Cagney always trained hard for pictures in which he had to box or dance – as these rather obviously posed pictures attempt to prove. They were taken in 1933.

some of the niceties that could not be picked up between blows on the curb exchange. His mother, however, noticed something different about his appearance and challenged him. 'I was getting thinner, and she said, "What are you doing . . . getting up at six o'clock in the morning and – what are you doing?" So then I told her I was training. You got ten bucks a fight at a club nearby. She said, "Going to be a fighter?" I said, "Well, for the time being." She said, "Can you lick me?" I said, "No, Mom, and I'm not trying." And that was the end of the fighting thing.'

But there were plenty of other outlets for his exuberance, baseball in particular. With his fireplug frame, he had the build of a catcher, if not quite the heft to block the plate. But he liked the position, he once said, because it was at the center of the action, therefore at the center of attention, and he was good enough to play with the 'Nut Club', a well-respected team drawn from the Yorkville neighborhood. Even on the diamond he found moral instruction, for one time the team was invited to Sing Sing, to play the prison team, known as the Mutual Welfare club. When the Nut Club came to bat in the first innings, Cagney trotted down to the third base coach's box and received a greeting from the Sing Sing player at the hot corner: 'Hey, Red, go down to the Eastside House anymore?' he asked, referring to a settlement house. The player was a neighborhood acquaintance. And that was not the end of it. 'When we got playing the game the greetings came from all sides.' Cagney would estimate that there were at least a half-dozen neighborhood boys on the prison team or in the stands – plus two more he was told were in the prison hospital that day. He said everyone on the Nut Club team discovered he knew at least one inmate, and he would recall that one of the lads who greeted him that day died in the electric chair one night a decade later when Cagney was running in a show on Broadway. He has said he came away from that prison baseball game 'depressed'.

Did Cagney regard his presence on the Nut Club team instead of their opponents that day as a lucky near-miss? It is hard to think so, given the strength of his mother's values. And yet, superficially there was not that much to distinguish the Cagneys from their neighbors. In background, in economic and social status, in manners, everyone was pretty much alike, and Cagney has never passed any judgment on those who did not escape poverty's cruel determinism. Like Father Jerry in *Angels with Dirty Faces* he knew all about boys who couldn't run as fast as he could.

But it wasn't merely a question of running fast. Cagney ran intelligently. Unlike other youths in his circumstances he never denied the impulses of talent, never said to himself that as a poor kid he dared not aspire. Take a very simple thing, his taste for the countryside, his desire to live there someday. He traced it back to a visit to an aunt when he was perhaps five years old. She lived in Greenfield, Long Island, then a rural retreat. His mother took her boys there for a week or two one summer. It was 'beautifully green, and that's when I first fell in love with the country . . . where I first learned the glory of morning glories. The fence in front of the house was full of morning glories. I remember that well . . . . From that point on I was a country boy.' It was, one gathers, something to work for, to sacrifice for – a positive goad to self-improvement, supplementing all the negative ones he had already begun to absorb.

Not long thereafter he discovered drawing. He had a natural aptitude for it, and he would keep working at it throughout boyhood and adolescence. It was, in fact, what led him to his earliest stages. His mother conceived that if his brother Harry was going to become a doctor – a decision he apparently reached when he was twelve – he ought to learn to express himself in public. So she enrolled him in the drama classes at the Lenox Hill Settlement House, with James tagging along. He discovered an outlet for his skills with pencil and brush by painting the scenery for shows that were constantly being put on by the dramatic society there. And he drew covers for the settlement house magazine as well. As he tells it, those activities were far more interesting to him than the time Harry was taken ill and James had to replace him in some play or other. By this time, he says, the brashness of his earlier years, his love of playing the show off, had been replaced by shyness. Nevertheless, he seems to have done a number of roles there, among them some leads – and a turn as a faun in a woodland fantasy.

It was also at the settlement house that he learned his first dance steps. Or so he would say in his later years. There exists some early publicity that attributes another nick-name to him, 'Cellardoor Cagney', given him for his boyish habit of tap dancing the resonant wood of the doors leading to basements. If so, those first steps were all improvisations. He did not then, or ever, have any formal training. What set him to dancing as a child, if indeed he did, must have been nothing more than a natural aptitude, goaded on by his own restless energy, which no amount of toil or sport could completely discharge. But he is very precise about who taught him his first professional combination. It was a boy named Joe Hevron. And what he taught him was something called the Peabody, an intricate set of moves that, it is said, was first put together by a policeman from Boston (hence its impeccably WASP name).

It would be some time before he put that modest attainment to use. He was graduated from Stuyvesant High School and, still working part-time, went on to Columbia University as a member of the Student Officers Training Corps while the U.S. was engaged in World War One. His hope, besides getting a college degree, was to broaden his skills as an artist, and so he enrolled in the camouflage course offered by the training corps. He was also a member of the college band, a bass drummer. He could not read music, but he did have rhythm. A story frequently told was of a speech course in which the professor, despairing of getting a student to read aloud properly – slowly, in pear-shaped tones – asked Cagney to take the book. To his dismay, he got yet more pace, that speed of delivery that, like his rhythm, would eventually become an internationally recognized trademark.

It was while James was at Columbia that his father, weakened by years of alcoholism, succumbed to influenza during the great postwar epidemic of the disease. With his older brothers already enrolled in college and determined (as Cagney was not) to train for a profession, it was logical for him to drop out and find a full-time job, especially since the last of the children, Jeanne, who would become a dancer and an actress and work frequently in her brother's films, was born shortly after his father died. It would seem that he went back to Wannemaker's store, though in a capacity slightly more elevated than package-wrapper. He had a friend there who was a vaudeville fan, particularly of the dancing acts, and he and Cagney would pass the time talking about them. Inevitably Cagney demonstrated his Peabody for him and it was he who heard of an opening in an act called *Every Sailor*, then appearing at Keith's 81st Street Theater, and urged Cagney to audition for it.

'I was nineteen years old, needed a job. Needed it badly. When they said, "Do you hoof, do you dance?" I said, "Sure. Oh, of course." Couldn't do a thing, couldn't move a leg, not and have it mean anything.' With a pause no longer than there must have been when he responded to that crucial question at his job interview, he added: 'So I got on and did it.' And got the job. As a chorus *girl*, wearing a wig, tights and a tutu. The following Monday he went on with the troupe in Philadelphia. The pay was $35 a week, 'a mountain of money' to him in those days.

The show had been put together by a small-timer named Phil Dunning, who found himself serving as a petty officer during the war, and somehow talked the brass into letting him create a 'morale-building' vaudeville act using shipmates aboard the *George Washington*. Now he was trying to keep the act together. It was, apparently, nothing much, but it was fun for Cagney, possibly more fun than he had ever had while drawing a pay check – 'a knock-about act, pure burlesque'. He frequently said that part of the show business's appeal for him was that once he got into costume, make-up and character, he could set aside his natural shyness. 'I am not myself. I am not that fellow Jim Cagney, at all,' he once told an interviewer, and he was perhaps less Jim Cagney in this first professional appearance than he ever was later.

Still, after four or five weeks he tired of *Every Sailor*. His mother was almost as dubious about show biz as she had been about boxing. And besides he was in constant pain from having to dance in high heels. He would later say that his characteristic walk, knees stiffish, his upper body canted forward, his butt sticking out, developed in part from this experience, which perhaps exaggerated a natural tendency. Still, the attempt to return to more normal employment – he worked in the backshop of a brokerage firm – he found notably unexciting. So in 1920 he auditioned for the chorus of, and was cast in, *Pitter Patter*, then running at the Longacre on Broadway. He stayed with the show, which had received no better than mixed notices, after it ended its thirty-two-week run in New York and went on tour. His pay was $50 a week, but for that he understudied and served as dresser to its star, Ernest Truex. Somewhere along the road he graduated from the chorus into a specialty routine.

It is astonishing – the suddenness of this transition from amateurism to professionalism. It bespeaks a natural gift of a very high order. It also perhaps says something about the level of standards for dancers then pertaining in the musical theater. 'We didn't have schools then,' Cagney would say to me. 'You'd see somebody's stuff and you'd steal it and use it.' Sometimes, of course, knowledge was openly swapped.

But *Pitter Patter* was something more than the instrument of Cagney's emergence into full-fledged professionalism. For in it with him was a young chorus girl named Francis Willard Vernon, known as 'Bill'. She was from Iowa, and she was – and remained – a bright, chirpy woman whose youthful energy must have been more than a match for Cagney's. Moreover, she was a dancer whose skills he greatly admired. 'I learned from her . . . she could do steps that I couldn't do. She was a natural winger.' By this he meant that those steps hoofers refer to as 'wings' and 'half wings' and are, of course, integral to that most familiar of the basic tap routines, the buck and wing, came more easily to her than to him. They were in love by the time *Pitter Patter* closed on the road, but they split up for a while in order to accept work. Bill went into a 'sister act' while Cagney during this time worked in an act called *Dot's My Boy*, in which he played a Jewish kid who gets a job in a show in which he must impersonate an Irishman. It is his stage mother, of course, who utters the tag from which the piece derived its title. The Cagneys married in 1922 and were able to find work together in two of the shows the well-known Lew Fields packaged for the vaudeville circuits, his *Ritz Girls of 1922* and his *Snapshots of 1923*. It would appear that both Cagneys did specialty routines in these shows. Somewhere along the line he and Bill decided to try the West Coast, where he and a male partner tried out a new song and dance act that failed in San Pedro and where he also looked for work in the movie studios, to no avail. They had to borrow money to get back east.

There, as Cagney would later tell it, life was a succession of cheap furnished rooms with one-ring burners to cook on. He often wanted to quit, but Bill believed he could only be happily at work in show business. At one point in this down time, Cagney would always remember, he ran into an old friend from the neighborhood, Artie Kane, on a bus, and invited him home for dinner. Kane saw, it

Family album. Cagney's beloved wife, 'Bill' welcomes him back to New York after finishing *Hard to Handle* in 1933 (below). Opposite, clockwise, they pose informally in an unspecified California setting, show off their dog, 'Reddy' in 1936, don Edwardian costumes for a fancy dress gala in 1933, and share the joys of country living.

would seem, a poverty deeper than they had shared on the East Side, and insisted on giving the Cagneys half his paycheck – his loans came to about $20 a week – for the next several weeks until they could get a job. When Cagney could pay back the debt, Kane refused it. They would remain friends the rest of their lives.

Cagney was, in the show biz phrase of the time, a 'ham-and-egger' who spent more time than he cared to on 'Panic Beach', the corner of 47th and Broadway, where out-of-work vaudevillians hung out exchanging gossip and job tips. He would later write that the difference between him and the others on the beach was that they would only go to calls where their speciality seemed to be in demand, while he would try for anything. But he admired the craftsmanship and dedication of men and women who devoted ten or fifteen years to perfecting their routines. In a way, of course, that was analogous to what movie stars with highly defined screen personalities were starting to do.

He would claim later that he always thought of himself as a vaudevillian, that is, as a perfectionist always trying to please an audience by honing his routine to an ideal state. But he would also remember comedian Will Mahoney in this regard. The end of his act consisted of an 'off to Buffalo' – a dancing exit – which he did 'higher and higher until finally he fell flat on the floor and looked at the audience: "There must be an easier way to make a living." And he was right, there was.' So Cagney kept looking for it. 'If there was a job to be done, we did it, regardless of what it was. When there was a vaudeville act where there was singing and dancing, we sang and we danced. When we did a straight act, no singing, no dancing, we did that, too. It was all a matter of a job.'

One of the engagements he managed to get, in 1924, was as a replacement in a dancing and comedy act known as Parker, Rand and Leach. It was the last named who had decamped, and Cagney took over for him in 'a turn without the semblance of a punch' as *Variety* would put

it. 'Small time is its only chance.' Still, as a footnote in show biz history, the act is not without its interest, for the first name of the departed Leach was Archie, and he would soon enough become better known to the world as Cary Grant. How curious it must have been, later in life, for Parker and Rand to contemplate the vagaries of fame and the might-have-beens of their careers.

Like Leach, Cagney was about to go legit. Maxwell Anderson had adapted sometime-prizefighter-hobo Jim Tully's book, *Beggars of Life*, for the stage (it would later be one of director William A. Wellman's early screen successes) and Cagney was given the second lead, playing 'Little Red' opposite Charles Bickford's 'Oklahoma Red' in the off-Broadway production that Anderson also directed. The play was a hit, in part because Tully had been taken up by the New York literati as an intriguing exotic, and it was moved uptown. On opening night there, Cagney would remember, Anderson came backstage at the end of the first act to tell everyone in the company to talk twice as loud and twice as fast as they had been – 'Everybody, that is, except you,' he said, fixing Cagney with a stern directorial eye.

The show ran for a few months, and then Cagney and Bill went into a vaudeville act called *Lonesome Manor*, for which he did the choreography and in which he played a character who seemed to be a city slicker, selling out of town newspapers on Broadway, trying to impress a girl who turns out to be from the same small town he came from – Kokomo, Indiana. They toured the south with this act, where Cagney claimed they laid an egg, mainly because no one could understand his fast city patter.

After that tour ended, Cagney drifted back in the direction of legit – and a major disappointment. He was up for a play called *Broadway*, which his first producer, Phil Dunning, had co-written with George Abbott. It is about a hoofer who gets involved with criminals, and when the legendary producer William A. Brady had it, it seemed to Cagney that he would be cast in the lead. But then the play was taken over by the equally legendary Jed Harris, and he gave the role to Lee Tracy, who was right for the fast patter dialogue, but did not have a dancer's moves. After the shows opened successfully, however, a London company was planned, and Cagney was offered the lead in it, with Bill getting a role as a dancer. He rehearsed and even gave a performance before

an invited audience of actors one night. But throughout he felt uncomfortable. The director wanted him to imitate Tracy and this was something Cagney could not – or more likely, would not – do. Just before the company sailed he was replaced by Tracy. He had, however, an unbreakable contract, and so was frustratingly employed to understudy Tracy's replacement in the Broadway company – until, at last, he replaced the replacement. The salary was good, $150 a week, but recounting this incident a rare note, something like bitterness, breaks through in his autobiography.

He was, however, on the move. He would never go back to vaudeville. Instead he went into *Women Go On Forever*, a possibly ill-advised attempt by Mary Boland, the delightful scatter-brained comedienne (see *Ruggles of Red Gap*), to do a straight drama. This is the play, directed by John Cromwell, whose Hollywood career would be distinguished and underrated, on the pre-Broadway tour of which Cagney met Pat O'Brien. Cagney would claim that on opening night in New York the audience broke into laughter on Miss Boland's entrance, and that it was never the same play thereafter. It ran for better than four months, but, it would seem, with the actors going for what laughs they could get. Around that time, Cagney and a partner opened a dance studio in New Jersey, and he found himself for the first time feeling overworked, as he raced between jobs. He soon abandoned teaching.

His next Broadway venture was much happier. It was *The Grand Street Follies of 1928*, a topical revue, in which Cagney shared choreographer credit with no less than Michel Fokine and received praise for his own dancing, especially in a tap-tango finale. He went into a second edition of the show, *The Grand Street Follies of 1929*, which the critics decided was a tired imitation of the previous success, though a Cagney turn as a dancing traffic cop was well received. The show closed soon enough for him to be at liberty for *Maggie the Magnificent*, which, though it closed even more

quickly than the second *Follies*, Cagney would later judge to be the best break he had had.

That was because it put him in touch with George Kelly, who was, to put it simply, Cagney's kind of man. G.K., as he was called, was Grace Kelly's uncle, and he was of that breed of thoroughgoing Broadway professionals who, like the lively, fecund and prospering theater they served, has now vanished. He had won a Pulitzer Prize for *Craig's Wife*, a serious drama about a cold, house-proud wife, but was better loved, perhaps, for *The Show-Off*, a comedy about an inveterate prankster and egotist and, latterly, for *The Torchbearers,* about an amateur theatrical company trying to bring a little culture into the life of an American small town. In other words, most of his work was aimed at the deflation of pretense, and Cagney would find that as a director he was of the same mind. He encouraged his actors to be what they were. That, after all, is why he had cast them in the first place – for looks, manners, vocal tones that matched the characters he had imagined at his typewriter – and he saw no reason to interfere with their natural bent.

As it happened, the play was a flop. It ran for only thirty-two performances. But since it was a George Kelly play, reviewers took it more seriously than anything Cagney had ever opened in in New York before. At long last he was widely noted not just as an actor, but as a singular presence, a young man who could handle the 'gashouse lingo' his part called for with an easy naturalism. There can be no doubt that he got his next – and last – Broadway role

Early stages. On the opposite page Cagney poses with
Mary Law and Mary Boland of 1927's *Women Go On
Forever*; and with Sophia Delza, his dancing partner in
The Grand Street Follies of 1928. Below he is seen with
Shirley Warde in *Maggie the Magnificent*, the 1929
George Kelly play he regarded as his best Broadway
break. The same year he starred with Joan Blondell in
Penny Arcade, to make the movie version of which Warner
Brothers brought both of them to Los Angeles.

at least in part on the strength of the notices he collected in *Maggie the Magnificent*.

This was as Harry Delano, a brash, briefly charming, ultimately tragic weakling in Marie Baumer's *Penny Arcade*, a melodrama that looked both forward and backward in Cagney's life. As the title implies, it was set in a Penny Arcade, on a Coney Island-like board-walk, populated by people of the class in which Cagney had grown up. Indeed, the play's central relationship was between Harry and his mother, who can perhaps be seen as a dark version of Cagney's own mother. That is to say, Ma Delano was the most powerful force in her son's life. The difference was that she was a smothering presence, a woman who instead of thrusting her son out into life could not let go of him and who, in the course of the play, tries to pin the blame for a murder he commits on an innocent party. This relationship also, of course, prefigures another, and more famous, fictional mother-son relationship that involved Cagney, the one between Cody Jarrett and his Ma in *White Heat*, nineteen years later. There were other coincidences as well. His girlfriend here was played by Joan Blondell, who had been with him (in a small part) in *Maggie*, and would accompany him to Hollywood to do the film version of *Penny Arcade*. Finally, the director was William Keighley, who would also accept a Warner Brothers contract and direct Cagney in four of his pictures there.

Penny Arcade would run only twenty-four performances, Cagney's shortest Broadway engagement ever, but again his reviews were excellent. More important, smart Al Jolson, star of the picture that had begun the sound revolution, *The Jazz Singer*, and a good judge of what Hollywood required in this difficult transitional moment, bought the motion picture rights to the play and resold them to Warner Brothers. The studio, in turn, offered Cagney and Blondell term contracts to come west and repeat their stage roles before the cameras. Cagney had no hesitation about accepting. After all, it was a job.

A QUALITY OF SOME KIND

'SHE WAS JUST A KID, AND I WAS JUST A DOPE, you know. I didn't know what was going on. Imagine that – seven years with a six-month guarantee. And we thought we were on velvet.' Thus James Cagney on the subject of Joan Blondell and himself heading for Hollywood under contract to the movies for the first time. All he could see at the time was that his salary was, as he now remembers it, $500 a week, though both that figure and the length of the contract vary in other accounts. But no matter. It was more than he had ever earned before, and for a longer period of time than he had ever before been able to count on. It was at least velveteen.

Not that *Sinners' Holiday*, the somewhat peppier title Warner Brothers gave to *Penny Arcade*, was of much consequence to the studio. The director assigned to it was John G. Adolfi, whose chief claim to fame is as George Arliss's kept director, guiding that silky, stentorian English actor through many of those shrewdly heart-warming displays of ageing benevolence that made him an Academy Award winner, a short-lived box office favourite and something of a joke historically speaking. To work with its unknowns, Cagney and Blondell, the studio employed Evalyn Knapp, Grant Withers and Lucille La Verne. The first named, a rather bland blonde who passed most of her career in low budget films, played Cagney's sister, who must finally betray him as a murderer in order to prevent his crime being charged to her fiancé, a logical fall guy since he was an ex-con. That role was essayed by Withers, essentially a B picture leading man, rugged and stiff. La Verne played Cagney's mother, she who attempts to implicate her daughter's lover rather than permit her beloved son, Harry, to suffer the consequences of his impulsive act. She had frequently been used by D. W. Griffith during the 1920s and this very year would do a small role for him in his first talkie, *Abraham Lincoln*. But, aside from her memorably evil Mother Forchart in *Orphans of the Storm*, she had never made a truly strong

impression. In short, *Sinners' Holiday*, which had a running time of only about an hour, was an inexpensive enterprise, never designed for any place more grand than the bottom of the bill.

It has not improved with the passing years, despite its obvious historical interest as Cagney's début film. Turgid and lugubrious, it is bound to a single set – an amusement parlor and its immediate environs, the boardwalk of a rundown seaside resort, which the director utilizes in perfunctory fashion – nothing here excites his camera's interest. And La Verne, in her crucial role, is hopeless; she has the manner of an opera singer trying to do jazz. She woefully overacts and, in her last scene with him, forces Cagney to do the same if he is not to be overwhelmed. In fact, it is Blondell who emerges from *Sinners' Holiday* most attractively. Pretty and lively, she is already what she will remain, a solid naturalistic actress, particularly believable and sympathetic as a good-natured, common-sensical woman, of the sort heroes tend to reject for something more glamorous in the first reel and then live to regret (or happily rediscover) in the last reel.

As for Cagney, something of what was shortly to make him a star is visible in the film, especially in its early passages. Despite the fact that he was thirty-one years old at the time, Cagney played Harry Delano as a juvenile delinquent, almost premoral in his inability to separate right from wrong. For him, we are made to feel, crime is a kind of pranksterism, and his amazement at discovering that it can have serious, not to say deadly, consequences, is, in a way, rather poignant. It prevents Harry from being just another punk, and this, more than any allusion to his father's alcoholism, redeems this character for our sympathy. Beyond that, and before he must surrender to the grinding mechanism of the plot, Cagney invests him with considerable wayward charm. There is, for example, a little scene with Blondell where, separated by the boardwalk, they arrange a later meeting through pan-

tomime. His deftness and confidence at least suggest what Blondell's character sees in a man who is, at heart, supposed to be a sneak and a weakling.

Not that one can fault his performances in the big scenes, where his mother confirms her suspicion that he is a murderer, and where he begs her to help him cover up his crime. As there would be occasion to observe later on in his career, Cagney could be, when he needed to be, a great sniveller. No one was better at allowing a hard case to crack open suddenly and let a coward's guts spill forth. He may have less control here than he would show in later, similar scenes. But screaming and whimpering, writhing and clutching – prefiguring a similar, more famous scene in *White Heat* – he reverts quite effectively to a parody of childhood, his head burrowing into his mother's lap, as if he were, perhaps, ten years old and was afraid of bullies picking on him on the way from school, not a murder rap. It's startling, since nothing

going before it in this flat little picture prepares one for such a torrrent of emotion.

One must not claim too much for Cagney at this point. The promise of things to come is more visible with hindsight than it was at the time. We see here the pathos that Cagney would evoke in later films. But not yet his manic wit, little of the capacity to beguile kinesthetically. And none of the quality that people would come to think of first when they thought of Cagney, his emblematic toughness. Oddly, of his character's salient qualities, this would appear on screen last. Certainly it cannot be said that either the public or the critics sensed, when *Sinners' Holiday* went into release, that simply because of Cagney's presence in it, this curious little program picture represented a consequential moment in the history of the cinema. Nor could it be said that the studio bosses divined, on the basis of the evidence *Sinners' Holiday* placed before them, precisely what was singular about him. Still there was obviously something there, something worth hanging on to in order to see what would develop. Or as Cagney was to say, many years later, 'There was a quality of some kind that they saw . . . and they liked . . . and kept it'. They would renew his option and throw him into all kinds of movies – seven of them in his first year and a half on the lot. Some of them were good, some of them were bad, some of them provided him with plenty of screen time and some of them would dispense with his services in a wink of the camera's eye. But one of them, to the surprise of everyone, himself included, would make him a star.

These arrangements suited Cagney – for the moment. Years later, asked what advice he would give a young actor, he would respond: 'Go where it's being done and hang around until they decide you're able to do it. "They" being the producers . . . If they see you often enough they kind of buy you at face value.' His attitude, in turn, suited the system of the moment. Or perhaps one should say the non-system. In those days, happily, there was no such thing as market research or product testing. They simply tried ideas, styles and people and judged the results by the crude, immemorial standard of show biz: did it work or didn't it? In the case of performers who might or might not have star potential their cases were judged slowly, after the box office returns from a half dozen or more pictures were toted up and roughly analyzed.

All Warner Brothers could safely say at this early stage of Cagney's movie career was that he was an obviously useful type to have around the studio, for in the few years since the talkies had arrived, the content and the style of movies had changed noticeably, and there was a need now for new kinds of stars to fit these new kinds of movies. Basically what was required were men (and women, too, though the need was less difficult to fulfil) who were capable of portraying urban types, suggesting rhythms and manners less obviously romantic than most of the leading players of the silent era had pro-jected, and suggesting backgrounds more citi-fied than the movies had heretofore implied for their central figures.

The movies were responding to two forces as they made this switch. One, obviously, was technological, and had to do with the kind of material sound pictures could – and could not – persuasively handle in their infancy. The other, less obvious perhaps, but also pro-foundly significant, had to do with the chang-ing nature of the movie audience. In fact, the movies had begun to respond to this sociologi-cal revolution before they began addressing themselves to the purely technological revolu-tion that generally gets more attention in the standard film histories.

It is impossible to say which of these two forces was the most significant in reshaping film styles and content. But it is clear that they reinforced one another and accelerated the process of change that – taken together with the beginnings of the Depression – buffetted Hollywood in the early 1930s. The shift in the composition and interests of the audience was presaged by the 1920 U.S. census, which very simply noted that, for the first time in the nation's history, more Americans lived in cities than on farms and in small towns. The census defined any hamlet whose population exceeded 5,000 as a city, and so one must cloud any con-clusions drawn from its statistics with ambi-guity. Still, journalism in its many new and expanding forms – not to mention the evidence presented to any intelligent observer's eyes – confirmed on an almost daily basis the fact that in the third decade of this century the popu-lation balance of the United States was in the process of shifting decisively to the big cities.

In the narrowest terms this meant that the basic movie audience had relocated. And since the rise of organized crime, coincident with prohibition, was a large, or at any rate vivid, part of this new reality for them, and was wonderfully melodramatic and photogenic as well – ideal motion picture material – it fol-lowed that the studios would turn gratefully, hungrily, to this subject. This they had begun to do before sound pictures arrived. The beginning of their preoccupation with criminal life is conventionally dated from a silent picture, Josef von Sternberg's *Underworld* in 1927. The genre would quickly encompass the first 'all talking' picture (prior to it dialogue was included only in isolated sequences), *The Lights of New York* in 1928. It opened on the same day as *The Racket* in New York, and within months reviewers would be complaining of a surfeit of gangster movies – though to little avail. For the genre was now established, and though it would wax, wane and change its moods over the decade to come and would greatly subside when World War Two provided movie-makers with a topic equally relevant and action-packed, it would never entirely die out. Unquestionably, though, its peak was in the early 1930s when the criminal element provided the movies with a subject that rivalled the backstage musical as a surefire attraction, not only because it provided sensational, exploitable material but because it seemed to suit the microphones so well.

The silent cinema had developed in the 1920s – when production moved off the streets and the other 'found' locations where movies had at first been made into the confines of the studios – as an essentially romantic, even poetic, form of expression, visually more venturesome than the movies had been before or have been since. If it was ever correct to refer to movies as dreams, to their stars as gods and goddesses, it was during this period. In all innocence, the studios, which could abandon habits no more easily than any other human institution, attempted to maintain some conventions of the silent film in the early sound era. No one, at first, understood that the addition of sound was not a mere enhancement of the medium, but a factor that would reconstitute it as something essentially different from what it had been – a prose medium, not a poetic one.

It was the stars who felt the impact of sound first, as the legendary case of the legendary

John Gilbert proved. It may be that his voice did not 'mike' as well as it might have (though it actually appears to have been a pleasant light baritone that just a few years later would have caused no comment). It may also be that the M-G-M sound department sabotaged his first talkie by turning up the treble in order to chastise him and make him more malleable to the executive whims of Louis B. Mayer. But the main problem was that the poor man was, in effect, forced to speak subtitles, and a literary style that had entered the mind more or less comfortably though the eye rang ludicrously in the ear. Similarly, his screen persona, as set forth in a variety of romantic excesses during the high silent period of the middle and late 1920s, needed to be toned down and resituated in the more humble venues that were more appropriate to sound film production. Nor was he singular in this need. All of Hollywood required the same treatment if sound pictures were not to be laughed off the screen, as many of the more sophisticated movie-goers and critics – committed to silents as a form with the potential of high art and convinced that sound was merely a novelty to amuse the *hoi polloi* – were prepared to do.

Not so the shrewdest studio bosses, who were, as always, at one with the mass audience, at odds with the self-consciously tasteful minority. They could not be said to have formulated any conscious aesthetic regarding their transformed medium. As usual, they were operating on instinct. But it was not lost on them that the first (sometimes) talking picture, *The Jazz Singer*, was the story of a Jewish lad, the son of immigrants whose father was a cantor, and who was torn between duty to the religion (and the social values) of his parents and his burgeoning career in the occupation specified by the film's title. It was, in fact, a sentimental, non-violent version of the tale that so many gangster films, past, present and future, told – that of a young man in a new country hurrying, perhaps too rapidly, to take advantage of opportunities alien to the old country values by which he had been raised. It may have been no more than a coincidence, but the success of this picture suggested a linkage between subject matter and the new technology that was extraordinarily powerful. It is not too much to say that the central subject of the American sound film in its early years was city life, and that the basic story it worked and reworked dealt with young men and women trying to rise to power in the urban jungle by fair means or foul, from humble, humbling circumstances.

These films were romances no less than the most Graustarkian of the 1920s concoctions. But they obviously had about them a realistic air. And it quickly became clear that if the fantasy element in movies was to be more subtly insinuated into them, so that it appeared in the guise of realism, then a new sort of performer was required. Suddenly players who were not perfectly handsome or perfectly beautiful could aspire to movie careers. Or even if they did not so aspire, they could find themselves swept up by the studios and shipped westward anyway, along with the stage directors who were thought to be able to handle dialogue more gracefully than the silent picture directors could and the playwrights who had proved their ability to write the stuff. Think how many young actors, falling short of idealized, or collar ad, good looks might have become only occasional character players in silents, yet became major figures in the early years of sound production. In addition to Cagney and his pal O'Brien, one might list Edward G. Robinson, Paul Muni, Spencer Tracy and probably Clark Gable as well.

What they all had in common was the capacity to both look and sound the part of contemporary urban males of less than elevated status – out-and-out criminals sometimes, but more often con men, shysters, small timers on the hustle, politicians and newsmen of dubious ethics. All of them could act tough, of course, but that was the least of their abilities. George Bancroft had already established himself as a tough guy before this crowd arrived on the

scene. George Raft arrived at the same time they did. (Both would twice play in support of Cagney.) And so what? Toughness when it presents itself in a new form can be intriguing for a moment or two. But it is perhaps the least interesting of human qualities in life or on the screen. We instinctively turn from it in the first instance when nothing is revealed beneath its crust, in the second when it has served its function in the plot. You cannot for long hold the attention of anyone but male adolescents if that is all you have to offer.

In fact, Cagney did not get a chance to offer it – not in its purest, hardest form – until *The Public Enemy*. For the moment, his opportunities were extremely modest. There were no leading roles. There were few chances even to make a strong impression on the audience. Immediately after *Sinners' Holiday*, for instance, he was assigned to a gangster picture, *Doorway to Hell*, but as the second lead. Lew Ayres, of all mild-mannered actors, was mis-

45

Lew Ayres had the starring role in *Doorway*, and the attention of Dorothy Mathews in the scene above. But Cagney got to wear the smart polo coat. He was elbowed to the edge of the picture (left) and the film as a whole by Grant Withers (center), well supported by familiar supporting actor Walter Long in *Other Men's Women*. A a fast-talking insurance salesman he was the liveliest thin about *The Millionaire*, for the cast of which he was personally selected by George Arliss (opposite).

cast as the Capone-like gang boss, with Cagney as the henchman who attempts to usurp his position while he is otherwise engaged in Florida. His casting is at least explicable, for his big scene in *Doorway to Hell* was analagous to his big scene in *Sinners' Holiday*: under pressure he again must break down and confess to a crime. The difference this time was that it is a full scale police third degree, not a desperate mother, that causes his loss of nerve.

It was, at least, a scene that some people noticed and remembered. It is said, in fact, that among those noticing and remembering were Kubec Glasmon and John Bright, contract writers at Warner's, who were just then working up the first draft of the screenplay (based on an unpublished novel of theirs called *Beer and Blood*) for *The Public Enemy*. They would later say that they wrote with Cagney in mind for the central role from the time they saw

Doorway. Maybe so, maybe not. Many would claim credit for the ideas that gave that film its vivid singularity.

Meantime, for Cagney, there were more minor chores to attend to. He had a small part, scarcely more than a bit, in *Other Men's Women*, a love triangle in which the two men in pursuit of the same woman are best friends. What was significant for him was that it was directed by William A. Wellman, who would shortly be responsible for the picture that would make Cagney a star. Cagney probably did not have any more total screen time in his next picture, which was a George Arliss vehicle (directed by Adolfi) called *The Millionaire*, but it was all compressed into a single scene, and a pivotal one at that. In the title role Arliss plays an ageing plutocrat for whom life has lost its savor. How to reinterest him in existence? That's where Cagney comes in – as a life insurance salesman, full of bounce and confidence, telling the old boy that he wouldn't 'sit around and wait for the undertaker' if he had as much to live for as Arliss's character does. Until Cagney's entrance, the film is a rather languid affair, and one can't help but be grateful for the rude life he gives to it. Moreover, he is the spring that propels both Arliss and the plot forward; the picture seems to live off his energy even after he has disappeared.

Arliss would later write that he had interviewed several young contract players for the role, but felt the moment Cagney walked in that he was perfect for it. As they talked, the older man found 'He wasn't acting to me now; he wasn't trying to impress me; he was just being natural and, I thought, a trifle independent for a bit actor; there was a suggestion of "Here I am; take me or leave me; and hurry up."' He would claim that he ordered Cagney to work in the film in his own wardrobe and without make-up. In effect he said to Cagney what George Kelly had said to him, 'just be yourself'.

He wasn't quite, of course; no actor ever is. On camera he affected a pipe and whistled through his teeth a lot, for the first time bringing to the screen those bits of behavioral business he was always trying to invent or to recall from his observations of other people's mannerisms. They were his way of getting a handle on a role. Sometimes it would seem that from one or two such actions he would build an entire characterization. Not that Cagney has ever admitted psychologizing a character. He always said that all he was looking for was a kind of trademark for each role he played, something that would catch in the viewer's memory. 'Doesn't matter [what it is] as long as it is something that is particularly personal. That became a kind of a stamp . . . The idea was that if you could give them something to remember, use it.'

People would, indeed, remember him in *The Millionaire*. Again, the analogy with Kelly recurs. As the playwright had given Cagney his first 'classy' stage role, so George Arliss had given him his first 'classy' screen role, something in a project the better critics, the tonier audiences, felt duty-bound to attend alertly. Cagney's response to this opportunity, his creation of a confidence man utterly confident of himself, is, in effect, a first sketch for an aspect of his screen character that was to become vital to his success. Up to now, he had demonstrated his vulnerability, but had not had a chance to show his cheeky, bustling side, to cut loose that excess of energy which, since it gave every evidence of being preternatural, seemed to excuse the excesses of ambition that were also so much a part of his *persona*.

What he needed now was a picture that would permit him to exhibit his full range, which assuredly included that hard core of hardness – the spine of his character – that he had not yet had more than a fleeting opportunity to demonstrate.

More important, to put the matter simply, he needed a major role, something that would give the audience a chance to take stock of him, to get to know him, or at least to partake of the illusion of knowing him. It would not hurt,

48

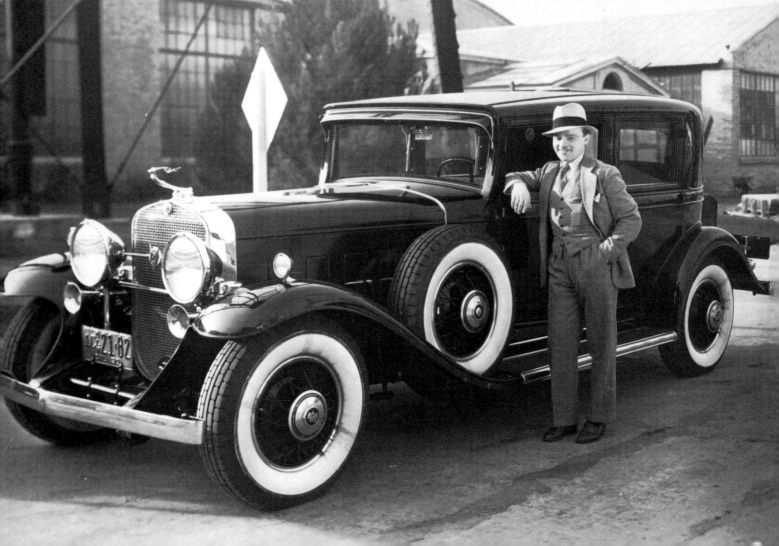

of course, if that role could be in a hit movie.

And to think that he almost missed his chance. *The Public Enemy* has become, by now, one of those Hollywood legends, a picture that was almost not made in the first place, that was almost sabotaged by miscasting, that was rewritten extensively as it was being made, and was finally made both famous and infamous by the success of its many improvisations, credit for which various hands continued to claim for years. To begin at the beginning, it seems likely that Bright and Glasmon's *Beer and Blood* script would never have been made had they not approached William A. Wellman, the director, on his way to lunch one day and asked him to read their story. Something they said piqued his interest and he invited them to join him at table, where they convinced him – always an important point with him – that the story was based on reality, a reality they had come to know as young men in the early 1920s in Chicago hanging about on the fringe of criminal life. He took their story back to his office and read it that afternoon. 'I went crazy about it', Bill Wellman would say to me many years later, and that was in character. He was a man of vast and sudden enthusiasms. He got an appointment with Darryl Zanuck, Warner's chief of production, and talked the story to him. 'I've got the script, it's wonderful', he said. According to Wellman, Zanuck replied, 'Bill, I can't do another one. I just did *Little Caesar* and *Doorway to Hell* . . . Tell me why I should do it?' At this point in his recital Wellman paused dramatically, then continued, his voice lower, slower, more intense. 'Because I'll make it the toughest one of them all.' To which, Zanuck being an extremely intelligent executive, there could be only one reply: 'Okay, you got it.'

For it must have been obvious to Zanuck that the picture lay squarely at the center of the country where the director was most happily at home. As Manny Farber once said, Wellman was at least four different directors rolled into one – 'sentimentalist, deep thinker, hooey vaudevillian and [the one Farber and those who followed him in creating the mystique of the American action director most admired] an expedient short-cut artist whose special love is for mulish toughs expressing themselves in drop-kicking heads and somber standing around.' There is not a lot of standing around in *The Public Enemy*, but as it finally worked out, it became a compendium of Wellman's other virtues as Farber memorably put them: 'A low-budget ingenuity, which creates flashes of ferocious brassiness, an authentic practical-joke violence . . . and a brainless hell-raising.'

The question is whether these qualities would have been as apparent, or as richly realized, in the film, if it had been shot as originally cast. For as just about everyone knows, once a writer named Harry Thew had done a polish job on Glasmon and Bright's original story, the picture started shooting with an actor named Edward Woods in the lead, as Tom Powers, and Cagney in the secondary role of Matt Doyle, his best friend. Precisely how the decision to have the two men switch roles came about is now impossible to say. It has been claimed that Glasmon and Bright objected to this casting from the start and, based on the quality of the early footage, finally won their point. In his autobiography Jack Warner himself seemed to imply that the decision to make the change was his. But Cagney, in his autobiography, credits Wellman with the idea, and it must be said that it was the director who offered the only recollection of the incident containing persuasive details. One suspects that he, along with the writers, may have argued for giving the lead to Cagney before production and that at that time Zanuck may have countered, as some accounts have it, by saying he did not want to give so important a role to Cagney after only four pictures. Certainly, he may have hoped that Woods would succeed as Powers because he was engaged to marry the daughter of Louella O. Parsons, the powerful Hearst gossip columnist, whose favor

51

studio executives were ever eager to curry. But faced with hard facts Zanuck did not hesitate to rectify his mistake. And it was Wellman who offered the clinching argument. As the director put it: 'We did two or three days' work and Zanuck was in New York and I didn't look at the rushes until the weekend. But when I finally looked at the rushes, I said, "Good God, we've got the wrong guy in the wrong part." It was so evident. So I went into his [Zanuck's] office, got him on the long-distance phone and told him. And he said switch, and we did.'

Cagney, naturally, affected that the whole business was a matter of indifference to him. 'When they handed me the first part it was all right with me, and when they made the switch, when Zanuck said to me, "We're going to change this around," I said, "yeah." That's about it.' He conceded only this much: 'Well, my background was a city tough kid... and I can understand the boys deciding they wanted me rather than Eddie, who was a straight man, really. Eddie wasn't tough at all: small town boy.'

There was, of course, more to Cagney's astonishing success in the role than the appropriateness of his background and temperament for it. To put the matter simply, he was Wellman's kind of guy – direct and forceful, of course, but with his enormous energy focused and, indeed, mentally choreographed with such precision that his several unforgettably brutal outbursts of violence seem to be over almost before they start. The paradoxical result of this premeditation was a sense he conveyed that his explosions were entirely *un*premeditated, instinctual. Thus beyond moral censure. Indeed now, if not then, he collects awed and envious laughs for them, partly because of his infectious joy in his own audacity, partly because he is able to accomplish what everyone would like to do under pressure, namely respond viscerally, instantly, to taunts and frustrations, cutting boldly through all the constraint, all the hesitant *politesse*, that rules the rest of us. Moreover,

the lack of calculation in his cruelty frees Tom from the taint of sadism, where pleasure derives from anticipation of the victim's pain and from prolonging his or her anguish. He is all brisk business when he decides to mete out justice as he sees it, setting aside, perhaps, one scene in which he toys with a stool pigeon, permitting the poor fellow a moment or two of hope before he is rubbed out.

In later years, Zanuck would claim that he was responsible for making Cagney's viciousness seem acceptable; in script conferences he insisted that Tom be given one redeeming characteristic, namely his love for his mother. And, literally, it is so; he is always coming home for dinner with Mom, and even as he hands over money to her he is at pains to disguise the criminal source of the sudden wealth he is sharing with her. But motherhood was not one of the subjects Wellman enjoyed sentimentalizing; that approach to it was too conventional and witless. So he cast an actress named Beryl Mercer, floppy-soft and round-eyed, the very picture of innocent Irish saintliness, and clearly instructed her to play dumb. The result is that Cagney's relationship with her becomes a near-parody of what was then, in popular culture, the most sacred of human connections, and that adds to the half-mad humor of the film. Tom's older brother, a streetcar conductor who has never so much as short-changed a rider, and who goes through the movie registering disgust with his sibling's ways, and lecturing at him, is made to seem, in Donald Cook's playing and Wellman's direction, as stupid as their mother. Indeed, every law-abiding citizen is shown to be slightly brain-damaged by respectability. As a result, in the closed world of the movie, we are given no reasonable alternatives to Tom's behavior, nothing against which to measure it. If we were thrown into the life of this picture we would try to behave like Tom, if only because all the other choices are so stupefying.

Even in its most famous moment, which is also one of the most famous moments in all of movies, when Cagney shoves the grapefruit into Mae Clark's pouting face, we are on his side, not hers. Tom has been living with her plain, dull character, Kitty, and he's getting bored with her, especially now that he has risen in the underworld and has met flashy but sympathetic Gwen (Jean Harlow, also establishing herself with this picture). She likes him for what he is – a sexy punk without redeeming social value – and she wants neither to reform him nor even to improve his manners. When he stumbles out of the bedroom in the apartment he shares with Kitty asking for a drink instead of a respectable breakfast, and Kitty whinily attempts to dissuade him, the scene already had a parodistical air about it: gangster as weary businessman

about to face another high pressure day and in need of a little comfort; gangster's moll as helpmate, proposing that booze before breakfast is not only unhealthy but, well, *infra dig*. 'I didn't ask you for any lip. I asked you if you had a drink,' Tom snarls. 'I know dear, but . . . well . . . I wish . . .' 'There you go with that wishing stuff again. I wish you was a wishing well, so I could tie a bucket to ya and sink ya.' Sensible people, of course, back off at moments like these, but Kitty, as simple-minded as any one Tom encounters, persists: 'Maybe you found someone you like better.' Expressions of weariness and disgust chase across Cagney's face. The grapefruit is picked up, slammed into Kitty's face and – sometimes overlooked – given a vicious little twist before he exits fuming.

Of course it is sexist. Of course it is degrading to women. But it is also a marital squabble settler that members of either sex might well envy. Above all, it is one of the very few scenes about which one can literally say that it made an actor a star. Without it, of course, Cagney's performance in *The Public Enemy* would have established him as a force that would have to be reckoned with at the studio, in the industry. But with it the picture shocked and titillated the press, and its reports of this amazing moment stirred the curious. It *sounded* good, different, not like the other gangster pictures. In a stroke people were made aware of both Cagney's singularity and the singularity of *The Public Enemy*. More than that, with its peculiar vividness, the scene came to symbolize for moralists and social commentators a shift in the relationship of men and women as depicted in the public media in this era. Cagney himself, reacting to the talk generated by the scene, would later point out that men began slapping women around in the movies well before he tried his hand at it. And that was true; it was all part of the pseudo-realism of sound pictures.

But a smack is just a smack. As time goes by, the fundamental thought applies – a grapefruit is a unique and startling weapon. At once

A Public Enemy's private life. Or the grapefruit that made him a star. Below, at a party celebrating Cagney's 30th year as an actor, he and a dubious Mae Clark recall their most famous screen moment for a photographer who obviously came prepared to make a saleable snap.

homely and rather exotic – a little touch of the subtropics that somehow arrives at our breakfast table each morning – it is the product, stop to think about it, of the same geography and climate that the Hollywood movie is. Be that as it may, the grapefruit, especially in the context of a table laid for a gangster, is a symbol in a way that a sweeter fruit could never be. It is, above all, healthy food – loads of vitamins and no calories. To use so beneficial a product – a thing that in its natural, unsugared state actually tastes rather medicinal – as an instrument of battery is to travesty all bourgeois good intentions, all that class's aspirations to austerity and self-improvement. Besides which, we are used to pursing our lips and squinching up our faces a bit when we take a bite of a grapefruit. We can only imagine what it would be like to be slapped in the face by one – the squish and splat and sting of it. Oh, what an inspiration it was!

But whose? In his later years Bill Wellman used to have grumble fits when Darryl Zanuck claimed credit for the invention. And he was not entirely certain of the claim Glasmon and Bright laid to it, on the basis that a real-life Chicago gangster had once administered a citrus facial to one of his girl friends. He didn't outright deny the writers' contention or the possibility that polisher Thew might have come up with it. He seemed to recall, though, that an early draft of the script specified a plate of eggs as the treatment of choice for nagging dames. But that, he thought, was too much – the runny aftermess would have been so unpleasant to gaze upon that it would have shifted sympathy away from Cagney for the rest of the film.

In other words, the cleanliness of the grapefruit also helped to recommend it to the director once he got to staging the scene. That, and a little trouble he was having at home:

'I was married to a very beautiful girl who was an aviatrix ... and whenever we had an argument she had a wonderful way of handling it. This wonderful, beautiful face became like a sculpture. There was no movement in it all, it just was beautiful and dominant .... And it stayed that way for two or three days and that's a frightening thing to have to overcome, you know. You go absolutely crazy. And many a time when we had breakfast and we used to have grapefruit, I wanted to take that grapefruit and mash it in her face just to make her change just for a minute ... But fortunately, this scene came and I said, "Oh baby, I can get rid of it here. I won't do something that will cost me money [in heightened alimony payments]", so I did it and Mae Clarke became the recipient of the ... grapefruit.'

This squares with the recollection of at least one of the scene's principals, Mae Clarke, for whom this moment would become, to her chagrin, her chief claim on immortality. 'I'm sorry I ever agreed to do the grapefruit bit. I never dreamed it would be shown in the movie .... Bill Wellman thought of the idea suddenly. It wasn't even written into the script.' She claimed it was all done in a single take, but since there are three different angles in the sequence as finally cut, it would seem that a little more calculation went into the invention.

But no matter. If man does not live by bread alone, this movie does not live by a grapefruit alone. Indeed, this scene is virtually a throwaway in comparison to some of the longer, more worked out sequences in the film which, seen much later, continue to carry an emotional power that this purely iconographic moment cannot possibly have. Tom Powers' downfall comes when he makes the mistake of succumbing to a decent impulse, the need to avenge the rubout of his pal Matt by a rival gang. He goes alone to their lair one rainy night, enters and while the camera waits passively outside the entrance, we hear a wild exchange of shots, at the end of which Cagney, carrying two enormous pistols, staggers back out, near-mortally wounded. He throws the guns away, reels, seemingly endlessly, along the sidewalk, before sinking into the gutter, where he whispers a line very similar in its amazed

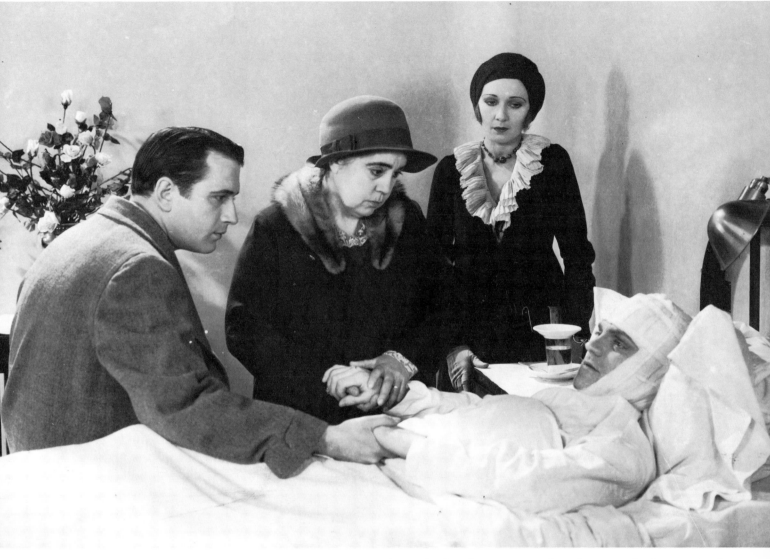

tone to Little Caesar's famous, 'Mother of Mercy, is this the end of Rico?' Tom Powers' epitaph is, 'I ain't so tough'. For a moment one almost believes he may have belatedly learned his lesson. About that we will never know, for these are the last meaningful lines Cagney speaks in the picture. He is seen next in the hospital, swathed in bandages, virtually immobilized. The scene after that finds his family at home, where they receive a phone call, purportedly from the hospital, telling them Tom is about to join them. Among their other defects must be a belief in miracle cures; how can they imagine that the living corpse they just left could arise and walk?

But never mind. A cheerful bustle ensues as poor simple Mom prepares a bed for Tom while on the phonograph the movie's ironically appropriate theme song, 'I'm Forever Blowing Bubbles', plays merrily. The doorbell rings, the brother opens the door and there stands Cagney, wrapped like a mummy. He teeters and then falls face forward to the floor – his death, and this cruel trick on his family, both arranged by the mob he had assaulted, the brutal ironies of this conclusion courtesy of a strong script and a fulfilled promise: 'I'll make it the toughest one of them all.'

That final scene, as surprising as the grape-fruit bit and infinitely more powerful – and just possibly an invention that can be credited to Zanuck, who worked it out with witnesses present – almost didn't make it to the final print. At the first preview *The Public Enemy* was a smash with the audience, but Jack Warner, sitting in a row with Wellman, Zanuck and Michael Curtiz, the director, hated it. 'You've got to cut it out. It made me sick. It'll make everybody sick.' But, as Wellman would tell the story, Zanuck fought the boss, who turned for support to Curtiz, who was puffing on his habitual large cigar. 'Don't you agree with me, Mike?' The answer, perhaps inevitably, was yes. Whereupon 'Zanuck hauled off, knocked the cigar right down his throat. I'm not kidding. That's what made pictures [in those] days. They don't do that anymore. And, by God, it scared Warner and we had no argument about it, it stayed in the picture . . . .'

And it went forth and made money, huge amounts of it, especially in relation to its cost, which was only about $125,000, and despite shocked reviews. In this instance, popular opinion was correct, as it so often was in this period, when reviewers tended to apply genteel and rather literary standards to movies – implicitly urging them to be more like the theater, now that they could talk – culturally aspiring and issue oriented. But *The Public Enemy* succeeded then, and continues to succeed now, rather better than the other members of the Big Three of the gangster genre's early years (1930's *Little Caesar*, 1932's *Scarface*) precisely because it avoided their evocations of the higher things. The former showed a criminal rising much higher than Tom Powers ever did, and demonstrated that he could not have done so had he not been implicitly encouraged by the élite of his city. Taking nothing away from Edward G. Robinson's fine, brooding performance, it suffered from an excess of social awareness. *Scarface*, on the other hand, suffered from a surfeit of perverse sexual awareness, particularly in its implications of an incestuous relationship between Paul Muni's protagonist and his sister. Moreover, with many shots portentously angled and shadowed, director Howard Hawks uncharacteristically insisted with almost every foot of film that you could make a movie about the rise and demise of a punk and still keep your mind (and at least one eye) on 'art'. By contrast, Wellman's steadfastly objective camera insists on nothing. Literarily, perhaps, Tom can be seen as a naturalistic figure, his behavior ruled by those instinctual forces that typically define the fates of Dreiser's characters, and James T. Farrell's among the contemporaries. But even that point is only lightly pressed.

Nor does *The Public Enemy* comfortably fit Robert Warshow's famous definition of 'The Gangster as Tragic Hero'. That piece now seems to be all generalizations and no specifics in any case. More to the point, it seems to refer mainly to the other pictures composing this trilogy. Maybe we can read Tom Powers as Warshow reads Rico and Scarface, 'doomed because he is under the obligation to succeed, not because the means he employs are unlawful'. Maybe his career – nasty, brutal and short – does prove, as the critic would have it, that 'In the deeper layers of the modern consciousness *all* means are unlawful, every attempt to succeed an act of aggression, leaving one alone and guilty and defenseless among enemies . . .' But don't count on it.

What we really have in *The Public Enemy* is not a version of a tragic hero in the classical vein, but of an existential hero in the modernist vein. That is to say, we witness a shrewd but essentially thoughtless man making himself up as he goes along, composing a character for himself out of a succession of heedless actions and then getting himself rubbed by an answering heedlessness. The point here is really the pointlessness of it all. We never see Tom hobnobbing with the political and social swells of his town, as Rico gets to do. And we don't understand him to be shadowed by the dark sexual drives of Scarface. He simply lives his little while and then dies, not having learned a thing in the process, thus being in no position to let his life teach a lesson. Primitive and uncalculated, he seems to prematurely define those qualities Norman Mailer later identified for us in his famous essay on 'The White Negro,' in which he saw the psychopath as 'the frontiersman of American night life,' he who 'murders – if he has the courage – out of the necessity to purge his violence'. In that crucial sentence Mailer adds that this emptying of hatred is a necessary precondition for this character's mobilization of the capacity to love. On this last point, obviously, *The Public Enemy* is silent, though one could possibly interpret Tom Powers' mad invasion of his rival's head-quarters as purgative in something like the sense that Mailer means. But of the Cagney figure being a 'frontiersman' in the Mailerian sense there can be no doubt. What the roots of his hatred are, whether they are social or purely pathological, we cannot say. But it is there, and poised – hypnotically – on a hair-trigger.

As for Cagney's performance, it seems, in retrospect, a marvel of incaution. It is difficult, in fact, to think of many like it anywhere in movie history. For its charm – and charm, however perverse, it does have – lies entirely in its unmediated unpredictability. One never knows, watching him, when or in what manner he is going to unleash his fury. All we know is that it will be sudden and, by normal stan-dards, excessive. What we are seeing for the first time is the absolutely basic nature of what would become Cagney's screen persona, with nothing redeeming or softening added, no special pleas entered on its behalf. It is, there-fore, as courageous and as challenging as any movie performance can be, especially since it appears so early in his career, before he had built up that residue of familiarity and affec-tion that allows older actors to play against agreeable type and win our admiration for their 'courage'.

But there is more than courage to this per-formance. There is sheer astonishment in it. Perhaps Cagney managed something like the remarkable combination of coldness and murderous abandon he exhibits here in one of his stage roles; it is impossible to determine that from the reviews. But it is perfectly clear that in the movie work that preceded *The Public Enemy* there is nothing comparable to this detached monstrousness. Nor is there any-thing in his biography to suggest what he might have drawn on to inform this role. A few bad boys observed – they might have suggested some behavioral bits, but not the prodigies of psychotic self-interest here manifested. No, all one can certainly say about Cagney in *The Public Enemy* is that something in the role, something in the opportunity that was so sud-denly offered him, unleashed some pure and terrifying instinct in him, a furious blur of energy and movement that was yet never fuzzy or generalized, that was like a well-choreographed dance because it built, out of a succession of precisely calculated movements toward well-defined ends, an overarching, overwhelming emotional line.

So vivid was this work that, in a sense, it would dictate much of his future work, forcing some acknowledgement, however brief, of this characterization in subsequent roles, some hint to the fans that he remembered what they would always remember, and cherish, from the moment when they first met him and fell under his thrall. In other words, it would distort his films, therefore his career, in various and curious ways. And one cannot help but believe that the sense of alienation from his past that so marked him as an old man comes from his sense of having travelled under false colors more often than he wanted to – maybe even needed to – from this point onward.

Be that as it may, he was perhaps luckier than he knew. In our own time, when actors often have to wait a year or two between roles, it is possible that something like *The Public Enemy* could have been a career ender rather than a career starter, for the delay in launching a film to counter the image it created might have been too lengthy. But here the thing that Cagney would find so offensive, the studio's habit of grinding out picture after picture without surcease, in order to satisfy the implac-able release schedule, which required the studio to deliver to the theater chains they owned (and the ones with which they had block booking agreements) an entirely new program every week, worked in Cagney's favor. It has been reported that he was at work on his next film, *Smart Money*, even before he had completed

Dark stars. Coming off his success in *Little Caesar* **Edward G. Robinson was paired with Cagney, coming off** *The Public Enemy,* **in** *Smart Money.* **The latter's was distinctly a supporting role, but it was the only time the screen's most famous gangsters ever appeared together. As** *The Racing Form* **attests, Robinson played a professional gangster. Cagney was his shrewd assistant.**

his last scenes in *The Public Enemy*. Even if that is an exaggeration, he surely went into *Smart Money*, in support of Edward G. Robinson, almost without pause.

This film would do more for Robinson's image than for Cagney's, since he would have the lead and since it was obviously designed to smooth the rough edges off the character he had exposed in *Little Caesar* and in *Five Star Final*, in which he played a too-tough newspaper editor, insisting on going after scandalous stories even if they were erroneous and victimized their subjects. Not that *Smart Money*, which was also written by Glasmon and Bright (as Cagney's next two pictures also would be), could be mistaken for a comedy of manners. Robinson plays Nick, a small town barber with a penchant for gambling, who comes to the big city looking for action and becomes notoriously successful with his wagering. Cagney plays his tough friend, Jack, a sort of valet-enforcer who is more cynical, less trusting than his boss. It is he who suspects that the woman Nick rescues from suicide may be a police informer who has chosen this method of establishing a relationship with him. His suspicions prove correct. At the climax Jack slugs the girl. Nick slugs him. Jack dies as a result. Nick goes to jail, insouciantly wagering that his manslaughter rap will not result in more than a five-to-ten stretch.

That natural graciousness, verging on the courtly, that marked Robinson's mature style begins to emerge here. No more than Cagney was he merely a hard guy. And he was perhaps quicker to shed that image than Cagney. In this film the latter was perhaps more cat-like than he had been. He seems to lurk in the shadows of the movie, leaping forth to grab a scene or two in a picture that lacked the usual Warner Brothers snap, crackle and pop, perhaps because no-one could seem to decide whether the film should be a flat-out melodrama or whether it should aim for a different set of values. One could imagine it, perhaps, played for a certain wistful, even romantic quality –

but at another studio, where snarls and sharp blows were less highly prized. Still, stolid as the picture was under the direction of Alfred E. Green, a man who made over 100 films in a career that stretched from 1917 to 1954, not one of which was distinguished, it did no harm to either of its principals and it made money for the studio because it featured its two hottest stars and the public came anticipating fireworks. It was also a turning point for Cagney: except for some short (but strong) roles in his late years, he would never again appear on the screen in anything but a leading role.

If however, that was the good news, the bad news was that for the next four years, when he was to make nineteen movies – one third of his filmography – his leading roles would almost all be in pictures very like the one he was now told to turn to immediately, which was called *Blonde Crazy*. Not that it was bad, not that all, or even most, of the pictures Cagney would do in this period were. On the contrary, a case can be made that, taken as a group, they represent perhaps the most interesting and – surely – entertaining work of his career. But, from his point of view, they were degrading. They were made too fast, they often did not draw on the best production talent, or the best supporting casts, available at the studio. They were not B pictures; they were intended for the top of the bill. But they were, for the most part, routine programmers, nothing the studio staked any prestige upon or promoted as anything special. And that clearly annoyed Cagney.

Blonde Crazy, in which he co-starred with Blondell under the direction of Roy Del Ruth, was neither the best nor the worst of these films. In it Cagney played a cheerfully larcenous bellhop working various petty swindles with Blondell as his chambermaid partner. Forced to flee, they extend their operations on a cross-country spree of schemes and scams. It is all a little too tough-talking and tough-minded to be thought of as a screwball comedy, but it has a lot of fizz. Most important, it began the process of establishing Cagney's

character as durably lovable. Most of the money-making schemes he imagines in the course of this plot are immediately apprehendable by the audience as foredoomed, and because we are one step ahead of him most of the time it becomes easy to feel a little sorry for him. He's so eager, so chipper, and (despite his manner) so incapable of thinking more than one move ahead. On those occasions when he actually pulls off one of his cons it is always against a mark so easy that the audience feels superior to the victim, thus not particularly sympathetic to him. One feels, looking at this picture today, and being aware of what was immediately in store for Cagney, that one is watching a performer take his first steps along a tightrope that would stretch from here to the end of the decade – and possibly to the end of his career. Heaven knows, the public quickly learned to like him as a comical con man and unconsciously they were pleased to have before them, at last, what Lincoln Kirstein presciently noted Cagney to be in this very year, 'the first definitely metropolitan figure to become national'. But that was not enough. They wanted more. They wanted to see him lash out at someone. And in the psychopathic manner. That is to say, his public got a thrill out of it when, having failed to wheedle or bamboozle something out of someone, he would suddenly strike out – hard and fast and with that karate-like precision that he so marvelously deployed. Maybe they did not want a movieful of this stuff (he would not do anything quite comparable to *The Public Enemy* until the quite differently toned *White Heat* of 1949), but they did want to be reminded that his screen character's temper had a hair-trigger, that there was in it an element of anarchy or, less fancily, plain nuttiness. Thus in *Blonde Crazy* there is a scene where he enters a pawn shop all false innocence, asking to see some revolvers. He keeps asking to handle larger and larger weapons until he is holding the biggest one in the store. Then he asks for some bullets to see how to load the thing. Then he says 'stick 'em up'.

Whereupon the man behind the counter laughs at this little joke. Whereupon Cagney slaps him silly and walks out with his gun.

It is a great little scene. It gets its laughs precisely because we know – or hope we know – what's coming. We delight both in our anticipation of the pay-off and in the pay-off itself. But the scene is also wildly out of keeping with the light mood of the film and with Cagney's character as he has previously been established. And the scene is both curious and memorable because it betokens no change in that character. He will walk away from this flash of brutality seemingly unaffected by it, putting it out of mind the moment it is over. And there will be a scene like it in almost every film thereafter, some small reminder of what he has been and perhaps what he might become again. These moments are weird, almost surreal. But if, in conventional dramatic terms, they are inappropriate, they are also a vital element in the formula for Cagney's success.

Their recurrence in so many Cagney films provides another clue to the actor's latter-day ambiguities and silences about his career, for they are something he would prefer to forget or deny, impositions by the studio in some instances, improvisations made in haste in order to improve a flagging scene in others. But in either case they represent compromises of his integrity as an actor and as a moral man who despised the glamorization of the criminal and the brutality.

Assuredly, he was right. These scenes do form a link between his character and the mostly repressed, but omnipresent, American fascination with the anarchical and the psychopathic, a link that was becoming more and more visible elsewhere in popular culture beginning with the pulp detective magazines of the 1920s, continuing through the hard boiled detective novels of the 1930s and surfacing more insistently in the post-war *films noirs* and paperback originals. While we are about it, we

In *Blonde Crazy* Cagney played a larcenous bellhop ever on the alert for scam, con or hustle. He was actually crazier about money than he was for the blonde, who was played by Joan Blondell.

might also remind ourselves that, like Cagney, most of us like to pretend that we are superior to this stuff, that only truck drivers and professors of American studies take it seriously. In other words, our middle-class denials of the junk pleasures match Cagney's refusals to acknowledge what he was up to in these years. We conspire in the fiction that he was just Jimmy, just our Yankee Doodle Boy all along. In so doing, of course, we trivialize him, and ignore the most forceful and memorable aspects of his instinctive artistry.

Caught up as he was in the scuffle and distraction of building his career, he has a better excuse for this lack of self-consciousness than we did, watching objectively in the shadows. For example – the first of several – *The Public Enemy* was in the theater by the time his work on *Blonde Crazy* was complete. At which point Cagney perceived a certain disparity between his salary and what the profits were on the earlier film. Indeed, at some juncture he had

taken a cut in pay, from $500 a week to $450 a week, receiving in return longer term options. Now, not illogically, he sought to redress this grievance. The studio, which knew a bargain when it saw one, was not entirely receptive to his pleas. And so he went on suspension, telling Jack Warner he would not return until he received a salary commensurate with his new worth. It was unprecedented – a hold-out by an actor with so few pictures to his credit, and with fewer still that he had carried. Nor did he loll about Los Angeles, waiting for the phone to ring. He returned to New York and waited the studio out for several months before it capitulated. When it did it was announced that henceforth he would be receiving $1,000 a week, less than he had asked for, but with a written promise of periodic reviews of that figure. That was good enough for Cagney, who saw his personal new deal not as a surrender but as a truce in the long war of attrition he was now fighting with his bosses.

FACTORY WORK

4

'WHAT IT AMOUNTED TO, REALLY, WAS DOING factory work, and . . . we just did it . . . . We worked all the time, six days a week, sometimes seven . . . . See, the misapprehension people labor under is that they think they were all great, well written, whatever. Not so. They were cuff operas, that's all. And as these holes appeared, or seemed to appear, we would adjust and do something else.'

Thus Cagney on working conditions, and working methods, at Warner Brothers as he had found them when he first arrived at the studio and as he rediscovered them, entirely unchanged of course, when he returned from his first brief suspension in 1932. He was no less alienated from them now that he was a presumptive star than he had been as a starlet. But he recognized, naturally, that there was nothing he could do to change the overall functioning of the system. In particular he realized that there was nothing he could do to change his type or the type of films in which he was asked to display himself. The machines in this factory were set to run at too fast a pace for that; you would have to shut them down entirely and retool, in the process depriving the theater chains of their weekly change of bill, the studio of its cash flow. Particularly at this moment, when all the studios were beginning to feel the pinch of the Depression (somewhat later than the rest of the economy, the novelty of sound and the inexpensiveness of the escape movie offered having carried them unscathed through its first years), that was simply not going to happen. What he could do, what he did do at the cost of much work and anxiety to himself, was to humanize and particularize the basic character he was required to play. There is scarcely a picture he made in these years that does not bear the mark of his inventions – lines of dialogue or whole scenes that were worked up on the set with fellow actors or with the kind of *laissez faire* directors he preferred to work with, unpretentious craftsmen like Lloyd Bacon (nine films), Roy Del Ruth (four) and a little later, the more gifted Raoul

Walsh. These people encouraged him to 'adjust' his scenes by inventing bits of business or adding details of costume and makeup that would fill 'the holes' as they were observed looming before him.

These activities were entirely natural to him. He probably would have undertaken them if he had been completely happy with every aspect of his working conditions. He was a busy actor. That was his nature. He once told his brother Bill, when he attempted his short-lived acting career: 'Never settle back on your heels, never relax. If you relax, the audience relaxes.' He said to me: 'That's the essential – to understand what the requirements of the part are and then go at it with everything you have.' The only way he knew how to do that was physically, working from the outside in, through movement and mimicry and makeup.

But there was more to it than that. There was his understanding of himself, and of his new position at the top of credits, to consider. He might be, for the moment, a valuable property to the studio, but he could see that its leaders were careless and profligate with even their greatest treasures. They would use them up thoughtlessly in order to keep the machine humming along profitably. Or to put it another way, only he could defend his long-term interests, because only he had any concern for the condition in which he might find himself in a few years.

Among the most illuminating things he said to me in the course of our talks was something he remembered saying to John Travolta, then a hot young star who had admired Cagney since he was a child watching old movies on television. He had sought Cagney out to express his admiration and he had been favored by this advice: 'I said, start with one thing – that they need you. Without you, they have an empty screen. So when you get on there, just do what you think is right and stay with it . . . . If you listen to all the clowns around, you're just dead. Go do what you have to do.' Speaking these lines, all vagueness, all benignity suddenly dropped away. The jaw jutted out, the eyes glittered, the voice was that of the young Cagney – harsh and precise in its enunciation. For just an instant one caught a glimpse of what Jack Warner and the rest of his bosses had to deal with when he was a bouncing boyo. Oh, no, there was nothing modest about this workman, nothing about him that was grateful to his employers for his big chance.

Of course, he was lucky in his timing. He was, literally, a little man, compensating for smallness of stature by largeness of spirit, and in the depths of the Depression people welcomed that. He did not directly confront the system, but he was seen in the majority of his first films standing outside it, playing various shady, nervy games by his own rules, not someone else's, and that, too, appealed to a nation that had too complacently accepted the assurances of its leaders that everything would come to those who behaved themselves. Above all, he created an impression, when the plot got him into trouble, that he was gripped not by irredeemable evil but by irrepressible high spirits, and that was a tonic in a time when it was all too easy to be gripped by hopeless low spirits. Three decades ago Kenneth Tynan captured much of his essence in one of his characteristically graceful sentences when he wrote, 'Cagney, even with sub-machine gun hot in hand and corpses piling at his ankles, can still persuade many people that it was not his fault'.

But this was hard work, harder work than the public could see. For the majority of the scripts he was handed in this period, if played literally, without the transforming charms he brought to them, would have been rather unpleasant tales of mean and driven spirits, human marginalia, whose tales, in other hands, might have been grim and cautionary instead of infectious and exemplary.

Another way of putting this is to say that whatever the ostensible subject of a movie was, Cagney, with his subtle tuggings and patting and twistings of the basic material, made

certain that its true subject was his personality. Few stars have ever worked at it as consciously and determinedly as he did. And few have done it as effectively, so that in a strange way the many little films of the 1932–35 period tend to merge in one's mind, no matter who directed or wrote them, becoming one large epic of personality, requiring of the viewer a real effort to recall which great bit, which memorable line, belongs to this film, which to that.

Still, it was exhausting, frustrating, and ultimately alienating work. He might be implicitly encouraged by his generally pliable directors, he might draw sustenance from the acting pals he worked with on picture after picture, permitting him to function as a sort of gang leader, but in the end his position was always adversarial. The studio never seemed to see what he was trying to do, never seemed to offer him material he did not have to fight. He was always the touch-up artist, never the designer, never even the chief engineer once construction

began. One can see why, looking back, his remembrances are touched by weariness, cynicism, the defensiveness of his 'just a job' line.

But he started out with a will. Returning from his holdout, he knew he had at least a little clout at last, that he could, with relative impunity, rewrite a scene on his or somebody else's cuff. It was not an opportunity he was slow or diffident to use. In fact, his first movie after his return, *Taxi*, contains, besides the tag line that – inevitably misquoted – launched a thousand nightclub impressions of him, two notable autobiographical contributions by the star. Essentially another Warner Brothers working stiff story, about cabbies organizing to protect themselves from a mob-controlled fleet that threatens their independence, its first major scene has Cagney picking up a fare who is an old-world Jew, dressed in black and capable of speaking only Yiddish. Cagney surprises his customer, and the audience naturally, by speaking Yiddish himself. An Irish cop, watching this exchange, glances at the cabby's hack license, and comments: 'Nolan, eh! What part of Ireland are you from?' Big grin, and this response, suitably accented: 'Delancy Street, tank you'. It was very endearing, and authentic, since, as a boy, 'Just for fun I picked up Yiddish as I went along, cause all the boys in the class were Jewish.' He added characteristically, 'No strain, no stress. It was easy'.

Taxi also provided Cagney with his first opportunity to dance on screen, with him and his co-star, Loretta Young, cutting a fine figure in a dance contest. Their chief rivals turn out to be a couple whose male member was George Raft, just months away from establishing himself with his role as the coin-flipping thug in *Scarface*. Proving its devotion to realism, the script had the Cagney-Young team, despite their status as leading players, lose to Raft and his partner.

An even better creative decision was to have Cagney play off his reputation as a belter of women. Loretta Young is not quite the passive little creature most of his leading ladies were in this era. She could take and hold screen against him, so theirs is a fighting love story. In their first scene Cagney comes on fresh with her, and she comes back feisty, 'For two cents I'd knock the ears off ya,' he snaps. 'For less than that I'd slap your face.' 'Go ahead, I'll give ya first punch.' And, to everyone's surprise, slender, lady-like Loretta Young takes him up on the offer – pow. Needless to say, it's love at first blow. It also sets up an opportunity for Cagney to delve into his autobiography for material again. For, at the end of the picture, when she is bringing him down a peg or two – good naturedly by this time – he cocks a fist at her and says, 'Why, if I thought you meant it'. This was an habitual phrase and gesture of his father's when one of the kids sassed him.

In the end, though, it was not a line that Cagney wrote that gives *Taxi* its place in dialogic history. This movie, for all its low-life comedy and bantering romance, is rather more sober than the average of Cagney's early star vehicles. It may not have been *Waiting for Lefty*, but it took the issue of the corruption and ordinary people organizing to fight against it seriously. It has a dark middle passage wherein the younger brother of Matt Nolan, Cagney's character, is killed by a drunken soldier in the gangland army and Matt runs quite mad in his need for revenge. The murderer finally barricades himself in the bedroom of the apartment, and it is through its locked door that Cagney screams what would become the tag line for his entire career at the justifiably cowering killer. His exact words are: 'Come out and take it you dirty yellow-bellied rat, or I'll give it to you through the door.' Mostly the impressionists have rendered that line, 'Come on out, you dirty rat', making it the most familiar misquotation of a movie line this side of the never-quite-said, 'Play it again, Sam'.

What almost no-one, impressionists or anyone else, remembers is the tone of the scene, which is total hysteria, or the lines Cagney screams at Young when she prevents him from shooting by placing herself between his gun and the door through which he is aiming it. 'Get away from me,' he cries. 'Get away from me. I can still give it to you, too. Get away from that door.' We are a long way from affectionate banter at this moment, a long way from comically stated romance or even socially-conscious melodrama. We are again in the dark land of temporary insanity, or worse. And this sequence is much longer than that little outburst in the *Blonde Crazy* pawnshop. In fact, the movie never recovers its former equilibrium afterward. Everyone, not just Cagney, this time, must appear affectless in its aftermath. Young's character is required to treat this outburst as just one more eccentricity, one more rough spot in need of a good woman's reformist touch.

Of course, hers was but a variant on what was, and would remain for many years, a highly conventionalized female role in movies, that of the tamer of the wild man-child. There was a crude shrewdness in placing this type in juxtaposition with Cagney. It had always worked before, hadn't it? Yes. It had. But Cagney's wildness was of a new and quite demented kind. It did not express itself as, say, that of the western hero's had, in a shy preference for open spaces and far horizons. Nor could it be likened to that of the conventional movie womanizer who, in his secret heart, wishes to be lured to a cottage small by a waterfall. To quote Kirstein again, 'no one expresses more clearly in terms of pictorial action, the delights of violence . . . the tendency toward destruction, toward anarchy, which is the base of American sex appeal'. Or anyway, of American sex appeal as Cagney and the rest of the new breed of talking picture leading men were redefining it.

In other words, *Taxi* applies a traditional solvent to the male's hard case without quite acknowledging that the shell on which it is being dripped is made of a new alloy, a metallurgical miracle as it were, impervious to old-fashioned chemistry. It remains impossible, in fact, to recall any film, before or since, in which the leading man, no matter what the provocation, actually threatened the life of a woman who was not visibly a *femme fatale* and then, a few minutes later, found himself marrying her within the chucklesome conventions of romantic comedy. It is simply too preposterous. It requires of the audience both emotional amnesia and a blind faith in the come-right-at-all-costs conventions of traditional movie construction that passeth all understanding. All one can say for this business is that it betokens a conscious awareness by the producers that Cagney's singularity, which was of course the source of his commercial strength, was also a potential source of trouble. 'We're working on it', *Taxi* seemed to say. And a public, still excited about their latest discovery, seemed to reply, 'Take your time, we're having fun'.

And they were. Beyond the fact that overall *Taxi* played as an entertaining and well-meant little picture, rather good in its willingness to find drama in ordinary urban lives, frequently rather clever in its naturalistic blend of melodrama, comedy and romance, it suggested a truism, which is that in the city our emotional weather changes rather more quickly and violently than it does in the country, and that must have been a boon to those at Warner Brothers charged with developing properties for their new star. They could see that in the context of fast-changing, ever-changing city life it was possible to slip the Cagney character back and forth across the line dividing right from wrong with no loss of his appeal. In short, he did not have to dwell forever in darkness. In three pictures they had moved him from killer to con man to hero-with-flaw. And the public was, if anything, more fascinated than ever.

Emboldened, they would take him into what amounted to entirely new country, for both him and the studio, in his next film. This was *The Crowd Roars*, a story about race car drivers. Lack of sound, lack of the ability, that is, to place on film that element of auto racing which is one of its most characteristic aspects,

Before he could acknowledge the The Crowd's Roars (below) Cagney first had to learn to control his temper – Frank McHugh is the one preventing him from slugging Eric Linden – and to expiate his sins. Ann Dvorak is the actress providing the shoulder for him to cry upon.

had prevented Hollywood from exploiting America's fascination with a sport that had been growing from about the same time that its fascination with movies had been growing. Howard Hawks, the director, had been racing cars at the semi-professional level longer than he had been around the movie business, and, for him, the opportunity to make *The Crowd Roars* was a great one. It was, he would say to me years later, 'the first picture that I made where I did something that was fun for me'. Much of it shot on location, at little dirt tracks and major speedways, the film is wonderfully flavorsome in its gritty, oily evocations of life in the pits, in the drivers' hangouts, and, of course, on the track itself, behind the wheel. Hawks liked to talk about the several top drivers who drove for him in the movie, of how Augie Dusenberg, builder of the famous cars, invented a tow bar for him so he could release the car at will and thus stage crashes at high speed on cue. All in all, the race footage is terrific, and it still plays authentically today, after it has been duplicated many times, using much more sophisticated technology.

The story, too, is flavorsome, with Cagney as Joe Greer, a tough and cocky competitor, convinced that a man of his talents does not require love or even friendship to sustain him. Winning, he implies, will satisfy all his needs. He refuses to surrender his independence to elegant and sympathetic Ann Dvorak, and becomes outraged when his younger brother, an aspiring racer, falls in love (with a Joan Blondell character), distracting himself from his career. Then, in a race, Joe's ruthless need to win results in the death of one of his best friends (played by Frank McHugh, who he met for the first time on this picture and who would become one of Cagney's lifelong intimates). Greer quits driving but haunts the tracks, almost a derelict, too proud to admit his guilt, but unable to transcend it either – until, finally, Dvorak manages to break him down. This is a powerful scene, with Cagney sobbing wildly, clinging desperately to her, almost as if – dare

one say it – she was his mother. Emotionally purged, he is able to return to driving, but, of course, with a new spirit about him.

Hawks would later claim that the script had not called for Cagney to cry, but that he proposed it to the actor. 'I've seen plenty of men cry. When I get somebody who was good enough – I tried it with Dick Barthelmess in *Dawn Patrol* and he sounded like a cow mooing. So I said, "This isn't gonna work very well, you're not a good cryer". But Cagney was great . . . .' To interviewer Joseph McBride, the director was all admiration for his star's working methods. 'Jim Cagney worked with movement. He didn't work with lines. I don't ever remember him suggesting a line – it's the way he does a line . . . . Cagney had these funny little attitudes, you know, the way he held his hands and things like that. I tried to make the most of them . . . even though I didn't know how he worked.'

The result, in this case, was a movie that stands somewhat outside both the Cagney and the Hawks canon. The picture has a somewhat more leisurely, almost contemplative, pace than was customary with them, Hawks' male bonding theme was present but muted, and the process of civilizing the Cagney character seems more thorough-going than usual – a matter of morals rather than of mere manners. More important, there is a spaciousness to the movie, and of course spectacular elements in it, that are entirely missing from the studio-bound and less expensive films that dominate Cagney's filmography in this period. Above all, there are no violations of his character's inner logic requiring lengthy and desperate rationalization. His climactic breakdown here is well prepared and it is not, as it was in *Sinners' Holiday* or *Doorway to Hell*, an acknowledgement of weakness, but a signal of maturity.

Cagney seems to have recognized that this was an unusually strong picture, and he may well have regarded his next assignment, *Winner Take All*, as a reversion to the studio's old cheap ways with him. In any event, he could

Winner Take All. **And he certainly did – including beatings in and out of the ring (Guy Kibbee and Clarence Musel are with him in the barroom) and insults from society swells like Charles Coleman. Virginia Bruce is the lady offering a restraining hand.**

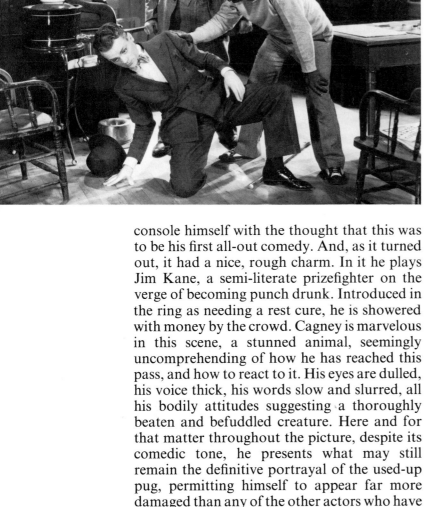

console himself with the thought that this was to be his first all-out comedy. And, as it turned out, it had a nice, rough charm. In it he plays Jim Kane, a semi-literate prizefighter on the verge of becoming punch drunk. Introduced in the ring as needing a rest cure, he is showered with money by the crowd. Cagney is marvelous in this scene, a stunned animal, seemingly uncomprehending of how he has reached this pass, and how to react to it. His eyes are dulled, his voice thick, his words slow and slurred, all his bodily attitudes suggesting a thoroughly beaten and befuddled creature. Here and for that matter throughout the picture, despite its comedic tone, he presents what may still remain the definitive portrayal of the used-up pug, permitting himself to appear far more damaged than any of the other actors who have essayed similar parts in films more consciously cautionary in their attitudes toward boxing. His boxing sequences are similarly persuasive. Kane's fighting spirit, Cagney wants us to

know, is not damaged. Whatever else has happened to him, he is all killer instinct on the job, a bouncing, wind-milling fighter, quick to scramble up when knocked down, eager for his opponents to recover from their knockdowns, so he can start mixing it up again.

Cagney remained proud of his ability to persuasively portray a boxer almost a half century later. One of the professional fighters who had been engaged to play an opponent was impressed not so much by his work with his fists (though Cagney had trained hard to give and take pulled punches authentically), but by his footwork. 'I said to him, don't be surprised, I'm a hoofer . . . a dancer . . . I did something with my feet . . . without even knowing I was doing it.'

It is the contrast between Jim Kane's physical competency and his mental fogginess – all he has going for him in this department are instincts of another kind, decent instincts – that makes him a poignant figure. Once again the sheer courage of Cagney, his willingness to try anything in order to stamp his characters with both singularity and humanity, astonishes.

Without his presence *Winner Take All* would have been the most routine kind of prize fight drama with its protagonist caught at the apex of the most familiar kind of triangle, between a good girl and a bad girl. The former appears when he has taken the money the crowd has thrown at him and repairs to a western dude ranch to rest and recuperate. Her name is Peggy (Marian Nixon) and she is down on her luck and has a young son to support. He helps her anonymously and, when she finds out about it, he shrugs off her gratitude, but not the affectionate support she offers him. When he returns to the East, and the ring, however, he is taken up by a society dame (Virginia Bruce) who represents false values as surely as Peggy represents honest ones. She and her effete friends treat Kane sometimes as an amusing peasant, sometimes as a kind of court jester. Or would if he would permit it.

Some of the film's best comedy arises out of his refusal to be patronized by them. For instance, at a white tie party one of the swells asks Jim what he thinks of Russia's latest five year plan, and he replies, 'Oh, I think anybody's a sucker to tie up with those installment terms. Five years is too long. I pay cash for everything.' Needless to say, everyone laughs at him. Needless to say, Honest Jim brings a haymaker up off the floor and punches out his questioner. Eventually, of course, Kane comes to his senses, deserts his false friends and returns to his true love. And wins the big fight at the end.

Taken together with *Taxi*, and with two or three subsequent films, *Winner Take All* helped establish Cagney not merely as a comic figure, but also as a democratic one – a spokesman, if you will, for aggressively unpretentious urban populism. And this picture, too, was a hit – perhaps from Cagney's point of view, too much of one. Like the equally modest *Taxi* it did somewhat better at the box office than the more expensive *The Crowd Roars*. The message was clear to the studio: the closer you kept Cagney to his native streets, and the lighter you kept his material, the more successful it seemed he would likely be. No need to go to a lot of expense and bother with him.

In line with that policy Cagney immediately began shooting something called *Blessed Event*, in which he was cast as a fast-talking, shifty-thinking newspaper gossip columnist, a Walter Winchell type. Sounds like his kind of stuff, doesn't it? But something went wrong, and Cagney walked out – with film in the can. That was a real challenge. It was one thing to go on suspension because you didn't like a

script or the way they treated you in the commissary. But to quit a picture after it was rolling, when money had been spent and other talent engaged – that was not done.

There is no record of what, specifically, Cagney objected to in the film. In his autobiography he records that around this time a producer asked him to read a script which turned out to be so bad that he inquired of the executive whether he, too, had read it. The man said he had and agreed with Cagney's judgment, but he reminded the actor that the picture was in profit before shooting began. It had already been sold to the theaters, probably on the basis of Cagney's name, for advances totalling around a million dollars. Also at this time, according to Cagney, a theater owner told him that under the block booking system – later declared illegal by the courts – he was forced to take five indifferent pictures in order to obtain a Cagney title. The evidence that he was worth far more than his new contract paid him was accumulating. It may well have been that he was the single most valuable asset the studio had, even though other players, among them Dick Powell, Ruth Chatterton, Edward G. Robinson and Douglas Fairbanks, Jr., none of them any more potent than he was at the box office, were receiving $4,000 to $6,000 a week, while he had worked his way up to only $1600 a week.

Ironically, *Blessed Event* was completed with Lee Tracy in Cagney's role – the same Lee Tracy, of course, whom Cagney had once understudied and who took his job in the London company of *Broadway* away from him, the same Lee Tracy whose Hollywood career would mostly be passed as a sort of second-string Cagney (he could talk twice as fast, but he was only half as charming). And it is reportedly an entertaining and interesting movie – probably something like *Taxi* or *Winner Take All* in brash spirits and quick-step pace. But at this point, Cagney didn't care if it was a masterpiece of world cinema. He told the press he would be glad to make three pic-

80

An actor's life. At a 1934 film star frolic (below) Jimmy Durante was on Cagney's right. To his left were Eddie Cantor, Ann Harding, Adolphe Menjou and Robert Woolsey. At right he casts a dubious eye on the boss, Jack L. Warner. Cagney's mood appears to have been sunnier when Frank Capra and Darryl Zanuck joined them for lunch.

tures for Warner Brothers for nothing if, thereafter, they would release him from his contract. He also told them that he might soon re-enter Columbia to study medicine, it being a tribute to his acting that he made people believe that one. What gave him credibility where it counted, in the eyes of Jack Warner and his staff, were the lengths to which he would go to make his point stick – six months to be specific, six months once again back on his native New York ground.

Finally, they were persuaded he meant what he said. And the Academy of Motion Picture Arts and Sciences, which in pre-union days frequently acted as a Hollywood labor arbitrator, appointed Frank Capra to referee his case. The director eventually settled it by proposing a new contract calling for a $4,000 weekly salary for Cagney, which at least placed him at the lower level of the studio's upper echelon of contract players. The deal also specified that he would not be required to work in more than

four films annually.

For three years they worked him to that limit and – to their ultimate sorrow – beyond it. There appears to be, in retrospect, a pattern to Cagney's work in this period, though perhaps it was not consciously apparent to him or to his bosses at the time. He would do two of three pictures that appeared to him distressingly routine and then, as a reward, or as a response to his restlessness and ambition, he would be given something a little different, something with more production values or with a more consciously 'significant' theme. After which he would return to the programmers for a while.

It is curious, however, that, again in retrospect, the little pictures are generally more appealing that the big ones. This is true of not just Cagney's work, or of Warner Brothers', but of most American studio releases of the 1930s and 1940s. Film makers tended to choke when they addressed major topics or tried to convince middlebrow critics that the humble

movies were capable of being an art form. Because these films required larger than usual cash outlays the moguls generally assigned them to cautious directors and to hover anxiously over both scripts and dailies, in the process managing to congeal them with self-consciousness and self-importance. By contrast, the program pictures, relying heavily on generic conventions and type casting for their appeal, and as we have seen often profitably pre-sold on that basis, rarely occasioned much anxiety in the front office. This is not to say that all or even most of these pictures have stood the test of time brilliantly. Yet many of them retain their capacity to delight in a way that the Oscar nominees do not. And it is astonishing how many of the directors we now think of as the best of this period – Hawks and Walsh and Ernst Lubitsch, John Ford, Fritz Lang and (a little later) Preston Sturges – worked in this less grand, but generally more glorious, level of the business, ringing their subtle changes on convention, indulging their lively, often lunatic sense of pace, creating those stylizations by which now, after the fact, we recognize not so much a vision of life but of the movieness of movies. Cagney was actually the beneficiary of this attitude toward the less significant movies in which he starred. The 'fixing up' he insisted on and the fierce energy he brought to this task – the product of intense and conscious thought if we are to believe witnesses like Pat O'Brien – would not have been tolerated if his pictures had seemed more artistically consequential to the studio.

It is too bad Cagney could not see this at the time or, for that matter, recognize it later, when passions had cooled. But he was very much a man of his time and most people who thought of themselves as serious-minded, devoted to the traditional values of the theater and literature, not to mention the view that the world was a seriously troubled place in which no institution as powerful as the movies should devote itself exclusively to 'escapism', had trouble avoiding a certain feeling of contempt for Hollywood, contempt for themselves if they were involved with its works.

Cagney was himself of a leftist persuasion in these days – was even occasionally accused by the loopy right of being a Communist, and the attitude of the executives around the place did nothing to persuade him that his politics were misguided. In 1933, he was one of the several stars who began the process of organizing what was to become the Screen Actors' Guild, in the process forging his lifelong friendship with Robert Montgomery, the Guild's first president. Ultimately, he would follow him and such later Guild stalwarts as Ronald Reagan rightward, in part because of their disgust with Communist tactics in union matters. But perhaps more telling about his mood of the moment than his political activities is a curious little piece of film, a promotional short subject in the 'Intimate Interviews' series. These featured a starlet-type pretending to be a girl reporter who penetrated the stars' lairs to give the fans a glimpse of how they lived and their 'intimate' views on various weighty matters.

In Cagney's instance, he is discovered in his backyard, in shorts and sweatshirt, working out. He does not look happy to see his questioner, and throughout he speaks in toneless monosyllables, his eyes dead, his face expressionless. If anything guarantees the truthfulness of his statement that he could only overcome his natural shyness by hiding in a role, this film is it. Glumly he complains about being 'fixed in the public's mind' as an underworld character. Not very confidently he suggests that he will try to do fewer of these figures in the future. Modestly he proposes an ambition to return to the stage. 'I'm a ham at heart,'

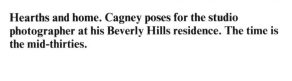

he says in his least hammy manner. 'I like to feel the boards under my feet, to have contact with the audience.' So far what we have here is your standard serious actor interview, a self-portrait of the star who is not to be understood too quickly as a mere entertainer.

But among the amenities of his backyard is a little putting green, which one suspects may have been hastily installed as a prop for this film, so unkempt is it. Anyway, the conversation turns to the subject of his having reached the top, or close to it. Does that satisfy him? If not, what further ambitions might he have? He rejects the notion that he has arrived in a rather surly fashion. 'Where's the top?' he asks wearily. It appears to him to offer little more than the opportunity to 'just keep on working indefinitely' – a prospect he views ambiguously at best. As to further ambitions, he has only one – 'to put this little ball into that little hole'. It is that on which he has been working all day until the reporter interrupted him. For the camera he makes a couple more attempts to hole out – unsuccessfully. Whereupon his interlocutor picks up his putter and smoothly strokes the ball into the hole, for a cute ending. If they had played this scene in one of his movies, one imagines the script calling for him to punch her after she sinks her putt. In fact, he permits himself only a look of sour surprise.

We are a long way from the bounding energy Cagney was mobilizing in the movies of this time. We are very close to the depressed evasiveness of his later interviews. We are yet closer to that instinctive existentialism that informed his screen character, not to mention the weary sadness that marked his scenes on the skids in *The Crowd Roars*, and which would come more and more to the fore in pictures lying just ahead. And that says nothing about the persuasive manner in which his screen character often accepted, almost seemed to welcome, the way grim chance sometimes worked against him.

The antidote to depression is activity, and one cannot help but think that the pace of his

83

His co-star in *Hard to Handle* was Mary Bryan, who did duty in one scene as a marathon dancer. The picture sparkled most brightly, however, when Ruth Donnelley, playing her mother, joined them.

work, the ferocious concentration it required of him, the opportunities it afforded him to discharge physical energies that might otherwise have been turned inward, were good for him. The infectious joy of his comic portrayals in this period may well stem from a need to bury the brooding side of himself in work of a highly kinesthetic kind.

That was never more true than in his first two pictures after his return to work in 1933 – *Hard to Handle* and *Picture Snatcher*. The former is, in fact, one of his best comedies, about the cynical adventures of one Lefty Merrill, who is discovered promoting a marathon dance contest, for which he cannot pay the prize money because his partner has skipped with it. This puts asunder his romance with the female winner of the contest (Mary Brian) and her mother, played with her patented sweet acerbity by the gifted Ruth Chatterton. He pursues them to New York and into adventures in the reducing cream trade. He has one of the funniest sequences he ever did persuading a rich society matron to endorse this preparation, earnestly enlisting her on the side of 'the tragic fat people of the world'. He finally scores – obvious reference to *The Public Enemy* here – as a promoter of the beneficial effects of grapefruit in the diet. Co-written (as was *Winner Take All*) by Wilson Mizner, sometime newsman, full time raconteur and beloved Hollywood character, directed with unassuming alacrity by Mervyn LeRoy, it was, possibly, the breeziest comedy Cagney ever did, unshadowed by social conscience, untroubled by ambiguous violence.

Picture Snatcher is a darker affair, and somewhat muddled in intent. The title precisely states Cagney's occupation herein. It is among the most distasteful in journalism – sneaking pictures of the suddenly bereaved or embarrassed or threatened. One of Danny Kean's chores for the tabloid presided over by Ralph Bellamy, another actor who would become a lifelong crony, duplicates a famous stunt by a New York *Daily News* photographer who

'Cuff operas'. Alice White co-starred with Cagney in *Picture Snatcher*: Robert Armstrong, the immortal King Kong's captor, played a more minor role in *The Mayor of Hell*.

sneaked a mini-camera (strapped to his ankle) into the Sing Sing death chamber to capture the death throes of murderess Ruth Snyder. Later, Danny talks his way into the hideout of a pal who is a cop killer in order to take pictures of his last stand against raiding policemen. In short, Danny is anything but a savory figure. But, it is explained, as an ex-con, this job is the best he can hope for – and be glad to have it, fella. Once again, society can be blamed for his troubles; he is trying to go straight but the only available work bends him back toward the crooked path he would like to abandon. Meantime, he is gutty and funny as he pursues his nefarious activities – except when he's batting women around. Both his leading ladies in *Picture Snatcher*, Alice White and Patricia Ellis, feel the sting of his wrath.

The former, Cagney has recorded in his memoirs, forgot to duck one of his masterfully thrown near-miss punches, despite careful rehearsal by director Lloyd Bacon, and actually landed on the ground, seeing stars. The latter interrupts him at a pool game for some sober chat and receives a rather shockingly staged lesson in the virtues of silence. On the whole, the film has the bitterest tone of any Cagney had made since *The Public Enemy*, a cynical and anarchic air that was the glory of the newspaper yarns the movies liked to tell in this era.

On the whole, the cheerful amorality of something like *Picture Snatcher* is more appealing, and more honest, than something like *The Mayor of Hell*, which immediately followed it. In this Cagney plays Patsy Gargan, a small-time mobster who does small-time favors for a political machine, and is rewarded with a post at a boys' reformatory, the warden of which (Dudley Digges at his meanest) is both corrupt and a sadist. Patsy, however, falls in love with the institution's idealistic nurse

85

Chorines: they adorned the lobby cards, they surrounded the star for publicity purposes. But it was sweet Ruby Keeler (opposite) who shared *Footlight Parade*'s most memorable moments with Cagney.

(Madge Evans), who dreams of turning the place into a sort of Boys' Town with walls, the inmates governing themselves in democratic fashion. The fundamental goodness of bad boys being one of the 1930s' prime articles of faith, this concept appeals mightily both to Patsy and the audience. And all goes smoothly until Patsy must take it on the lam for a former crime. The bad superintendent returns, a youth dies as a result of one of his draconian punishments and the kids riot, causing the death of their oppressor when, attempting to escape them, he tumbles on to an electrified fence and is electrocuted in a good, grizzly, morally satisfying scene. His troubles with the law solved as if by magic, Cagney is last seen embracing the nurse while some of the boys sneak a peak at their love-making through a window. He catches, them, whistles warningly (but cheerfully) at them through his teeth and makes a cut sign with his hands while giving them a big brotherly wink. Once again a light jollity too soon replaces scenes of stark violence. The desire of the studio to have it both ways at the same time – to grab the masculine audience's attention with brutal action while not neglecting the ladies, God bless 'em, and their need for light romance – was truly astonishing. And, it would seem, insatiable.

If *The Mayor of Hell* was arguably the weakest picture of this period, Cagney was quick to claim his reward. *Footlight Parade* is one of his best. An expensive (by Warner Brothers standards) musical, with its dance sequences staged by the great Busby Berkeley, with the likes of Blondell, Dick Powell and heavy-footed but agreeable Ruby Keeler co-starred, it presents Cagney for the first time in an utterly unambiguous light, as a totally above-board producer-director of Roxy-like stage shows to accompany first-run movies in lavish theaters. He has three such extravaganzas in rehearsal, two women in love with him, an ex-wife clamoring for increased alimony, a partner about to abscond with their funds and, at the film's climax, a lead dancer

who turns up drunk, forcing Cagney to replace him in the production number which brings the picture to a smashing climax. He is manifestly too busy for criminal activity, or to knock a dame around. His only sin is workaholism, which any American can understand and forgive. Writer Patrick McGilligan has advanced the amusing argument that, in 1933, Cagney's character, Chester Kent, symbolized the newly elected president, Franklin D. Roosevelt, also an energetic man attempting to solve a multiplicity of crises simultaneously. It's a nice thought and some credence is lent it by the film's concluding images when Cagney is leading a chorus of sailors on to a ship. At a certain point they pause for one last full-throated chorus of 'Shanghai Lil', the camera goes to an overhead shot, and they display cards that first form the famous symbol of the National Recovery Act, a sternly stylized eagle, then flip the cards to create a portrait of FDR. It's lovely stuff, but not, perhaps, as lovely as what preceded it, a tap routine of Cagney's and Keeler's, with the former dominant, and at his best.

It was the first time he had a chance to display in movies his singular dancing manner and every time one looks at it again one has to wonder why the studio did not put him in more musicals. Cagney has always said he would have been willing. 'The inclination was that I was a hoofer, born with it,' he would say to me forty-eight years later. 'When we touched on that in a picture, I stayed with it.' By that he meant that he willingly spent arduous weeks in rehearsal and, more remarkable for him, was willing also to look at the dailies, something he claimed he never did when he was working on straight dramatic sequences.

His work in *Footlight Parade* was well worth studying. His style was generically known as 'eccentric', and sometimes referred to as 'legomania'. It involved very little movement from the waist up and, as a rule, his arms were loose at his sides, perhaps outflung very occasionally for emphasis. Poised on his toes, which had the effect of canting his body eagerly forward, he kept his legs quite stiff, except when he did one of his loose-kneed high kicks. In effect, his style focused all our attention on his feet, tapping out their dizzying combinations. There was nothing elegant about Cagney's dancing, nothing like the entrancing total line that Fred Astaire achieved with the flow of his body, the flow of his choreography. This was hoofing, 'laying down iron' as it used to be called in Britain. But proud of it. No dancer has more delightfully asserted the glories of the pure vernacular tradition of tap or more seductively invited us to partake of his pleasure in it. It had something to do with the attitude of his body: there was just something jaunty and endearing in the way Cagney held himself when he was dancing. It had something to do with his attitude of mind as well: Cagney sometimes seemed to regard the sublime flash and chatter of his taps with a sort of bemused objectivity, almost as if they had a life of their own for which, since this gift of his was inborn, he could claim no special credit, yet in which he could find enormous pleasure, a pleasure akin to our own, since he was, like us, an innocent witness to something wonderful.

Looking back, *Footlight Parade* seems a significant moment in Cagney's career. For if *The Public Enemy* starkly set forth the darkest side of his screen character, then this picture offered an entirely unclouded view of his nature's

Rising star. In *Lady-Killer*, Cagney played Dan Quigley, a crook on the lam who gets discovered by movie talent scouts. In the films within the film he played an Indian chief, an 18th Century dandy and a convict. In the end he and Mae Clark got to play a sweeter scene than their famous breakfast table squabble in *The Public Enemy*.

sunny side, bravely banishing from the proceedings all references to that mean and crazy guy, Tom Powers. By chance, this was the first Cagney film the great critic, Otis Ferguson, ever saw, and having no knowledge of what had gone before caught unblemished his vitality and that easy conspiracy of his with the camera that puts him in the company of the few who seem born for pictures. What he glimpsed here, in its purest incarnation so far, was that characterological subtext that was the true source of Cagney's appeal. He wrote: 'this half-pint of the East Side Irish somehow managed to be a lot of what a typical American might be, nobody's fool and nobody's clever ape, quick and cocky but not too wise for his own goodness, frankly vulgar in the best sense, with the dignity of the genuine worn as easily as his skin'.

One would like to think that the scales fell from the executives' eyes when they saw the first answer print of *Footlight Parade*, that they told Cagney he could unclench his fist and hang his gat above the mantlepiece because he wouldn't be needing it any more. Who knows? They might have done just that had there ever been any time to stop, take stock and think. But time was precisely what no one around the studios ever had in those days. Before *Footlight Parade* went into release Cagney was at work in another quickie.

Lady Killer was one of the better ones, with Cagney as Dan Quigley, a minor hood forced to flee New York for Los Angeles where he lands up on the skids. A couple of talent scouts looking for 'types, new faces, tough guys for a gangster picture' spot him and offer him a job. 'Who are you trying to rib?' he replies. 'Do you want it or don't you?' 'What's in it for me?' 'Three bucks a day and a box lunch.' 'I'm on,' says Cagney.

There follows a nice sequence, montage-like in its pacing, showing Quigley's rise from the ranks to stardom. He calls attention to himself in a prison rebellion scene where he's the only extra who knows how to throw an authentic looking punch, survives miscasting as an Indian chief (atop a mechanical horse in front of a process screen) and as an 18th-century fop. He enhances his standing by writing fake fan letters to himself, and he falls in love with a movie star. In the picture's funniest nasty scene, he corners a movie critic in a men's room and forces the wretch literally to eat some unkind words he has printed about Cagney's lady friend. He treats the scrivener like a bad boy, twisting his ear to force him to open his mouth, ordering him to swallow like a mother pushing spinach down junior's throat, checking to make sure he's swallowed the whole mouthful. Whereupon – and here the scene goes over the top – he shoves the writer into a stall, shoves his head into the toilet and flushes. His exit line is: 'Now if you write any more cracks about Lois Underwood I'll cut off your ears and mail them to your folks.' In the picture's nastiest nasty scene, Cagney once again gets tough with Mae Clarke – far tougher than he did in *The Public Enemy*. This time he drags her the length of a room by her hair and then tosses her out the door. The scene is played for laughs, but given its duration it is the one treat-em-rough scene in the Cagney canon in which bad sexual temper shades over into sadism. And once again one must pause to contemplate the lengths to which the studio would go to satisfy what may have been by this time an entirely imaginary public desire to see Cagney act tough.

Yet one's memory of the movie is an agreeable one for Quigley is ultimately offered the opportunity to redeem both his bad past and his bad manners when his former mob appears *en masse* in Hollywood with a plan to rob the movie stars' houses, which, of course, he foils. Before the picture has finished there is a lot of good-natured satire of Hollywood pretensions (most especially of a European director with misplaced passion for realism) and some good cautionary satire of the American dream of being discovered and becoming an overnight star.

90

Jimmy the Gent was perhaps a more seamless affair. In it he co-starred (the first of two times) with the studio's other leading rebel, Bette Davis, who was unhappy to be doing a low-brow quickie, but whose impatient air gave a crispness to the picture Cagney's other leading ladies rarely imported. This is the picture that is famous for a haircut. Cagney arrived for the first day's shooting with a bowl cut. That is to say, all the hair on the sides and back of his head had been shaved off, leaving only an upright stubble – almost a flat-top – on his scalp. It is safe to say that no one billed above the title of any picture ever made ever appeared with such a tonsure. The director, Michael Curtiz, was reportedly ready to abandon shooting until time had repaired this travesty, but Cagney insisted on it – one of his more daring inventions and a great sight gag. For it suits his Jimmy Corrigan, who is a terrible-tempered character, we understand to have no time for such niceties as a hair stylist.

In his rages Jimmy is always contriving to break the pebble-glass panel in his office door. In fact, much of the picture's suspense derives from waiting to see it shatter again and wondering how the gag will be accomplished. Corrigan's business is finding the lost heirs to fortunes and getting a percentage of the estate when he succeeds. He has a rival in this peculiar trade, a smooth-talking fellow named Wallington, whose upper-class accents are near to Anglified and who is expertly played by a nearly forgotten actor named Alan Dinehart. He not only makes off with Jimmy's clients, he has also made off with his assistant (Davis) who Jimmy loves in his rough way. There is a wonderful scene where Corrigan invades Wallington's office and is forced to take tea with them. It's all raised pinkies and genteel talk – 'I tell Joan putting sugar in this jasmine tea is a minor blasphemy.' 'Yeah, sure, that's what I think,' replies Cagney in the thickest, dumbest acent he has used since *Winner Take All*. 'A biscuit, Mr Corrigan,' the oily Wallington persists. Cagney takes it, eyes it dubiously, and mumbles, 'Didn't turn out so good, did it?'

What turns out swell (as Corrigan would doubtlessly have put it) is the story. Wallington, for all his airs, is a true shyster, while Cagney's roughneck democrat develops as we expect him to – relatively honest and totally lovable. Davis falls back in love with him and the picture ends with the promise implicit in the premise of all these early Cagney comedies – that she will have a lifetime to smooth him out. Along with *Hard to Handle* this is, quite possibly, the best of this breed, the one with the greatest unity of mood, the fewest improbabilities in Cagney's character to laugh our way past. Certainly it is the last of them.

He would not again appear in films of quite the same flavor. In the future his comedies would not tie him quite so tightly to the city's streets or to the city's scams. Once or twice they would be pure farces. Once or twice they would be exercises in nostalgia. But he would not ever be quite such a pure con artist with his beady eye fixed on the main, crooked chance. Rather he would be seen more romantically, as a rebel adventurer who must try to fit himself into the values of a complex and specific system, something like the military, for example, or else die trying. And he would be, on the whole, a sweeter character, far less muscular in his relations with women. In short, he would be universalized in the comedies to come, and they would be more leisurely paced, less nervous in manner. They would also be more infrequent in their appearance. The more characteristic Cagney film of the late 1930s would be a melodrama, often with tragic overtones.

This change in manner was not necessarily the result of nice aesthetic calculation. In some immeasurable measure it was imposed upon him by outside forces. Since 1930, responding largely to pressure from the Catholic Legion of Decency, the movies had been operating under a production code that, among many absurdities, insisted on the punishment of wrongdoing by the end of the final reel. No one

...e was Her Man – **Joan Blondell's, that is. But the picture**
...t that title was their last time together as co-stars. Below,
...me of the cast gathers on a fishing pier in Monterrey,
...ere they shot on location. Actress Sarah Padden is
...aring the checked apron, Cagney's most frequent
...ector, Lloyd Bacon – they did nine films together – is
the far right.

...ad paid it much heed, but in 1934, the movie
...dustry, no longer able to stay the moralists'
...amor, created a production code administra-
...on, which required the submission of scripts
...fore they were shot, finished films before they
...ere released, and its censors had the power
...o compel producers to bend to their absurdly
...iggling wills. That meant that a character like
...agney's could not claim reform and bounce
...untily away from his past transgressions at
...he end of his pictures. He would have to make
...enuine expiation. Had anyone been enforcing
...he code to its letter, every single one of his
...omedies to date would have had to conclude
...ith his character behind bars. What a
...owner! In the future, obviously, his crimes
...ould have to be crimes of heart, not crimes
...hat violated either the criminal code or the
...ovie code. That no harm came to Cagney as
... result of these new strictures may perhaps be
...id to a lucky coincidence; it was probably
...me to readjust his image somewhat anyway.

About that one cannot be entirely certain.
...'e may observe, however, that his next film,
...ade under the shadow of the impending
...oral dispensation, did offer a crude sketch of
...hat was to come and that it did not bode well
...or his future. In *He Was Her Man*, Cagney,
...earing a moustache for the first time on
...creen, played a safecracker named Flicker, on
...he run from a vengeful rival gang. Along his
...ay he meets Rosie, a sometime prostitute
...layed by Joan Blondell (this would be their
...st film together) who is unhappily en route
...o a mail order marriage. A brief, bright flame
...s kindled, but Flicker is killed by assassins and
...he must proceed alone toward her depressing
...estiny. There is some tough-tender, rue-laden
...alogue in the picture, but it has an enervated
...r about it, and it was Cagney's first distinct
...ox office failure since he had achieved
...ardom.

If its disappointing commercial performance
...enerated any anxiety around the studio, it was
...uickly dissipated by *Here Comes the Navy*,
...hich, unprecedented for a Cagney film, actu-

ally received an Academy Award nomination
for best picture, the year Frank Capra's *It Happened One Night* won the Oscar in all five major
categories. If the Cagney picture was not quite
as charming as Capra's, it can certainly stand
comparison with such other light-footed
nominees as *The Gay Divorcee* and *The Thin
Man*, and like them it remains infinitely more
watchable than such other contenders as

A perfect palship. Cagney and Pat O'Brien met in the theater in 1927, and eventually made nine movies together. They were part of the 'Irish Mafia', a group of actors including Spencer Tracy, Ralph Bellamy and Frank McHugh who, in the 'thirties and 'forties, met for dinner once a week when they were all in Hollywood. The first Cagney – O'Brien screen collaboration was 1934's *Here Comes the Navy* (right). Below left they are between takes of *The Irish In Us*. Both films were directed by ubiquitous Lloyd Bacon, shown with them on the *Irish* set (bottom left). In *The Fighting 69th* O'Brien was an army chaplain, Cagney a coward who learned bravery from him. Opposite, top left, Stu Irwin joins them in *Ceiling Zero*. *Boy Meets Girl* (middle left) was their funniest film and *Torrid Zone* (1940) was their last one together until *Ragtime*, four decades later. On its set they posed with Bessie Love (the reknowned silent screen actress) who also did a small role in the film.

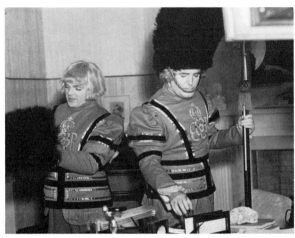

Here Comes the Navy was the most spacious movie Cagney had yet made, and its production values helped it win a 1934 Academy Award nomination as best picture. But it had plenty of comedy, which hammock-mate Frank McHugh (left) helped provide. *The St Louis Kid* (right) featured Allen Jenkins – on the floor – as Cagney's funny friend. The ladies are Edna Bennett and Patricia Ellis. *Devil Dogs of the Air* (opposite) in 1935 was essentially a remake of *Navy*. Here Cagney does a scene with Helen Lowell under the none-too-stern eye of director Bacon. His sympathetic co-star was Margaret Lindsay.

Cleopatra, Imitation of Life and *One Night* Love. Moreover, it has its historical signi cance for introducing Cagney to his perfect star, Pat O'Brien, with whom he would sha top billing in eight films not counting *Ragtin* in which O'Brien's role was distinctly min They were often, as Ferguson was to say, Fla and Quirt. But not always. Sometimes th were both Quirt. Sometimes they were fath and son, or perhaps one should say *a* fath (when O'Brien donned priest's vestments) a a wayward son. Once they were brothers. Pr ably the best way to generalize their screen re tionship – alas – is to resort to Freud terminology. O'Brien usually personified t superego, preaching duty and responsibili

Cagney usually personified the rampaging id, all for immediate gratification of his impulse toward egocentric adventure and the romantic gesture. But the main thing about their screen relationship was that O'Brien gave Cagney someone against whom he could test his mettle, as no woman ever could. O'Brien could talk as fast as Cagney and he could trade punches with him, too. Best of all, his bulk and his dead pan contrasted effectively with Cagney's size and animation. Those poor pallid girls could now be relegated to properly secondary roles. Finally, this rebalancing of forces generally permitted Cagney to introduce a little more psychological subtext in his roles. One might regret the passing of the heedless hoodlum sprite, that Caliban of the concrete jungle, but this revised character would be much less threatening to a much larger audience. Before he had fascinated with his strangeness. Now he would sympathetically seduce.

As for *Here Comes the Navy*, it had a certain scope – it got Cagney off the ground for the first time – put him at sea and in the air, far from the city's clamor. He is a shipyard worker who gets into a hassle with Chief Petty Officer O'Brien when he is making a dockside inspection tour. Shortly thereafter he is rendered jobless, joins the fleet and finds himself assigned to O'Brien's unit. To make things more comically binding he falls in love with the chief's sister. After much yelling and hitting, Cagney is given a chance to become a decoratable hero, at one point saving a gun crew from an explosion, at another helping to prevent a dirigible crash. He gains, besides his medals, two boons – the girl's hand in marriage and a chance to go on squabbling with her brother for the rest of their lives.

He was another kind of honest working stiff in *The St Louis Kid* – a truck driver who has a taste for country living (surely some of the scenes in which he romantically praises the bucolic life are Cagney inventions) but no class solidarity whatever. He scabs against striking milk truck drivers until he is falsely accused of murdering one of them. He then realizes that he is being used by mobsters in a war against his own kind and finds happiness as a unionist. Hollywood liked to place the blame for labor

troubles in the 1930s on the underworld when
it could, so that it did not have to confront corporate American responsibility for labor violence (the same evasion, of course, marks
Taxi), but the picture was lively and occasionally funny. As he had been off and on since
Hard to Handle, and most notably in *Jimmy
the Gent*, Allen Jenkins is marvellously funny
as Cagney's comically moronic sidekick ('ya
splitskull' Cagney affectionately addresses him
here). He was everything Cagney was, except
smart, and so created an engaging contrast to
the leading man.

The picture is memorable for two small bits
of invention. Cagney appeared for a slug-a-
thug scene with his hands bandaged and, over
the protests of director Ray Enright and the
producer, insisted on knocking the man out by
a new method; he bonked him on the forehead
with his own head. The blow, suitably
enhanced by the sound department, was surprising and funny, and Cagney would repeat
the bit later in this picture as well as in a scrap
with Bette Davis in *The Bride Came C.O.D.*
('They say that's the way Eskimos kiss', he
would tell her). At the end of the picture, when
he has married the girl (Patricia Ellis again, this
time as a country lass he has met by running
his truck into her roadster) and they have
checked into a hotel, a house detective knocks
on their door, suggesting their relationship
may be illicit. Cagney starts to go for him with
his fists cocked. But she heads him off, turns
sweetly to the intruder and K.O.s him. In all,
The St Louis Kid was modest, enjoyable and
undistinguished.

Devil Dogs of the Air, essentially a remake
of *Here Comes the Navy*, introduces him as a
man perhaps mistakenly looking for a steady
job. Tommy O'Toole comes stunting into a
Marine Corps air field in search of his old com-
rade from barnstorming days, Bill Brannigan
(O'Brien, naturally). He wants to join up. But,
great natural flyer or not, he has to learn to
fly the Marine Corps way – by the book. Needless to say, the attempt to re-educate O'Toole

has its comic ups and downs. And its melodramatic ones. Perhaps equally needless to say,
Tommy O'Toole eventually proves to be heroic
and amenable to discipline. Dare one suggest
it? These service comedies seem to partake of
a new spirit moving through the land. In the
earlier comedies Cagney virtually parodied, in
his occupations, and in his preoccupation with
cutting shady corners, old-fashioned *laissez-
faire* entrepreneurship. Not a few great and
once greatly admired American enterprises had
begun with the spirit Cagney demonstrated as
a ruthlessly self-promoting hustler or careerist.
But now, after a couple of years of the New
Deal, it was established that happiness was to
be found in the group, especially the group that
pulled together as a disciplined unit toward a
well-defined and socially acceptable, even
socially improving, goal, which the defense of

the realm by professional military men was assumed to be by most people in those innocent days. In other words, it was more than agreeable for audiences to witness their sometime causeless rebel, their dear Jimmy, signing on with an organization and suppressing his normally high spirits the better to fit in and do the job.

As witness his next picture, *G-Men*. What hoopla attended its release – the public enemy comes over to the side of law and order. And what success attended it as well – it is said that no Cagney picture of the period equalled its grosses. After the lunacies of the Federal Bureau of Investigation's history in the last decades of J. Edgar Hoover's reign, it is almost impossible to recapture the sense of awe and of glamour with which the agency was invested in the 1930s. Or the shrewdness with which Hoover promoted its image of incorruptibility and efficiency – so different from the national view of the typical local police force. In particular, its war against the famous hoods of the time, with Hoover himself often managing to be on the scene, when his agents closed in for the kill, was made to seem particularly dangerous and exciting – 'Just like the movies', people were wont to say. The director, with his fierce bulldog's countenance and his eagerness to put himself forward in the public prints, on the radio and in the newsreels, became a great media figure of the time. He was ever ready to open his organization's files to provide movie and radio people with 'authentic' story material, always obliging about permitting people to film at FBI facilities. He even sometimes permitted FBI employees to appear in movies in small parts. For him, *G-Men* was a major publicity coup, just as it was for Warner Brothers a major symbol of status to be associated with so august an American institution.

For Cagney it represented a first-class production, his first since *Footlight Parade*. The best things about it are the moody shadows cast on some of the sequences, particularly in a night assault on a gangster's hideout, clearly based, as much of the picture was, on an attempt to trap the notorious John Dillinger, whose success in evading capture had titillated the public in this period. It was Cagney's first collaboration with the man who had directed *Penny Arcade* for the stage, William Keighley, who did have stronger visual values than men like Del Ruth and Bacon did although he never mastered their ability to hasten past the weaker elements in a script or a characterization.

Of those there were many in *G-Men*, especially where Cagney's Brick Davis is concerned. In essence he was playing a tamed-down version of the figure he had played in service comedies. He joins the FBI for a selfish reason, in order to avenge the death of his best friend at the hands of mobsters. He needs to learn, once again, that the good of the organization must be placed ahead of personal needs. The superior officer in charge of teaching him this lesson is not O'Brien, unfortunately, but stolid Robert Armstrong, best remembered as the original captor of the original King Kong. Cagney also has his *de rigueur* romance with the rather boring sister of the Armstrong character. The situation, obviously, is a simple steal from *Here Comes the Navy*. She is played by Margaret Lindsay, who had done similar duty a little more persuasively in *Devil Dogs*. Her role is rendered particularly thankless in this case because Ann Dvorak is on hand, playing an old flame who has become rather tragically – and inexplicably – involved with Cagney's chief quarry, who is played with his usual lugubriousness by Barton MacLane, heaviest-handed of Warner's contract heavies. On the whole, aside from the novelty of observing Cagney firmly on the side of the law, and of observing what purported to be a documentation of FBI methodology in action, it is hard to see what the attractions of this picture were. But it maintains a surprising hold on latter-day critics, who mysteriously praise it at the expense of far livelier and infinitely more curious Cagney enterprises. Perhaps that is because, respectable as it is in

Cagney played professional prize-fighters three times and always came up off the canvas to win the big bout – as he did in *The Irish In Us* (opposite).

tone, and a bellweather for dozens of sober studies of law and order in action, it plays more comfortably on television than other pictures he made at this time. It requires no explanations, no imaginative leaps backward into the stylistic and narrative conventions of its period.

The Irish In Us, by contrast, represented the vanished realities of Cagney's boyhood in a form so stylized that even at the time critics found it preposterous (if entirely good-humored). There is a warm and indulgent mother (Mary Gordon) with an Irish brogue so thick as to be incomprehensible at some moments, and three rough-and-tumble boys – Frank McHugh as a fireman, O'Brien as a policeman and Cagney as the rebel who manages prize fighters who win few prizes. Most notable among them is one Carbarn McCarthy (Jenkins again), so punchy that if a bell of any kind – for example that of a telephone – rings anywhere near him, he goes into his boxer's stance and starts windmilling punches. Olivia de Havilland, of all genteel souls, is the girl who sews dissension in the family because she cannot make up her mind between the two of the brothers, the free-spirited Cagney and the four-square O'Brien. In the end Cagney has to substitute for Carbarn when he fails to turn up for his big fight. In an exemplary show of familial solidarity O'Brien serves as his cornerman, goading him to a come-from-behind victory in the fight, which victory also wins de Havilland's love at last. It could be argued that the institution whose imperatives Cagney has to learn to love, honor and obey in this one is the most basic of all institutions – the family. But if *The Irish in Us* can be made to fit this revisionary cycle in the Cagney character's development, no one at the time noticed or cared. With Cagney's entire Irish mafia present for the first and last time in the same picture, the spirit of improvisation was thick in the air, and ever-agreeable Lloyd Bacon was glad to give them their freedom. The picture has a raucous, larky air about it, winning and forgettable.

No one who has ever seen it will forget Cagney's next project, playing Bottom the Weaver in the richly anticipated, then much clucked over, Max Reinhardt production of *A Midsummer Night's Dream*. This was the kind of thing, lavishly literary, that Irving Thalberg, head of production at M-G-M, was trying to do in order to demonstrate that, contrary to prevailing middlebrow opinion, the movies could essay the classics. But even Irving had not yet attempted Shakespeare – his *Romeo and Juliet*, starring his wife, Norma Shearer, and Leslie Howard would not appear until the following year. Nor had he recruited anyone like Max Reinhardt, impressario of German theatrical impressionism and, stylistically, one of the most significant forces in world theater in the first third of this century, to produce it and co-direct it with William Dieterle, one of the several leading figures in the renaissance of German film-making after World War One who had trained with Reinhardt. 'The best actor in Hollywood,' Reinhardt proclaimed as Cagney went to work. 'Few artists have ever had his intensity, his dramatic drive.' And so on. Cagney himself was less impressed. 'Imagine,' he would say to me. 'A hoodlum actor doing a part among the classics. Well, they gave it to me and I did it, that's all.'

In a way it was a foredoomed project. Had it been perfectly realized, the self-appointed guardians of cultural purity could not have let Hollywood get away with it. As it was less than perfect, it was critically trounced – and ignored by the public. But with the passing years, the picture's wayward charms become more evident. There cannot have been a more delightful Puck than Mickey Rooney, who was fourteen at the time, but looked and acted like a pre-adolescent. And the sets and special effects were really quite wonderful – sophisticatedly unsophisticated, more often than not underwhelming rather than over. And there is something like the spirit of vaudeville in the playing of the rude mechanicals – with the likes of McHugh, Joe E. Brown and Hugh Herbert

A Midsummer Night's Dream, **or culture comes to Warner Brothers. Joe E. Brown was among the rude mechanicals who joined Cagney, playing Bottom the Weaver, in the play within the play. At right, Cagney prepares for his transformation scene.**

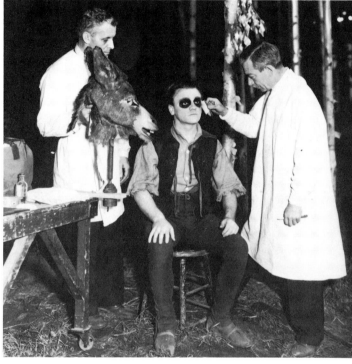

joining Cagney in the play within a play. The largest problem lay with people like Dick Powell and de Havilland in the major roles – somehow too insipid – and a camera and editing that seemed awed into stateliness by The Significance of it All.

Quick! Back to business as usual. Lloyd Bacon behind the camera, Margaret Lindsay as the love interest, a movie entitled *Frisco Kid*. It is Cagney's first period piece, about the era of the Barbary Coast in San Francisco. In it he plays a sailor who secures his reputation for toughness by killing a hook-handed brawler known as the Shanghai Duck in a bar-room. Soon enough he is duded out in a brocaded waistcoat and some of the sweetest curls you've ever seen, helping to manage an empire of vice. In something less than seventy-seven minutes he has made another transformation, enlisting on the side of virtue principally because it is captained by a newspaper editor (Lindsay)

with whom he has mysteriously fallen in love. Cagney would come to consider this utterly unfelt film as the nadir of this phase of his career, and it may have contributed to a new growth of restlessness with studio employment.

Nevertheless, he went more than happily into *Ceiling Zero*. In 1980, lolling around his dressing room, helping Pat O'Brien to help him kill some time until his next call, I idly asked them what they thought was the best of the pictures they had done together. O'Brien unhesitatingly named *Angels With Dirty Faces*, a logical choice, given the intensity and range of emotions it offered them, and the brooding quality of director Michael Curtiz's striking *mise en scène*. Cagney, surprisingly, named *Ceiling Zero*, which I have always thought of as one of Howard Hawks' lesser works, stage-bound and talky. But, as it turned out, that is precisely what Cagney liked about it. Based on a Broadway success by Frank 'Spig' Wead, a

Frisco Kid **Cagney considered to be the worst picture he made in the 1930s. But it was very atmospheric.**

sometime flyer who had been crippled in an accident but became a beloved Hollywood character because of his gallant conduct in his second career as a writer of aviation screenplays (and the subject of a mawkish John Ford film, *The Wings of Eagles*, where no less than John Wayne played him), Cagney admired it for its origins. No one at the studio had ever thought to buy him an expensive outside property before; originals from the less exalted denizens of the writers' building had been good enough for him. Beyond that, his role had been originated on the stage by Osgood Perkins, a distinguished actor of whom he thought well.

Be that as it may, one can see why the studio, acting on Hawks' shrewd suggestion, had acquired the play for Cagney. Except that it was a little more sober in tone, and has a tragic ending, it was in essence a version of the service comedies he had done with O'Brien. Indeed, O'Brien was still in uniform in this picture, that of a fledgling airline for whom he was managing a station in and out of which flew the air-

mail. Cagney makes his entrance as he did in *Devil Dogs* – stunt flying – and again sporting a sporty little mustache. This time there were executive objections. 'Jack Warner didn't like it. He said, "It takes away your toughness."' But, of course, that was fine with Cagney. By this time, he thought, 'the image had been well established', and he felt he could safely play against it. If, in the process, he could rile Warner a little bit – well, that was a fringe benefit. Or should one say, a benefit of the fringe?

Actually, that pencil-thin mustache spoke, if not volumes, then paragraphs, about Dizzy Davis, the dashing flyer he portrays. Cagney was trying to vary the character he had been doing since *Here Comes the Navy*, draining it of heroic overtones, and the facial decor said something about the childishness of his vanity. So did the inveterate womanizing the script called upon him to undertake. So did a line Cagney insisted on writing into a scene where O'Brien, as usual representing maturity and responsibility, is dressing him down. The script permits him to expose the fact that, without family, and given the wandering nature of his barnstorming career, the characters played here by O'Brien and Stu Erwin constitute the only family he has even known. 'I'd cut my heart out for you,' the script has him say. After which comes the line, lovely in the simplicity with which it reveals the permanent childishness of his nature and which, the minute he heard it, Hawks, himself an inveterate scribbler or improvised dialogue on the set, told Cagney to write in. It is: 'Please don't be mad at me.' And it is, of course, a line most of us start practicing on our parents almost as soon as we can talk, but which we hesitate to use once we've grown up. To hear it here, in this bustling, bristling all-male world is a shock. And a subtle blow for psychological truth in an unlikely context. '"Don't be mad at me."' Cagney would say to me. 'Just a question of writing in a couple of lines,' but it made for humanity in the picture.

In the end, after O'Brien as the embryo capitalist has delivered himself of a speech envisioning a new age of scheduled air traffic spanning the continent, Dizzy Davis recognizes that there is no place in that dream for a non-sked character like himself. And, anyway, it looks as if he's developing a bum ticker. So he takes up a suicidal flight, replacing a flyer with a brighter, longer future, and, naturally, dies, victim of his own nature. And of the changing nature of the world.

That ending is both neat and morally satisfying. And it permits Cagney the opportunity to consciously acknowledge, and ask the audience to contemplate, the essential childishness of his screen character. It permitted him to enunciate as well the self-destructive side of that character's nature – an aspect of him that would become more and more obvious in the years ahead. Indeed, *Ceiling Zero* represents the first – but not the last – of Cagney's screen suicides in aid of some larger good. But, for all its moral weightiness, and for all the flying scenes that were added, the film never really transcends its origins as a one-set theater piece the ambitions of which perhaps exceeded the reach of a writer with an unfortunate taste for he-man philosophizing. Hawks would do much better, four years later, with the similar *Only Angels Have Wings* which he turned giddy at every point where *Ceiling Zero* goes solemn.

As for Cagney, if the film offered him more satisfaction than most did, it could not mollify his overall sense of dissatisfaction with the studio. He had been readying himself for a walkout and *Ceiling Zero* provided him with an excuse. His contract had restricted his output to four films per year and this was his fifth of 1935 – and the sixth the studio had put in release during that year. Moreover, he discovered a theater where the marquee billed Pat O'Brien above him, and he contended that that, too, was a technical violation of the billing clause in his contract – though just how Warner Brothers could policy every theater manager, every kid charged with climbing a ladder to spell out names in lights is not entirely clear. At any rate, Cagney sued the studio for release from his contract – and damages – and once again decamped, this time for his newly purchased farm on Martha's Vineyard. The other studios were not interested in incurring Jack Warner's wrath by signing him. And even if they had dared risk it, they were not eager to encourage the example he was setting for other contract players. The major independent producers, Samuel Goldwyn and David O. Selznick, apparently expressed some interest, but they too were members of the moguls' club and backed off. Eventually Cagney would win a contract with another studio. But it was with a poverty row outfit called Grand National, which specialized in B pictures. Its managers advanced him $100,000 against his salary for two pictures and promised him veto power over stories. But, as it turned out, they could not recruit first-class craftsmen, or actors, to support him. This first bid for independence would turn out to be short-lived and no happier than his servitude at Warner Brothers.

SOMETHING TO REMEMBER

CAGNEY WAS INACTIVE FOR ALMOST A YEAR while the lawyers took his case against Warner Brothers to court and while his deal was being set with Grand National. But his return to the screen late in 1936 was anything but triumphant. The two movies he made for Grand National are among his feeblest. No different in kind from the films he had made at Warner Brothers, they were rather worse in quality – their writing and direction second-class, their settings and other technical work considerably less than that. The first, *Great Guy*, has him as a fighting deputy in a municipal bureau of weights and measures, crusading against consumer fraud. It is, to say the least, a comedown from the FBI. There is a difference in one's level of involvement when one is watching public enemies, men who have made the most wanted list, being run to ground, and when one is watching small time crooks, butchers who put their thumbs on the scale, for instance, or gas station attendants who give short measure to their customers, being brought to justice. As for Cagney, his Johnny Cove character is congealed by his desire not to resort to violence or even, it would seem, a wisecrack in fulfilling his duty to the public weal. Only Mae Clarke, who had suffered so grievously at the hand of Cagney in previous pictures, might be imagined getting some small satisfactions out of this picture. She plays Johnny's straight-laced girl-friend, insisting that they eat in a cafeteria when they dine out, so that they can save money for their nest-egg. This, like most of their other scenes, amounts to premarital hen-pecking, and one gets the impression that if any grapefruit are going to be flung about in this relationship, it is she who will do the flinging. In any case, *Great Guy* is that rarity in the body of Cagney's pre-war work, a film that is now almost totally unwatchable.

Something to Sing About is marginally better. In it Cagney plays Terry Rooney, a bandleader recruited for Hollywood stardom, who discovers that his new occupation is something less than glamorous, or even manly. No sooner does he arrive on the west coast than the movie people set about making him over, vitiating the very qualities that they hired him to display in the first place. He is mildly funny as he submits to make up, hair-styling, diction lessons, all designed to fit him to some imagined ideal of masculine charm. In a big brawl scene in Terry's first film he is supposed to play a victim, but he can't stand it, so he punches out everyone in sight and leaves the studio to marry the girl he has left behind, the singer in his band. She is played by Evelyn Daw, another of Cagney's evanescent leading ladies, and when they return from their honeymoon they discover that the director has left the cameras running during the brawl sequence, and that his performance in it has made him a star. Now, however, the studio places a new imposition on him. They insist that he keep his marriage secret lest he dampen the ardor of his female fans. An arranged romance with another studio player causes jealousy, his wife leaves him, but he comes to his senses and reclaims her. 'Get back in your cage, canary,' he says when he joins her on stage for a musical finale. That line is sure to set a modern feminist's teeth on edge, except that by the time it occurs in this dully staged film it is difficult to imagine it – or anything – arousing passion of any sort other than the home-going one.

If *Something to Sing About* can be said to have any interest at all, other than as a curiosity in a great star's career, it is for the conscious analogies it permits one to draw between Terry Rooney's fictional movie career and Cagney's genuine one. Terry may have been a tough guy who objected to appearing gentle and Cagney may have been, as he saw himself, a gentle man who despised acting tough, but in either case the message is the same: a man's gotta be what a man's gotta be, and it is foolish and demeaning to make him violate his God-given essence. If that happens, of course, the only honorable course is the one both the imaginary actor and the real one chose – the walkout. 'If you listen to all the clowns around you're just dead.'

107

Having gone to all that trouble, however, it is difficult to see why Cagney did not make a more radical departure in choosing material. Why do watery versions of the kind of pictures he had already done, by his own standards, far too frequently? Why not try to do something in an entirely novel vein? Here we come up against one of the ambiguities of his career, which is that whenever he had the opportunity to exercise free choice he almost always acted cautiously. It was as if he did not quite believe in the loyalty of his public. And that he believed, more than he dared let on, that the kind of type-casting his former bosses had insisted upon was responsible for his success. He would try to shade his character, but he would only occasionally and cautiously try to show it in an entirely new light. One can scarcely blame a man who had come as far, as quickly as he had economically for avoiding high risks. One might also observe that Cagney was never a generalizer, a man with a taste for large statements. The glories of his films are all to be found in breath-taking moments.

Still, his first solo flight ended in a safe landing. A third Grand National production was announced, but by that time the studio was in a parlous condition. And so, suddenly, shockingly (considering the amount of bad feeling that had been publicly vented by both sides), Warner Brothers and Cagney announced a new agreement. This was probably facilitated by the fact that Cagney had actually won his suit against his once and future employers. It had the effect of satisfying his honor and proving that his basic contention, which was that the studio had unfairly exploited him, was correct. As for the party of the second part, it now had abundant evidence that Cagney was perfectly capable not merely of walking away, but of staying away, accepting even worse working conditions, worse projects, in order to uphold his principles. Both sides could now reconstitute their former partnership on the only sensible basis – mutual wariness. Under the terms of his new contract Cagney would be paid

$150,000 per picture, with no obligation to make more than two of them a year. Beyond that he would have a large voice in the choice of scripts and co-workers and his brother William, who had come to Hollywood to try acting – a brief encounter it was – and had stayed on to become James's business manager, would work with him as a producer. It was, by the standards of the day, an extremely good deal for the performer, about as close as anyone came at this time to the sort of independent production arrangements that stars began negotiating with the studios in the 1950s.

And it worked out well. Between 1938 and 1942 Cagney would make twelve pictures at Warner Brothers, culminating with his most beloved work, *Yankee Doodle Dandy*. They would range the genres, they would be uniformly well produced, enlisting some of the best talent on the lot, and they would offer Cagney an opportunity to explore territories into which his screen character had never before ventured.

In its curious way, his first film on his return set the tone for what was to come. Like his last Warner picture, it was a good and pricey 'property', Sam and Bella Spewack's hit Broadway comedy, *Boy Meets Girl*, a loose and farcical rendering of the Hollywood careers of those self-consciously colorful screenwriters, Ben Hecht and Charles MacArthur. It was a piece that was very much of its moment, when the first group of Eastern writers, having digested the culture shock of coming west to write for the vulgar movies, were beginning to turn out their first plays and novels about that weird, wonderful (and highly profitable) experience.

The Spewacks' play no longer reads as humorously as it once did – it is an old-fashioned Broadway laugh machine, heavily burdened with contrivances. But the movie – considerably retooled – in which O'Brien co-starred, and which perfectly suited the bang-it-out style of director Lloyd Bacon, is quite another matter. It is almost impossible to recall the plot – something about making a star out

of the illegitimate child of a studio commissary waitress (played with a sweet unworldliness by Marie Wilson). But no matter. What remains are the brilliantly paced set pieces in which screenwriters Law (Cagney) and Benson (O'Brien) madly improvise plots, acting out all the parts and, when they are stuck, maniacally diverting attention – singing, dancing, doing skits, breaking up the furniture. Their prime audience is a dull-witted but egomaniacal western star (Dick Foran) they have to convince to play opposite the scene-stealing kid and (even funnier) their equally dense, but intellectually pretentious, producer. Said to be patterned on Walter Wanger, who was inordinately proud of his Dartmouth degree, and one of the few Ivy Leaguers in Hollywood's executive ranks, he was played by Ralph Bellamy, whose gallery of well-dressed, mannerly stupes and squares (c.f. *The Awful Truth* and *His Girl Friday*) is one of the small, authentic treasures of American film comedy.

For Cagney, *Boy Meets Girl* represents a complete novelty. He had never before played in a pure farce, but in this form he was as expert as he ever was on the screen. The speed and precision of his speech pattern, the inventive no-waste choreography of his movements are superbly calculated. And he makes a masterful lead dancer for O'Brien, setting the tone and pace for their intricate and dizzying verbal exchanges – and their pratfalls – with his pal following with his perfect professionalism and adding a few neat improvisations of his own. But it is the suggestion of cold reasonableness that Cagney brings to his performance that is a revelation. In his way Robert Law – wonderfully ironic name — is as much an anarchist as Tom Powers ever was. Perhaps more so, since as a literate man he would be familiar with that word, understand its meaning and its application to his own behavior. He may be, then, even less moral than the instinct-driven gangster. Cagney conveys that self-consciousness, that air of the put-on – which is not entirely dissimilar to what Groucho

Marx used to imply in his work – without ever choking off any of his laughs.

That Cagney could go from this to *Angels With Dirty Faces*, arguably his greatest performance, is evidence that he was, at this moment, at the height of his powers. The shrewd Warner Brothers had taken over the lovable juvenile delinquents of Sidney Kingsley's hit play, *Dead End*, which Samuel Goldwyn had turned into an equally successful, if stiff, movie under William Wyler's direction. The idea was to star the boys, led by Huntz Hall and Leo Gorcey, in a series of B comedies, but the pattern was interrupted for this sober, powerful and affecting film. Indeed, the only thing wrong with it is its title, which seems to imply a chucklesome, warm-hearted comedy about good-bad boys, which, of course the Dead End Kid series and its various spin-offs (The Bowery Boys, The East Side Kids, The Little Tough Guys) were. But under the direction of Michael Curtiz, whose mature style was all sinuous camera moves and *noir* lighting, the picture has a brooding quality unlike anything else Cagney had done, or for that matter, would do. The Kids who have been swept up off the streets and into the settlement house established by Father Jerry Connelly (who else but Pat O'Brien?) do provide some comic relief but their most profound function is to serve as a sort of chorus for the main action. It is for their moral edification, that, at the end of the film, Cagney's mobster character, Rocky Sullivan, must make a terrible decision. It is the process of bringing him to that point logically that consumes this very long picture.

It is important to understand that except for occupation Rocky is not Tom Powers. As Andrew Bergman has commented, 'Rocky is *the* most lovable gangster in all of movies'. And also one of the most consistent losers among them, really too nice a guy for this difficult line of work. And too much of a victim. When we meet him, returning to his old neighborhood and renewing his boyhood friendship with

111

Father Jerry, he has just been released from prison where he has taken the rap not only for himself but for his previous partner in crime, James Frazier, a crooked lawyer, played by Humphrey Bogart, in these days always a much more squalid criminal type than Cagney was. He has not only let Rocky suffer in silence, he has also kept for himself the proceeds of their activities. Revenge, or at the very least a settling of accounts, is very much on Rocky's mind. Redemption, of course, is on Father

Jerry's mind, but he treads cautiously on this point. In one of their first exchanges Rocky asks his old friend how and when he accepted his call to the priesthood. Jerry explains he was riding along on the top of the bus one day when it was passing a cathedral, and he happened to glance down and . . . 'That's funny,' says Rocky, 'I got an idea top of a bus one time, got me six years.' The two men laugh wryly. And Jerry gently steers Rocky toward involvement with his wayward boys and toward a love

fair with that cute little pigtailed, freckled kid who has grown up to be Ann Sheridan. Cagney terrific with the kids, a tough, funny, understanding older brother who is himself still an adolescent at heart.

The kids call to that heart. He sees his young self in them, can't help but reflect on how a little basketball under the church's patronage might have kept him off the streets and out of trouble. And the role obviously called to Cagney's heart. It is full of quotations from his memory.

For example, Rocky's habitual greeting, 'Whaddya hear, whaddya say', is a tag line borrowed from one of his own boyhood chums. Perhaps more famously, since it was picked up by all the impressionists and worked into their Cagney routines, was a curious little nervous tic, a hunching forward roll of his shoulders which bespeaks – what? Aggressiveness or defensiveness? A little of both perhaps, symbolizing the split nature of Rocky Sullivan's personality, good at the core, yet drawn

113

thoughtlessly toward the dark. 'I did that once, and they walked out of the theater with it', Cagney would recall, pleased with himself – no matter that he did it far more than once in *Angels*. It was a habit he had first observed watching a pimp when he was himself a dead ringer for a dead end kid. 'He had four girls working for him out of a Rathskellar on 77th and First Ave, and this is all he did all day long . . . . The extent of his activity.' Cagney grinned. 'The idea was that if you could give them something to remember – use it.'

But, of course, there is more to this deeply felt performance than remembered phrases, remembered observations. What it seemed to summon up in him was his old childhood sense of how close one was, every day, to the fatal mis-step that leads irresistibly to the next and the next until, at last, one is walking the last mile. As the movie makes clear, chance plays a large role in this matter. What if, when they were stealing coal, Jerry had been caught and Rocky had been the one to outrun the cops? It seems to prey on the latter's mind – and to motivate him in his work with the kids. If only that could totally occupy him. If only their awe of his criminal celebrity could be converted into something healthier, a kind of respect and love that will lure Rocky over to the side of goodness permanently. But he has other business in hand – old and deadly business with his former partner. Eventually he kills Frazier and is cornered and captured in a handsomely staged shoot-out sequence.

That action might have cost Cagney his life. In those days, before the effects men perfected the squib (a small charge of powder electronically triggered, so that a tiny explosion, like that of a bullet striking a solid object, could be made near an actor), the studios employed sharpshooters who fired live rounds that struck as close as possible to the performers. 'Stupid', Cagney would recall. 'They were dangerous, and I went on doing it for a long time, with the wild bullets flying in all directions.' In this instance Cagney was supposed to be at bay on the upper floor of a factory, tear gas pouring in, machine guns chattering. 'The fellow said, "Get the cue, fire a couple of shots and duck down below the window sill." It was one of those steel casement windows. Well, when they turned loose the machine guns one of the bullets hit and went right where my head would have been – right through – and the man doing it was an expert.' One can, in fact, see in the finished film Cagney's involuntary flinch and the quickly hidden look of amazement and fear on his face. But naturally, he goes on with the take although, perhaps, needless to say, no more live rounds were fired in his vicinity thereafter.

But it is not this bit of unintended realism that makes this scene so powerful. What does is the near-madness he conveys in his entrapment, the accumulated anger and viciousness that Rocky Sullivan, who always wanted too much to be liked, has never before expressed. Driven from his lair, making a last desperate dash for freedom down an alley, he finally finds

no place to turn. When a cop takes his gun away from him he says, 'empty'. To which Cagney, his face twisted into a sneer and starkly lit by a harsh uplight, makes this snarling response: 'So's your thick skull, copper'. It is a great moment, a wonderful astonishment from an actor who has been so ingratiating, so worthy of sympathy, for so much of the picture. In this time, only Cagney so readily dared these sudden transformations, these quick descents into a character's dark depths.

And there was more to come. The death house; the night of Rocky's execution; Father Jerry comes to him, asking for courage. 'You mean walking in there. That's not going to take much,' says the prisoner, who makes a little joking analogy between electric chair and barber chair. 'But you're not afraid,' the priest persists. 'No. They'd like me to be, wouldn't they? I'm afraid I can't oblige 'em, kid. You know, Jerry, I think in order to be afraid you . . . you gotta have a heart. I don't think I got one. I had that cut out of me a long time ago.'

Cagney plays this scene with great stillness, in the sharpest imaginable contrast to the preceding insanity, and to the careless bravado of the film's earlier passages. But now the good Father confesses his real mission. He does not want a stoic's death from Rocky. He wants him to die yellow, begging for mercy, so that in death he can set an example for the street youths that he never could in life. Or, as the priest puts it, 'You see, you've been a hero to these kids and hundreds of others all through your life. And now you're going to be a glorified hero in death and I want to prevent that, Rocky. They've got to despise your memory . . . got to be ashamed of you.'

The sequence is milked for every drop of suspense, not just by making the walk to the death chamber seem to take forever – it's one of Curtiz's greatest tracking shots – but by Cagney's enigmatic behavior. He will let his old friend accompany him down the last mile only if he promises not to pray. He lashes out at a guard who taunts him. He walks boldly past the witnesses, firm of stride and expression. Only at the last moment does he begin to whimper and cry for mercy: 'Please, I don't wanna die; oh, please don't make me burn now'. He sobs as he is dragged to the chair grabbing at anything and everything that will impede the inevitable. Much of the scene is shot in silhouette, but that does not diminish the power of Cagney's performance.

Nor need this high, rich melodrama distract us from reading this film's subtext. In effect, it is the same as that of service comedies, but put in bolder, more grippingly melodramatic terms. Once again the rebel is being asked to abandon his selfish interests, in this case not just his treasured individuality, but whatever hope he cherished for admired immortality in the memory of misguided youths. Yes, to be sure, God looking down will note his *beau geste*, but since Rocky has specifically rejected religious consolation, we know that he expects nothing from that quarter. And since his gesture will be rendered meaningless if the only man who knows about it ever tells the true story, he cannot hope for delayed recognition. No, such satisfaction as he can derive from his act must come from his sense that, at long last, he is enlisting in, accepting the values of, not just a military unit, but of the entire vast army of the anonymously decent, the gathering phalanx of the common man if you will, whose spirit by this time the whole nation, encouraged by the political rhetoric of the moment and by the media, ever ready to amplify the conventional wisdom, was learning to embrace.

Perhaps here, in 1938, as the Depression decade draws to a close, it is appropriate to observe how Cagney's screen character, whatever he thought of what he was doing, however the impositions of the studio may have occasionally distorted its outlines, nevertheless seems to have been borne along on the main currents of American cultural history in the period of its development. One can so easily read not merely his Tom Powers but all those desperately shady entrepreneurs and self-

promoters of the early comedies, as men panicked by the failure of traditional American individualistic values, flailing about, lashing out, hungrily groping for some piece of the wreckage to cling to as the economic seas rise alarmingly around them. But beginning with *Footlight Parade* and the Cagney character's orchestration of those perfectly rhythmic, perfectly in-step, marching feet, an alternative is proposed. It is, of course, the group, and no small group at that. The nation as a whole, the people, yes (to borrow a phrase) — they in their instinctively shared values could offer the troubled and wayward individual solace and, more important, the hope of progress toward a better world.

This is a theme the late Warren I. Susman, the distinguished cultural historian, developed at great length in his suggestive essay on 'The Culture of the Thirties'. He observes that it was not just in our political rhetoric, but in many other realms that the idea of a majoritarian community consensus was given the weight of a moral imperative, something the eccentric individual was not just merely foolish to oppose, but demonstrably wrong to resist. He suggests that the hidden agenda of cultural anthropology and the new pseudo-science of public opinion sampling, in which there was greatly heightened interest at both the élite and popular levels, was to support the legitimacy of community values at the expense of individual wishes and needs. And everywhere – in pop psychology, in pop religiosity, even in the mystery novels that began proliferating in this period – this stance was reinforced. As for the movies and the radio and the new picture magazines, it is obvious where they took their stand, given their need for the easily read, easy-to-agree-with symbol.

Now, in 1938, *Angels With Dirty Faces* makes us see how neatly the line of Cagney's character development compliments the developments of our social history. Here, at the end of the picture, he joins nothing palpable, dons no uniform. Rather he embraces a quasi-

116

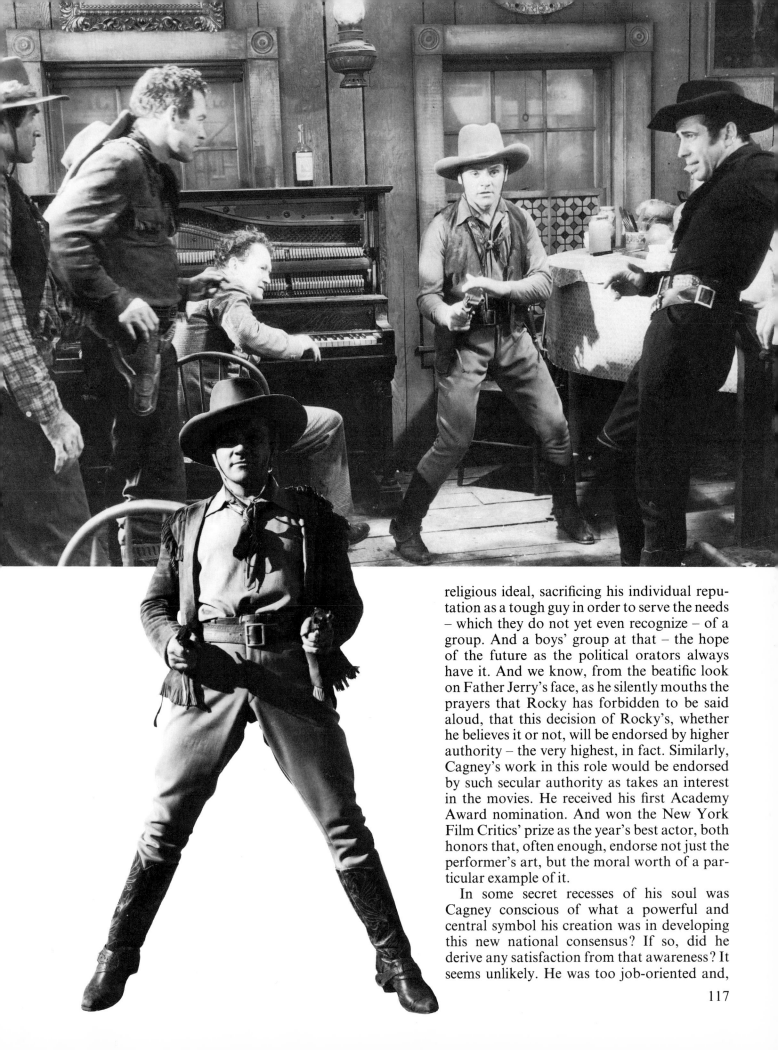

religious ideal, sacrificing his individual reputation as a tough guy in order to serve the needs – which they do not yet even recognize – of a group. And a boys' group at that – the hope of the future as the political orators always have it. And we know, from the beatific look on Father Jerry's face, as he silently mouths the prayers that Rocky has forbidden to be said aloud, that this decision of Rocky's, whether he believes it or not, will be endorsed by higher authority – the very highest, in fact. Similarly, Cagney's work in this role would be endorsed by such secular authority as takes an interest in the movies. He received his first Academy Award nomination. And won the New York Film Critics' prize as the year's best actor, both honors that, often enough, endorse not just the performer's art, but the moral worth of a particular example of it.

In some secret recesses of his soul was Cagney conscious of what a powerful and central symbol his creation was in developing this new national consensus? If so, did he derive any satisfaction from that awareness? It seems unlikely. He was too job-oriented and,

117

perhaps, when the glooms were upon him, too focused on his immediate artistic dissatisfactions. And he was receiving little enough help from outside in calculating the effect of his work. The studio could never see beyond the box-office returns and in selecting and preparing projects for him worked almost as much on instinct as he did. The shifts in his screen character's nature, and in the way he responded to pressure, were not in any sense consciously motivated or subtly planned. They just happened as a kind of instinctive response to a change in the climate. Certainly the critics of the time – with a few rare and honorable exceptions – did not notice what was happening. They may have admired his performance in *Angels*, but they did not fit it into any larger social context or make any observations about the changing nature of his screen work. For the most part in these years their attitude toward him remained what it had always been, hearty-jocular, affectionate but just a little wary of his explosiveness, which always carried with it, of course, the potential for offending a certain element among their readers.

Of course it could be argued that, from the standpoint of his craft, it was just as well that Cagney remained unconscious of the powerful psychic connections he had established with his public. It might have interfered with the operation of his instincts, a disaster for an actor who was all instinct. Probably just as well, too, that the studio did not grasp too firmly the source of his fascination for the public. A string of imitation *Angels* might have worn out his welcome. As it was, they kept finding new venues for him, and that kept the interest in him lively. In this period, particularly, you could never tell where he might turn up next.

For example, *The Oklahoma Kid*, which was greeted derisively. Imagine those two city kids, Cagney and Bogart, in a western! How silly can you get! No one will ever argue that it was a major work, and Bogart, dressed all in black, as the villain who, in the course of trying to become the vice lord of frontier Tulsa causes Cagney's father, a judge, to be lynched, never quite settles comfortably into his role. But Cagney, as the rebel son turned outlaw, dressed mainly in lightish clothes when he returns to avenge his father's death, is really quite interesting. He can't drawl like Gary Cooper, or move with the languid ease of the classic western hero, but he can walk quite close to a cheerfully parodistic line. For instance, he has trouble making one of the subsidiary villains reach for his gun in order to honor the convention that the western hero always draws last. The crook flat-out refuses to make his move. 'Why should I?' he inquires. 'Well, if you don't move, I can't shoot you', Cagney explains, all sweet and reason and amiable patience, something like a father trying to tell a balky child how the world is supposed to work. Naturally the man tries a sneak move, Cagney is ready for it and blasts him to kingdom come. After which, gently, almost quizzically, he blows the smoke out of his revolver barrel, acknowledging the hoariest of western clichés, and commenting on it with subtle satire. Elsewhere in the picture he can be heard to warble 'I don't Want to Play in Your Yard'. And he even sings a lullaby to a baby – in Spanish. The latter moment, in particular, seems to parody the tradition that the western hero is always, at heart, a gentle and reluctant hero, something like *The Virginian*. In all, *The Oklahoma Kid* is much airier – and much earlier – than such films as *Shane* and *High Noon* in its consciousness of what constitutes the classic tradition in western drama, and willing, as they were not, to make airy fun of that tradition.

By contrast, *Each Dawn I Die* is the most claustrophobic of all Cagney movies, which is only natural since it is the only prison picture he ever made. He is back on the side of the law in this one, as Frank Ross, an idealistic newspaperman crusading against municipal corruption. About to break the story of a dishonest district attorney, he is framed by the man's confederates on a manslaughter charge and sent to the state penitentiary. There he makes friends with another sometime slum kid, Hood Stacey, played by blank-faced, effective George Raft, whose contempt for bourgeois hypocrisy has led him to professional crime. Ross agrees to keep silent about a jailbreak Stacey is planning – if the latter, once he is on the outside, will track down the men who framed Ross. Once out, Stacey forgets his promise – it's all bright lights and loud music for him. Meantime, to break him down, Ross

is placed in the hole – solitary confinement – and break he does, in an outburst of hysterics beside which all previous Cagney efforts in this line pale. Finally, with a little prodding from Ross's girl, Stacey gets busy, discovers that the man who did the dirty work against Ross is actually in jail with him, and strolls back into the pen in time to participate in a prison riot – and get killed for his trouble. But not before fingering the finger man, which leads to Ross's pardon. In an epilogue, George Bancroft, playing the warden, gives Ross an autographed picture of Stacey which the con had entrusted him with before he died. The inscription reads, 'To Ross – I found a square guy', the reference being to Stacey's repeated observation that the reason he had turned to a life of crime was his inability to find an honest man anywhere.

Each Dawn I Die was reportedly Josef Stalin's favorite American movie – so he apparently told President Roosevelt at Yalta – and it is easy to see why. It is a perfect paranoid's nightmare – false accusation, false imprisonment, betrayal by a friend (even if it turns out to be only temporary), resolution of the situation only through what amounts to violent revolutionary activity. Underneath the melodrama – perhaps not far enough underneath it – lies the broadest indictment of the way things seem to work in America that Cagney was ever involved in, which doubtless contributed as well to Stalin's pleasure in the film. For remember, the corruption Ross is fighting appears to extend to the upper levels of government and the film insists on the connections between organized crime and elected officialdom.

No one – excepting the Soviet dictator, of course – appears to have noticed all that at the time. Nor was it observed that for the first time what had been only an element in Cagney's screen character, an implication of victimization, was now dominant in his portrayal. Aside from the Raft character's ambiguous friendship, he derives support in his lonely ordeal only from his customarily blond and faithful

119

The Roaring Twenties. **At the far left director Raoul Walsh (hands clasped) stages a scene with a little help from Bogart and Cagney. Frank McHugh joined the two stars in the publicity photo right, but in the end Cagney had to face his double-crossing former friend and his henchman alone and hung over. It was Gladys George (far right) who cried alone after Cagney died a martyr's death.**

girl friend (played this time by Jane Bryan) and his mother (Emma Dunn), who yields nothing to Ma Powers in her simple-mindedness. They are as impotent as he is, however, and the film can be read as a dramatization of the hopelessness of the individual when he tries to go it alone against evil.

If one thought that anything like the spirit of social criticism was moving through Warner Brothers when the year's release schedule was drawn up, one might see *Each Dawn I Die* as an effort to balance the implications of *Angels With Dirty Faces*. For if the earlier film suggests that even in death the individual may find a way to join with the idealistic spirit of common values, its successor suggests that that spirit is generally thwarted by the powers that be, that salvation from their machinations is pretty much a matter of chance, of making the right friend in the prison jute mill. No wonder Cagney goes bonkers in the middle of the picture. It is not just a matter of unspeakable physical torment in the 'the hole'. It is that hi

most fundamental faith in democratic justice, in the belief that right will somehow prevail, is shattered.

Each Dawn I Die was received as no more than a somewhat belated addition to one of the basic genres of the 1930s, the prison drama, which always revelled in the cruelty of conditions in our jails and made at least an implicit appeal for reform. But it did not represent a very distinguished contribution to that genre. It was Cagney's first collaboration with his old stage director, William Keighley, and stylistically they were not well matched. The director's style was a rather brooding one, unrelieved by the kind of grace notes someone like Curtiz generally brought to this manner. He tended to reinforce the intensity of Cagney's playing instead of working against it as the more relaxed studio craftsmen did. The result is perhaps the most hysterical film Cagney made in the pre-war period.

The Roaring Twenties was everything that *Each Dawn I Die* was not. Raoul Walsh was, heaven knows, a director who could drive an action sequence along at an absolutely furious clip, but there was a tenderness about him, too, especially when he got to thinking about the secret sentimental lives of guys who presented themselves to the world as tough. This was particularly so when they were Irishmen like himself and had lived long enough so that he could nostalgize the past that had shaped them. Unlike his friend and contemporary, John Ford, he did not romanticize the raucous, boozy side of Irishness – always the least welcome aspect of Ford's work. There was, rather, something wistful and gentle in the way Walsh showed these brawlers when they were off-duty. And by slackening his characteristically tense rhythms for these moments, letting the humor and the romance play at a leisurely pace, Walsh gained an element of contrast in his films that most of his action director peers never achieved.

In short, *The Roaring Twenties* was almost perfectly suited to bring out the best in a talent

that, when it was uninterested in what it was doing, would often preoccupy itself merely with brisk but unfelt staging. It also suited Cagney, allowing him to develop, to the furthest extent yet, the victim side of his personality. We observed earlier that Eddie Bartlett, the returning soldier, couldn't be blamed for going into bootlegging when the opportunity arose. Nor could he be entirely blamed for failing to observe that his old army buddy, George Hally (played by Bogart as an ever-sneering bully-weakling), was a thoroughly bad egg. Finally, it is difficult to blame Eddie for loving not wisely but too well the snippy little singer (Priscilla Lane, and where did they keep finding these dreary creatures for Cagney to have to fake a passion for?) the while ignoring faithful, lusty Gladys George as Panama Smith, a saloon keeper-singer clearly modelled on Texas Guinan. In short, Eddie's problem is that, for all his fast patter, for all his skill at creating an empire of crime, he is not a very shrewd judge of character. So Cagney plays him at any rate – much more wide-eyed, less cynical, even than Rocky Sullivan was.

Indeed, when the Lane creature jilts him for square, WASPY Jeffrey Lynn who plays Eddie's sometime lawyer, Lloyd Hart, it causes Eddie to lose his grip on his criminal enterprises, which are then totally devastated by Repeal. He sinks back to where he began, driving a cab.

And to drink. In the film's later scenes Cagney appears unshaven, dishevelled, shambling – more pathetic than he had ever previously appeared. When he discovers that George is planning to eliminate Lloyd, who has now been transformed into a crusading district attorney and implacable mob enemy, Eddie must try to protect him and the happiness of the woman he still blindly, obsessively loves. He goes to George, pleading for mercy. But the latter, paranoid enough to be premier of Russia, believes Eddie himself might rat on him in order to take the heat off Lloyd, and proposes taking him for a ride. Instead Eddie, pulls himself together, kills George and, in the great climactic gun battle, in which he races through the snowy streets exchanging fire with George's henchmen, is himself mortally wounded, staggering up the steps of a church before expiring at the feet of Panama.

It is only the plot of this movie, which was written by Mark Hellinger (the sometime newsman turned producer of crime pictures), Jerry Wald (allegedly the model for Budd Schulberg's Sammy Glick) and Robert Rossen (later a strong director, always a writer with a special gift for tough-romantic dialogue) that is complex. Emotionally it is very clean-lined, and quite touching. Its flavor is perfectly captured in the movie's great conclusion, one of the most powerful and memorable endings ever made. A cop, dumb and beefy, flatfoots it to Gladys George's side, hauls out a notebook and starts making inquiries for the record. 'Well, who is this guy?' 'He's just Eddie Bartlett,' says the tear-stained actress. 'Well, how are you hooked up with him?' 'I never figured that out,' she says softly. 'What was his business?' A beat for rueful emphasis, then: 'He used to be a bigshot'. Another beat, and then the camera begins a slow pullback until the figures in this tableau assume their proper perspective – sinking back into their littleness and anonymity, black shadows against white snow, the noble religious edifice huge and blank and silent behind them.

Oh, it's grand stuff. And, as a conclusion to the first phase of Cagney's criminal life, perfect. He is not an existential hero here, not in the customary sense of the term. Nor is he a tragic hero, not in the sense that Warshow meant, since Eddie never really overreached economically or socially. Nor is he tragic in the sense that *Angels With Dirty Faces* implied, either, where the failure of the individual and the community to make a compassionate connection – until it is too late – is the source of all misery. Maybe the beginnings of Eddie's troubles can be found in bad social policy – Prohibition combined with indifference to the working man's lot when the business cycle turns against him. But essentially he is undone by romantic obsession, by his hopeless, unreturned love for the singer who married the lawyer, who chose, that is, respectability and rectitude over energy, passion, and good old American hustle, which is almost always a little shady.

Here, indeed, was a new way to teach the lesson that crime does not pay, one that verges, it must be said, on the un-American. And what a downward path we have traced since the days of Caesar, Scarface and *The Public Enemy*, from the gangster as thrilling animal to the gangster as pathetic wimp. Or, to put the case of Eddie Bartlett less cruelly, as romantic loser. Which is to say that in less than a decade the movies had begun to turn a figure who had only recently been one of their most vital inventions into a figure of nostalgia, a figure this film sees as having been rendered redundant by politically conscious, socially aware figures like Lloyd Hart, who as he is presented here might as well have been an earnest New Deal lawyer.

Of course, this is nonsense. The movies were writing off the gangster just at the moment when, in reality, he was beginning to weave himself permanently into the fabric of American life, as a member of the Mafia. But be that as it may, *The Roaring Twenties* cannot be written off. It remains a permanently affecting movie, and the repository of one of James Cagney's best performances, one in that line

ne Sheridan came between O'Brien and Cagney in
rrid Zone (below). But nothing could come between
agney and a good smoke in *The Fighting 69th*.

iat, beginning with *Ceiling Zero* and ending
ith *Yankee Doodle Dandy*, secured him a
lace in the softest, most sentimental corner of
ie American heart.

Some of the pictures from here through the
'ohan biography would continue that insinu-
ting process – but not his next two, *The Fight-
ig 69th* and *Torrid Zone*. The former is, in fact,
ie most lugubriously pious work in his
lmography, with Pat O'Brien impersonating
'ather Duffy, the heroic chaplain of the
imous World War One unit, composed
iainly of New York Irishmen, Cagney imitat-
ig a coward – a man who loses his annoying
ravado once he finds himself under fire on the
Vestern Front. Again William Keighley goes
·lentlessly for the biggest, most obvious emo-
ons. Cagney is required to find his misplaced
·ligious beliefs before he can recover his
ourage, and his impression of a lost sheep
·andering into a Christmas Eve service in a
alf-bombed church just behind the lines in
·rance – the music swelling, every shadow
·regnant with symbolism, every light agleam
·ith the hope of heaven – is enough to make
nyone fear not for the immortal soul of Jerry
'lunkett, but for that of James Cagney, the
weetest little Mick ever to bounce down a
·nement steps. Well, he gets to do a couple of
10se screaming meemies scenes he loved so
·ell to do as an actor, to die a martyr's death
n the battlefield and to work in a picture doing
s bit for the preparedness movement that was
·athering momentum in 1940. But on the
·hole, *The Fighting 69th* is an experience best
·ft buried under fonder memories.

Torrid Zone, so obviously unpretentious,
·as, and is, infinitely more agreeable. It found
·agney and O'Brien in a mythical South
·merican country, working for a Yankee
·nperialist corporation mighty like that *bête
·oire* of the left, The United Fruit Co. They
·ad to get the bananas harvested and on the
·oat despite a recalcitrant labor force, revolu-
·onary activities, the disturbing presence of a
·tranded American girl – played by Ann

Sheridan, the actress who finally filled the void
in Cagney's professional life, a girl spunky
enough to allow one to imagine him actually
falling for her. The switcheroo here – in their
last picture together until *Ragtime* – is that Pat
is a worse con man than Jimmy. The latter does
all the work, the former gets all the credit – and
keeps preventing his pal from quitting and
improving himself. The crosstalk is as fast as
it was in *Boy Meets Girl* – right on the edge
of incomprehensibility – and with Keighley for
once bouncing the picture artlessly along and
Cagney again wearing his silly little mustache,

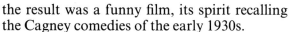

the result was a funny film, its spirit recalling the Cagney comedies of the early 1930s.

Cagney's next assignment, *City For Conquest*, unfortunately summoned up the less happy aspects of his early movie days. In outline it sounds like a typical Cagney project, more in the pathetic than the triumphant vein: good-natured, quick-fisted Danny Kenny takes up professional boxing at the behest of his ambitious girl friend (Ann Sheridan again) and is then blinded by an opponent whose gloves are treated with dangerous chemicals by mobsters angry with Danny for refusing to tank their bout. But there was more to the film than that, even in the apparently heavily-edited final release version. Based on Aben Kendell's well-received novel of the same title and directed by Anatole Litvak, who had come to Warner Brothers from Europe trailing an artist's repute behind him (he had directed the Charles Boyer-Danielle Darrieux *Mayerling*) the intention was to make something more than a boxing picture. It was to be a sort of 'Symphony of the City', which is, in fact, the title of the great musical work Danny's kid brother (Arthur Kennedy) dreams of composing, having had his musical education subsidized by Danny's pugilistic career. Beyond that, the picture offers glimpses of the city's show biz life – the Sheridan character is a dancer, who is seduced from true love by Anthony Quinn, in his youthful, Latin lover incarnation – as well as its criminal life, where we find Elia Kazan, quite memorable as a subsidiary hood.

But somehow it doesn't work as a whole, perhaps because the studio cut it ruthlessly, perhaps because it descends into the bathetic at its conclusion, with Cagney, reduced in his sightlessness to running a news-stand, listening to the première of his brother's symphony on the radio. And having his sometime girlfriend happen by just after the music has reached its triumphant conclusion. It has been said that Cagney and Litvak clashed repeatedly on the set over both the style of the production and

the tone of Cagney's performance. Nevertheless, Cagney apparently still felt good enough about it to set aside his rule of never looking at himself on the screen, and attended a preview of *City For Conquest*. After which, he later told Hollywood gossip columnist Louella Parsons, 'I sat there thinking, "Was that what it was about?" It didn't add up to the hours and days of work that had gone into it. It was all right, but it didn't represent the effort we'd all made.'

Decades later, he used almost the same words to describe his response to the film to me. 'I remember it well – yes, sure. The picture didn't turn out as I hoped it would, because I really worked on that one. I'd trained for 12 – 14 weeks to get in shape and did it, and after it was all over – so what?'

Somehow, *City For Conquest* seems to have been a turning point for him, renewing his old pessimism and suspicion about studio promises. Obviously he had sensed in it the oppor-

Anthony Quinn was the latin lover who wooed Anne Sheridan away from an obviously distressed Cagney in *City for Conquest*. The star had high hopes for the picture, and trained hard for its boxing sequences. He was bitterly disappointed when the studio carelessly shortened the picture, cutting its heart out. Still, he had some good men in his corner – among them Frank McHugh, Donald Crisp and George Tobias.

tunity to make a summarizing statement about the environment and the experiences that had shaped him – so much in the film analogizes to his autobiography. Who knows, perhaps he saw in that boxer blinded by criminals something of the actor whose gifts were being blunted, as he saw it, by the thoughtless studio bosses. And yet, set aside the clichés and the sentimentality of the story, and the inappropriateness of a few of Litvak's directorial 'touches' – distinctly alien corn – the picture is affecting. And Cagney is often astonishing in it, particularly in the later passages, after he has been blinded.

No one has ever more accurately caught the way the unsighted cock their heads when they are listening. Or the way they move through the world they cannot see, at once abrupt and tentative. Or, for that matter, the speech patterns of people who cannot see and thus judge the effect of what they are saying. To this Cagney adds a little mannerism of his own, a way of silently working his mouth between sentences or when he is in repose – exactly the sort of tic a man who cannot see himself might develop. *City For Conquest*, in its final form, may have frustrated his desire to make a grand and elevated statement about the world that had formed him, but it gave him a unique opportunity to physicalize the quality in which, at this point in his career, he was specializing: victimization.

That quality was also present, but muted, in *The Strawberry Blonde*. Indeed, so warmly colored with good humored nostalgia is this delightful picture, larruping along under Raoul Walsh's genial direction, that it requires an effort of memory to recall that Cagney is, in fact, sorely afflicted in its course. Mostly the mood Walsh creates is rather grandfatherly, that of an older gentleman comfortably settled back in his wing chair and yarning for the gathered grandchildren about the days of his youth – the Gay Nineties in this case.

This was a mood coming into fashion in the movies at this time. As the worst effects of the Depression faded a certain urgent, not to say desperate, need to entertain at all costs, and at a great pace, seemed to desert the movies. To be sure, the year was 1941, and not a few films hinted at new perils to come. But even after war came, the need to resort to more leisurely times, the gentle pleasures of strolling in the park or listening to the close harmonies of a barbershop quartet, persisted in the movies. Indeed, it often seemed, during the war, that when they were not lecturing us on the unredeemable beastliness of our enemies, or issuing gaseous promises about the restored brotherhood of man that was to come with the peace, American films were urging us to return to the simpler days of yore. Almost all of our musicals, and many of our comedies, invited us to contemplate the serenity of a moment when the largest available excitement was our first glimpse of a horseless carriage – or a female ankle.

The Strawberry Blonde stands at the beginning of this trend, and perhaps for that very reason it retains its air of freshness. The story is by two expert screenwriters, Julius and Philip Epstein (less than a year away from *Casablanca*), adapted from a play and an earlier Gary Cooper movie, *One Sunday Afternoon*. It recounts the life of feisty Biff Grimes (Cagney, of course) whose temper was comically hot (he was always putting up his fists in the manner of a daguerrotype boxer) but whose soul is somehow drawn toward the art of dentistry, which he learns by mail. In effect, Cagney is parodying his tough guy image as the film traces the history of two relationships, his with Amy (Olivia de Havilland), a shy nurse, and that of his friend Hugo Barnstead (Jack Carson) with Virginia Brush, the 'strawberry blonde' of the title (Rita Hayworth).

Hugo is everything Biff is not, bland and snaky in Carson's superbly disciplined comic performance, and on the rise in business and politics. The men meet the women on a blind date, a marvelous comic sequence, in which the former desperately pretend a *savoir faire* they lack and Amy pretends to be a liberated

125

woman puffing on a cigarette, even defending free love – in which she most assuredly does not believe. There is no sweeter comedy of manners in all of movies than these few minutes of muddled social and intellectual pretense, which no one is sophisticated enough to sustain. Biff at first is drawn to Virginia, which is understandable: Hayworth was never more attractive than she was in this film, pretty and straightforward, with no obligations to sex symbolism. But despite a night on the town that Biff cannot afford (they waltz to the title tune), Virginia elopes with Hugo and accompanies him on his rise to power, while Biff marries Amy on the rebound.

Eventually Hugo hires Biff to manage a construction business he owns, and permits him to take the blame for graft, which actually leads to the death of workmen in a building collapse. In Biff's leave-taking for jail, and in his return from it after serving a lengthy term, there is an unsentimental tenderness between him and his wife that is without precedent in any Cagney film. Had anyone bothered to write this kind of material for him, or regularly given him co-stars like de Havilland who, quietly, firmly, and with a humorously knowing gleam in her eye, asserts her right to share the scene equally with him, his image might have been a very different one. And he might have been a happier actor as well. At any rate, more years pass, and one Sunday Hugo comes to Biff with an aching tooth. Biff is tempted to revenge himself on him by employing an excess of anesthetic, but seeing that he and Virginia have turned into an unhappily bickering couple, he contents himself with a painful (but brief) extraction. 'I just realized', he explains to Amy, 'that I'm a happy man and he isn't.'

This picture proves Cagney could play in the middle range. If windmilling readiness for a brawl is a comment, good-humored and intelligent, on his own image, it is also a comment on standard masculine values as the movies have always put them forth. Similarly, his defeats lead to reconciliation, self-

understanding, instead of the tragedy that so often was the conclusion of a Cagney film. There is a calm sunniness, a lack of edginess in both his performance and its context that sets *The Strawberry Blonde* apart from almost everything else he did.

In effect, this picture was an attempt to relocate Cagney, to see if his character could live and breathe somewhere other than in a contemporary urban environment. He was older now, no longer quite a fresh mutt. Moreover, the issues his earlier screen character had illuminated – the failure of old-fashioned individualism, the need for a new definition of community – were no longer as pressing, as dramatically interesting, as they had been. The nation had recovered itself economically and psychologically, and the rebellious temptation was now muted. Entering the war years, our need seemed to be for heroes who had accepted all the givens of society before the movie began. The issue now was, or was about to be, acceptance of both fate and responsibility. *The Strawberry Blonde* gently prefigures that concern.

The Bride Came C.O.D. prefigures nothing; it is a backward-looking film. In it Cagney plays a pilot hired by a rich man (Eugene Pallette) to abduct his high-spirited (high-strung might be a better description) daughter (Bette Davis) and bring her home before she marries a bandleader (Jack Carson). He does so, but they have to make a crash-landing in the desert and in the course of picking cactus needles out of her bottom and helping her to be a good sport about the various other vicissitudes they encounter, they fall in love. It was obviously supposed to be an airborne *It Happened One Night*, but no one's heart was in it. Keighley's direction was something less than merry and Davis, who would later write that she had always wanted to do something 'fine' with Cagney, did not think this was it. There is something sour and grudging in her performance, and Cagney is really too forceful a performer for this kind of work, which requires

a certain distractedness of its heroes. The film has an almost brutal air about it when, that is, it does not seem merely tired and forced, as so many comedies made at the end of the screwball cycle do.

'So Full of Spectacle and Glory it Had to be Made in Technicolor' said the ads for his next picture, *Captains of the Clouds*, and indeed its only claim on history is as Cagney's first color film. He is Brian MacLean, a bush pilot in Canada who keeps disrupting the camaraderie of his fellow flyers by stealing jobs from them. When the war comes, however, they enlist as a group in the Royal Canadian Air Force where naturally Brian refuses to learn to fly by the military book and is cashiered. After a period of despondent isolation he gets a job ferrying unarmed bombers to England, and on his first flight encounters a Nazi fighter and eagerly accepts the opportunity for a hero's suicide, ramming the attacker so the rest of his flight can escape. The film obviously recycles elements of both *Devil Dogs of the Air* and *Ceiling Zero*, but without O'Brien, and neither color nor the addition of an awful title song notably freshen it. Indeed, its length and clumsiness place it among the most excruciating films ever made either by its director, Michael Curtiz, or by Cagney. And he knew it. He did it, according to producer Hal Wallis, only because Jack Warner persuaded him that he would be making a contribution to the war effort by accepting the role. But working conditions on the Canadian locations were terrible, and Cagney suffered a concussion when he refused to let a double substitute for him in a scene where he was knocked into the water by a wayward propeller. He might have been forgiven the thought that his was going to be a long war.

Still, he had hopes, right from the start, for *Yankee Doodle Dandy*. Cagney had seen George M. Cohan on the stage when he was a boy, and obviously felt an affinity for an ambitious and energetic performer who shared with Cagney not only an Irish heritage but the

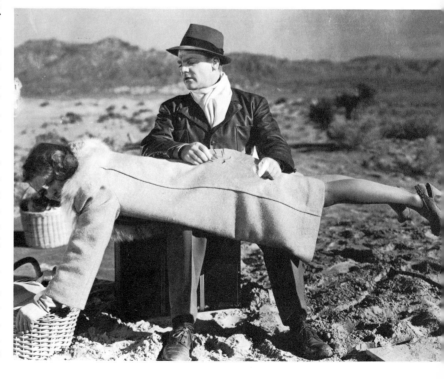

Captious in the cloud. Once again Cagney found it difficult to bear military discipline. This time the service oppressing him was the Canadian Air Force and the picture's title was *Captains of the Cloud*. It was a preparedness tract, not helped by its song score, a part of which played (below) by composer M. K. Jerome for character actor Alan Hale and Cagney as director. Michael Curtiz (wearing tie) looks on.

experience of rising from the humbler levels of vaudeville to a powerful stardom. In explaining why he would come to think of it as his favorite film, a choice that hardly needs an explanation, Cagney would quote a saying that Cohan himself was fond of repeating, 'once a song-and-dance man, always a song-and-dance man'. In that brief statement, Cagney would say, 'You have my life story: those few words tell as much about me professionally as there is to tell.'

His story of the picture's genesis is that Cohan's representatives took the idea of doing a biopic about him to Sam Goldwyn who was briefly interested because he had a commitment to make a picture with Fred Astaire, but that the latter, quite sensibly, turned it down as not right for him. The project was then offered to Warner Brothers with the stipulation that Cagney was the only acceptable star for it. He, naturally, wanted it – at least in part he admitted later – because he was at the time being accused of Communist sympathies, in part because of his union activities (he was now president of the Screen Actors' Guild), in part because of his very open support of the New Deal. He wanted to do an unimpeachable flag waver, and heaven knows the Cohan story offered him splendid opportunities.

The first script, however, he found awfully dour, and he insisted on getting an uncredited polish job from the Epstein brothers, who clearly contributed to the film some of the affectionate regard for times gone by that had marked their work on *The Strawberry Blonde*. The two pictures are, in fact, remarkable in their emotional kinship – there is something so easy and unforced in both of them. That was particularly valuable in *Yankee Doodle Dandy*, providing a gentle contrast for Leroy Prinz's wonderfully exuberant musical numbers, which evoked the spirit of the old time musical stage without becoming imprisoned in their sometimes congealing conventions. Similarly, Michael Curtiz was a fortunate choice as a director. His taste for shadowed lighting catches the flavor of Cohan's backstage world,

and the subtle flexibility of his camera imparts a musical flow to the piece even in its non-musical moments. *Yankee Doodle Dandy* has about it the air of legend, of fancy, and yet it never loses its realistic footing.

And whether it was the Epsteins or the credited screenwriters, Robert Buckner and Edmund Joseph, who devised its contemporary framing device, that simple idea was extremely important to the success of the movie, tying its nostalgic sentiments into high, current emotions. The picture opens with Cohan appearing in *I'd Rather Be Right*, a musical that satirizes President Roosevelt, and receiving, backstage, a summons to visit the White House. He fears that perhaps he has displeased the President and he approaches the meeting with trepidation. But no, he has been summoned to receive a medal for the contribu-

tion his songs have made to American patriotism, and Roosevelt (who is seen only from the back) requests a recounting of the performer's life and times. The tale he tells is of a show business family maintaining warm, decent, middle-class values despite the fact that they almost never stopped travelling the vaudeville circuit – very inspirational at a moment when so many American lives were being disrupted by the exigencies of war. It is also a tale of healthy first-generation American ambition, of a young performer determined to rise above his humble origins in two-a-day and make a name for himself in legit as a composer and playwright. And doing so by celebrating the most basic of American values – faith in the family, love of the country that permits a man to dream of transcendence. There is a cautionary element in work, too. Cagney's Cohan is seen

Our Yankee Doodle Boy. As George M. Cohan, Cagney worked his way up from humble showbiz beginnings (right) to smashing production numbers – left and overleaf. *Yankee Doodle Dandy* **was his favourite film – and everyone else's, too.**

as a workaholic, a man sometimes too absorbed in his work to actually practice what it preaches. But that is treated mostly as a forgivable and sometimes humorous foible, something to provide a little mild dramatic tension at midpassage when he retires prematurely and his wife joins in a benign conspiracy to get him back on his tapping feet, re-engaged with the world, which is, of course, what all Americans were supposed to be doing during the war, when self-absorption was a sin only slightly less horrifying than trading with the enemy.

But no one remembers *Yankee Doodle Dandy* for the issues, biographical and public, that it takes up. Its immortality rests on its songs – the title tune, of course, and all the rest – 'You're a Grand Old Flag', 'Give My Regards to Broadway', 'Over There', to name only the most famous. They are sung and danced with a full-hearted exuberance, a compulsive urgency, that finally turns the picture into a celebration that is almost orgiastic in its effect. And Cagney's work in the musical numbers goes far beyond the professionally expert. He conveys an emotional commitment to them, a transforming joy in what he is doing, that is simply overwhelming. There are moments in these passages that cannot be contained within any nice aesthetic discussion. Very simply, we are in that rare realm of performance here where the identification between performer and work is complete and seamless, a realm we occasionally are conducted to in theatrical performance – by someone like Laurence Olivier in *The Entertainer*, for example – but which is almost never to be found on the screen. No matter how often one sees Cagney fling himself into these routines the response is the same – a lump in the throat that can be dissolved only through a combination of laughter and tears, some strange kinetic charge that makes one want to leap up and try to join him.

Yankee Doodle Dandy is, in effect, a reconciling film. For just this moment in time all Cagney's doubts and disappointments about his life's work are resolved. This, he knows, is what he was put on earth to do, and no ambiguity is going to spoil his pleasure in it. And we partake of that sense of the moment too. In just a little more than a decade the Public Enemy has become a public hero, repository not of our worst fears about ourselves, but of our best sense of ourselves. All the goodness we always knew was in that boy, all the sweetness and energy that had drawn us to his character now, of a sudden, burst forth, unclouded by guilt, by moral qualms, by fear of its lunatic side. What a joy there was in this! And what a relief, too, to banish all those darkling clouds. From this moment on, Cagney's claim on our affections was complete. He could, and would, go back to doing wrong. But in the largest sense he could never do wrong again. He was, forever after, our Yankee Doodle Boy.

INSIDE, BLACKNESS

'I WASN'T AWARE OF ANY TOUGHNESS.' Of Cagney's several remarkable reflections on his first decade of screen stardom, this sentence, thrown away rather casually, with no hint of duplicity or false naiveté in his tone, is perhaps the most remarkable. It is actually difficult to credit, this failure to acknowledge what everyone understood to be his essence. Yet many of the most intense and memorable performances in movies and theater arise precisely because an actor is playing not merely (or necessarily) against physical type, but against his truest, deepest and possibly darkest sense of himself. For it compels him to mobilize his mimetic forces at levels of intensity those who merely play some version of their better selves never experience. There is in this a power to transfix an audience and hold it mesmerized, as Cagney did for so many years, no matter how dubious or even downright unpleasant the characters he was playing. It was a power he would resort to again in a very few years, and at new levels of dislocating intensity.

Now, however, in George M. Cohan, Cagney had played a figure that, as he saw it, he did not have to 'act' at all – not in the sense just described. Cohan was a character he could totally invest merely by being the song-and-dance man he was – or had started out to be. By so doing he created not only his most popular screen role, but his most generously acclaimed one, since he won both the Academy Award and the New York Film Critics' prize for *Yankee Doodle Dandy*. If ever the moment seemed right for him to strike out on his own, and to abandon the exhausting effort of not being his truest self, this was it. And so, with his brother William, he organized Cagney Productions, releasing its films through United Artists and obtaining its financing, for the most part, through banks. He was, indeed, so eager to be his own boss that he pronounced himself willing to defer, if necessary, his actor's salary, pegged at $150,000 a picture, the same as his Warners fee, hoping the films he made would recoup enough to repay him and, perhaps,

return an additional profit in which he would share as producer.

This venture was riskier than it appears to be now. For one thing, Cagney was quite distracted by his heavy commitments to the war effort. He made extensive tours entertaining troops at home and abroad and selling war bonds and in 1943 he made quite a powerful short subject in aid of civilian defense. Directed by Mervyn Leroy and entitled *You, John Jones*, Cagney appeared in it as an air raid warden, demonstrating what could happen to a peaceful, and achingly archetypal American, block should enemy planes manage to penetrate American air space.

Still, there were more important factors than Cagney's full-hearted response to the call of wartime duty at work in determining the fate of his new production company. One of these was his obsession with making a definitive break with his screen past. The other was the business climate in which the company was launched. Its press agent would say that he had been ordered not to stress the star's 'socko' image as he phrased it and both Cagney and his brother would tell interviewers that their productions would be thematically idealistic and uplifting. Said William: 'He was typed – typed exactly the kind of guy our mother had tried to push us farthest away from.' This was, of course, an exaggeration, as we have seen, but the brothers would seek material from more respectable and upscale sources than Warner Brothers had and Cagney would try to break out of the urban milieu in which he had mostly operated.

Unfortunately for their hopes Cagney Productions missed by a little more than a decade the first great era of independent production by star-entrepreneurs and preceded, by a shorter time span, the second such era. That first period had been marked by the foundation of United Artists itself by Douglas Fairbanks, Mary Pickford, Charles Chaplin and D. W. Griffith and had to all intents and purposes been brought to an end by the rise of an

And the winner is . . . Gary Cooper, the previous year's holder, presents Cagney with the 1942 Oscar for *Yankee Doodle Dandy*. **Below, he joins the year's other winners, Van Heflin, Greer Garson and Teresa Wright backstage.**

oligopolistic studio system and by the comi of sound. The new technology impose far heavier production costs on film make than silent films had, increasing the risks individual productions. These the handful major studios could amortize over many film something the independents could not d Moreover, the studios controlled most of t significant theater chains and imposed the brutal block booking system on the indepe dent exhibitors, which made it difficult even f United Artists, the main distributor for t independents, to secure profitable play dat for their films. This had the effect of makir

he Patriot. The Hollywood Band Cavalcade of 1943 took
agney to Boston in 1943. Among his fellow travellers
elow) were Groucho Marx, Art Jacobson, Frances
ongford and Charlotte Greenwood.
ou, John Jones, (right) was a short subject designed to
how it could happen here. Cagney played an air raid
arden trying to cope with the effects of a bombing run
n a typical American street.

the banks, the only source of financing for independent production, shy away from them. And U.A., chronically short of capital (a condition that had plagued it from the day it was created), was unable to offer its producers much help. In this period it subsisted on foreign pickups and on the activities of a handful of Hollywood producers who could not or would not work inside the studios. David O. Selznick and Walter Wanger had recently decamped, but the likes of Hunt Stromberg and Edward Small were still delivering pictures to its exchanges. At the time that Cagney went into business for himself, he was the only actor trying to function as an independent through U.A., excepting Chaplin, the last of its founders still active in movies, but completing a film only about once in five years. For all their complaints, no star had the gumption to attempt what Cagney was attempting. It was just too difficult in comparison to the comfortable entrapment the studio term contract offered.

In a few years, as everyone knows, all that would change. Before the decade ended the courts would force the studios to divest themselves of their theater chains and to abandon block booking, providing a wider opening for the independents. At the same time, television networking would begin and America would lose the habit of weekly moviegoing, replacing it with the more insidious television habit. Forced to produce fewer, riskier films, the studios ceased to offer long term contracts in the 1950s but vied with one another to offer stars with authentic drawing power independent deals very like the one Cagney prematurely obtained at United Artists – only much richer.

In other words, Cagney had seen the future. But it didn't work for him. His first independent project could not have been a greater departure for him. *Johnny Come Lately* was based on a Louis Bromfield novella that had run in the *Saturday Evening Post*, and as adapted for the screen by John Van Druten, a playwright whose middlebrow touch was generally as sure as Bromfield's, it was in a vein probably no one but Cagney could have imagined as suitable for him; it was pure whimsey. Or anyway, it started out to be, before it deteriorated into rather desperate melodrama. It is a turn of the century period piece, in which Cagney plays an itinerant newspaperman named Tom Richards. He is discovered by the audience and by a sweet little old widow who habitually befriends the friendless sitting in a park, reading Dickens, and in a wryly philosophical mood. The woman is played by delicate, genteel Grace George, a much beloved stage actress, making her first and last screen appearance – and a lovely one at that. In the film she owns an almost moribund newspaper and so it is natural for her to post bond for Tom when he is arrested for vagrancy and offer him a job editing her paper, which is staffed by adorable eccentrics and wistful has-beens. When Tom discovers his benefactress is being hounded by the corrupt local establishment he energizes his staff for a successful crusade for civic virtue. Having done some good, however, he remains true to his wanderer's code and hops a freight out of town. His freedom means more to him than a permanent job or the possibility of marriage to his boss's granddaughter.

In outline this is fine and, obviously, his character's desire to escape the routines imposed by conventional obligations spoke strongly to Cagney. The first hour or so of *Johnny Come Lately* has about it a sweet charm that is unlike anything he had ever done, except perhaps *The Strawberry Blonde*. A surprisingly handsome-looking Marjorie Main is very funny as the local madam, who enlists on the side of righteousness, and so is Hattie McDaniel, doing her expert routine as a spunky maid, more sensible than her employers. Such worthies as Margaret Hamilton and George Cleveland are splendid as the newspaper people invigorated by Cagney's presence. If the production has about it a somewhat frugal air it also has, in its early passages, lightness and grace – something of a departure from his usually more intense manner by the director, William K. Howard, a veteran craftsman who, like Cagney, had known difficulties in working under studio management. In short, as James Agee observed at the time, this 'tone and pace would never have survived a big studio.'

That agreeable mood is, however, broken in the picture's last third. Or as Agee put it in his review, 'It breaks down into a panic of melodrama and comic propitiation.' Especially the former, for suddenly blows and shots are being exchanged and Cagney is very much at the center of this action. But this is not at all where we were given to understand that his investigative reporting and his idealistic editorializing were going to take him – or us. On the contrary, the build-up was all in a different direction, towards a victory over rather comically presented wrong-doers through the exercise of a certain sly cleverness.

One cannot help but think that at some point during production someone suddenly observed that there was nothing in *Johnny Come Lately* to appease the more base members of the Cagney fan club, who expected him to swing lustily into action at some point in any picture he made. And so the film is wrenched around to fulfill their expectations, at whatever cost to carefully wrought mood, at whatever cost to the emotional logic of the film. Worse, these action sequences are perfunctorily managed by both the director and the star. They are distasteful obligations, not inescapable compulsions. If these scenes do not entirely spoil *Johnny Come Lately*, they do blemish it. Once again Cagney's attempt to express what he thought of as his best self on the screen was thwarted. But this time he could not blame Jack Warner.

Jimmy too soon. With his brother William, Cagney created an independent production company several years ahead of the fad, and suffered the consequences of pioneering. Their first film, *Johnny Come Lately*, flopped. Very mild love interest was provided by Marjorie Lord.

In any event, it did no good. *Johnny Come Lately* grossed only $2·4 million, returning at most only a modest profit to its producers. The immediate result was that the Cagneys turned to what must have seemed a more reliable subject, an espionage story called *Blood On The Sun*, which was heavier on anti-Japanese propaganda than it was on suspense. In it Cagney again plays a newspaper editor, this time running an English language sheet in Tokyo in the 1920s. He is rather well acculturated, among the quaint local customs he has acquired being an expertise in judo that will come in handy before the plot has entirely unwound. It revolves around his discovery of the secret Tanaka Plan for Japanese domination of Asia and his attempts to expose it, and the growth of Japanese militarism, to the sleeping world.

Blood On The Sun is in most respects a fairly conventional, not to say banal, story of spies and counterspies. It has Tanaka and his gang of conspirators, conspicuously including Colonel Tojo and Captain Yamamoto, not yet risen to flag rank, but instantly identifiable symbols in the war years of everything America was fighting against, perhaps more concerned than they needed to be about discrediting their newsman enemy (they attempt to falsely implicate him in a murder) and rather more reliant than one imagines the historical Tanaka and his cohorts might have been on the efforts of a Eurasian *femme fatale* (played by Sylvia Sidney) to advance their cause. Certainly, if these plotters were as clever as *Blood On The Sun* would have us believe, they would easily have discovered that she had family connections with their liberal and westernizing political enemies, and was thus a counterspy.

Her success in this line of work eventually leads to Tanaka's ritual suicide, though not before he has the opportunity to prove the depths of his vileness by insisting that his colleagues seek vengence on his betrayer: 'You will see that the woman is punished. Death that comes quickly is not punishment. There are other forms that must be more painfully absorbed.' This, needless to say, was a routine threat among Axis villains during the war years. But after he delivers this charge to his co-conspirators the movie gets down to its real propagandistic business. Tojo swears that his victorious armies 'will march through the streets of every capital of the world', while Yamamoto promises 'America will be crushed, never to rise again.' He will, he says, dictate peace terms from the White House. Both of these sentiments were widely attributed to these men by American propaganda during the war in an attempt to terrorize us into buying

ntleman of Japan. In *Blood on the Sun* Cagney was a
usading newsman ferreting out Nippon's secret plans for
orld domination in the pre-war years. Above left, he
cepts, but does not buy, their flimsy excuses. Below left,
a conversation with Rhys Williams passes over double
ent Sylvia Sidney's head. At right he hears the liberal
int of view from Frank Puglia.

Cagney learned Judo for his role in *Blood on the Sun*, and
his use of it in the film provided its most exciting moments.

ore war bonds. And it certainly worked on
kids: the *frisson* of fear as Japanese
uperialist or Nazi menace hissed or snarled
eir threats at decent folk increased your
esire to fight them however you could. Of
ourse, children are the most warlike of citizens
ad never need the slightest encouragement to
gn up for battle.

Encountering this movie again, four decades
ter it was first seen, is more than a little dis-
aying, especially considering its source, one
Hollywood's most liberal-minded and
escent-minded actors. To be sure, it offers
me minor pleasures. Sidney, another per-
rmer who had had her troubles with type-
sting – she generally appeared in 1930s
oblems pictures as a waif-like sufferer of
cial injustice – is astonishingly beautiful as
woman of mystery. One understands per-
ctly how Cagney the character could be smit-
n by her and why Cagney the producer,
oubtless remembering her striking appear-
nce in *Madame Butterfly*, a decade earlier, cast
er. Cagney himself has some moments that
e close to sublime. The dancer in him clearly
sponded to the opportunity to study judo for
e role, and to use it in the climactic brawl,
hich under Frank Lloyd's direction is one of
e best he was ever involved in, with Cagney
king on a hoard of policemen and besting
em through a combination of martial arts
id good old Yankee street fighting.

But even that has its obvious propagandistic
vertones, implying that one American is the
qual of at least a dozen 'monkeys', as the
apanese were ever referred to in wartime films.
ater, more dead than alive, he fails by a few
irds to gain entrance to the American
mbassy and diplomatic sanctuary. His
ountrymen rush out to him and confront the
ursuing Japanese who then offer a 'deal' for
is life. 'The American government doesn't
take deals', he snarls – a sentiment that would
oubtless surprise American governments
ast, present and future, but was of course
asily understood at the time as endorsement

of an oft-stated war aim: the Axis Powers'
unconditional surrender. This, in turn, was an
expression of the popularly held belief that we
would not be fighting this war if we had not
given our enemies such a sweet deal when we
made peace after World War One. Once the
Americans have glared the Japanese down and
brought him to safety, Cagney speaks the film's
coda, its moral: 'Sure, forgive your enemies,
but first get even.'

Perhaps the ideological high point of the
movie occurs in a scene where Cagney and Sidney reflect that though they only met ten days
before they had, in that short time, managed
to fall in love and to mount a conspiracy that
threatened the most powerful elements in
Japanese society. 'Ten days that shook the
world, eh,' says Cagney, quoting the title of
John Reed's famous history of the October

13 Rue Madeleine. **An obviously posed still. Symbolically tells the story of an espionage adventure. Villain, Richard Conte menaces Cagney and Annabella. Below, the trio join actor Richard Lattimore for an on-location musicale.**

Revolution in the Soviet Union and scoring a sly point for co-screenwriter Lester Cole, who like many of his Stalinist ilk enjoyed slipping 'revolutionary' tags into his scripts.

The phrase cannot be said to have rescued *Blood On The Sun* for the cause of enlightened humanism. And one would not dwell on this picture if it had been made at Warner Brothers or some other studio. It is not worse than most of the other examples of wartime *agitprop*. But considering its source one wonders why it is not better than it is. Or why it was not left entirely unmade. Like the last half of *Johnny Come Lately* it seems to betray the very principles for which Cagney formed his company. And to no avail. *Blood On The Sun* grossed about a million more than its predecessor, but it looks as if it cost a little more, too. Cagney was not getting rich as an independent – not yet, at least – and aside from the pleasure of making his own mistakes he was not achieving his other goals either.

Still, free to negotiate his own deals, he was in a position to command fees on the open market far in excess of what Warner Brothers had been paying him and now, perhaps pressed by the relative failure of his first independent pictures, he signed with Twentieth Century-Fox to make *13 Rue Madeleine* for the largest salary he had ever commanded, $300,000. The film was a stylistic sequel to a surprise Fox hit of 1945, *The House on 92nd Street*. Besides using an address in its title, the new picture also borrowed the semi-documentary technique of its stupefying predecessor. That is, it employed a voice-over narration to offer what purported to be an inside view of a secretive organization. The first showed the FBI's wartime anti-espionage activities – more Hooverian self-promotion of course. *13 Rue Madeleine*, also produced by Louis de Rochmont, late of the quasi-newsreel *March of Time,* and also directed by laconically impersonal Henry Hathaway, took us behind the shadowy scenes of the OSS, called in the movie '007,' a set of figures that would in a few years ring more

resonantly through popular culture. It traced the fate of one unit of American spies from training through their drop into France to the completion of their mission, which includes the martyrdom of their leader, Bob Sharkey, played by Cagney.

Sharkey's group includes a German agent (Richard Conte), whom Sharkey spots almost instantly because, on a training exercise, he proves himself 'too good', that is too smooth in his ability to talk his way out of a tight spot. 'A couple of American kids would have slugged the guard and fought their way out', says Sharkey, stating the film's main theme, which is that Americans are too open and generous of spirit to fit comfortably into the dark and devious world of espionage. It is the Nazis who have a natural bent for chicanery of that kind, and Americans have to undergo special and arduous training for this gloomy art. 'An American is a good sport, he plays by the rules,' says Cagney's character in his first speech to his charges. 'No secret agent is.' He adds, 'Years of decency and honest living – forget all about that or turn in your suits – because the enemy has.'

How Cagney's character, who is introduced as speaking five languages and having won at least that many varsity letters in college, acquired his cynical expertise in this field is unexplained. But the actor's screen past, in which his character had sometimes set aside his inherent decency in favor of expediency, helps lend authority to one of the very few conventionally heroic roles he ever played. Parachuted into occupied France, the unit is charged with spreading disinformation, namely that the Allied invasion of Europe will come through the Low Countries. But now the Conte character, whom Sharkey has refused to publicly unmask, waiting for a ripe time when some larger benefit may accrue from it, gets loose and must be stopped before he can inform the Germans where the main thrust of the invasion will strike. Cagney now follows his people into France, disposes of the informer but, with the

Nazis closing in on the Resistance group that has sheltered him, he eschews escape by air and helps fight a rearguard action that permits everyone else to get away. He, however, is captured and taken to Gestapo headquarters (at 13 Rue Madeleine, of course) where he is put to torture.

Walter Abel, playing 007's founder-leader, is now seen briefing the crews of a bomber squadron ordered to wipe out that house before Cagney's 'strong, tough Minnesota body' can endure no more pain and he breaks, telling the Nazis to strengthen their Normandy defenses. (The Abel figure's faith in precision bombing is near-to-touching.) This plan, however improbable, does provide Cagney with a great moment. We see German sadists, whips in hand, shaking their heads over the difficulty of their task as they take a break before returning to it. A door opens and we see a scarred Cagney, naked to the waist, stoically awaiting further punishment. We hear the sound of blows as the camera averts its eye from the torment. But then we hear the drone of approaching airplane engines and then the crash of bombs. Explosions flare and we cut back to Cagney laughing maniacally as a final blast ends his agony – and obliterates his torturers. There is nothing quite like it in any other American war movie, nothing quite so humanly heroic, so opposed in spirit to conventional movie bravery, which at the time tended either to the tight-lipped or to the loose-lipped, in which case impeding doom was greeted with rhetorical flights about the traditions for which we fought, the brave new world for which any sacrifice was worth while. Still, it is doubtful if *13 Rue Madeleine* as a whole is worth waiting through for those few frames of the pure Cagney spirit.

It was certainly worth making, however, from the star's point of view. He could now afford to defer salary again and return to Cagney Productions and its most ambitious and long-cherished project, a screen adaptation of William Saroyan's hit play of 1939,

Characters. Among the lovable eccentrics Cagney gathered around him in a San Francisco bar for his production of *The Time of Your Life* were James Bolton (right) and William Bendix (below).

The Time Of Your Life. This film is not quite lost – copies of it are known to exist – but to acquire their rights to the play, for which the author rejected the Pulitzer Prize it was awarded, the Cagneys had to agree to limit their release of the picture to seven years. By all accounts, their film, which was directed by H. C. Potter, a stage director who also directed a number of rather stagey movies, mostly comedies, is a mostly faithful rendering of the play. No attempt was made to open it up or to supply a more dramatically intense plot than Saroyan originally provided. Set in a San Francisco bar, where a number of whimsically eccentric characters gather to booze, banter and philosophize, it was well cast with the likes of Paul Draper, a fine dancer playing a dancer, James Barton as Kit Carson, crustily telling tall tales of the Old West, William Bendix as a grumbling bartender, Wayne Morris as an ageing *naif*, and James Lydon (the movies' Henry Aldrich), Ward Bond, Broderick Crawford and Cagney's sister Jeanne in somewhat less significant roles. Cagney himself plays Joe, a champagne-drinking, gum-chewing, long-shot playing character who reveals nothing about himself despite his philosophical garrulousness. Emotionally he correlates to Tom in *Johnny Come Lately*. It might not be too much to say that if Cagney was always the 'far-away fella' of Pat O'Brien's description, then these are the two roles in which he most closely played himself. And if that is true, then it is also possible to say that he would never have become a star without a studio's intervention, forcing him to reach for a different public definition.

Be that as it may, we do know that Cagney insisted on one significant change in Saroyan's play. Such dramatic tension as it contains arises from the intrusion of a thoroughly mean spirited character named Blick (played in the film by an actor named, of all things, Tom Powers). He represents nothing less than the snake in this boozy, woozy Eden, and at the play's climax he is killed, off-stage, by Kit Car-son. In the movie he does not die. Rather, Cagney's Joe, until then virtually immobilized in his chair – he even refuses invitations to dance – rises and beats him into a bloody heap. That Blick survives in the movie is sometimes taken as evidence of Cagney's humane sympathies, his determination, in his own films, not to play the killer. Maybe so, but the change also permits him to offer another sop to his fans, an extended, apparently well-choreographed, fight.

Few, if any, critics thought this change harmed the play. Saroyan himself wrote a fulsome letter to Cagney, after he saw the film with a paying audience in San Francisco. 'I was too busy enjoying it to care who wrote it,' he said. Agee, who called *The Time of Your Life* 'a blend of Nehi and sacramental wine', advanced the view that it could not really exist anywhere but on a stage, but thought this 'loving' production about as good as could be imagined or expected. He had particular praise for Barton and for Cagney's 'controlling, self-effacing' performance. Still, Cagney would complain about time and money lost because the director and the cameraman wasted two expensive weeks blocking the film, then reversed most of those decisions when shooting began.

This lack of decisiveness was not responsible for all of the half-million dollars that was lost on the picture, but of course it did not help. Neither did some unpleasantness that developed over the release of the picture, with the Cagneys desiring to give it to Warner Brothers to distribute, U.A. executives insisting it should be theirs even though they had not yet contributed to its financing as they were contractually bound to do. That company, once again standing on the brink of failure, finally was allowed in – just in time to lose its entire investment in the film. At which point, the Cagneys, who had talked bravely of making up to fifteen films for U.A. release, decided it was time to shut up shop, at least for the moment. In the end, *The Time of Your Life* grossed only

145

$1·5 million for its producers, and with the Cagney's rights running out in the mid-1950s the opportunity for further recoupment, which television would surely have provided, was also denied them. Their company would co-venture on some later films, but this was the disappointing end to the bid for untrammelled independence. One suspects the outcome was more embittering to Cagney than he ever admitted, especially since ironies abounded in his next venture.

'He'll find out that he needs me as much as I need him,' Jack Warner had been heard to mutter when Cagney left him in 1943. And now his eagle was coming home to roost. Yet again. Under the terms of an agreement the actor signed with his old studio, he would make a certain number of pictures Warner Brothers wanted him to make in return for the studio financing some projects the Cagneys initiated. And he would be free to undertake a limited amount of freelance assignments. It was by far the best of his many arrangements with Warner, but it still must have been galling. Especially since the first movie the studio wanted him to do was, of all things, another gangster movie, and the most brutal one he had been asked to undertake since *The Public Enemy*. Nor was *White Heat* to be a very grand production.

'It was really essentially a cheapie,' Cagney would say to me. 'It was, you know, a one-two-three-four kind of thing.' He may have been pleased to have Raoul Walsh behind the camera again, but he also felt the studio was stinting in other ways, especially on casting, though, in fact, most of his fellow players turned out to be excellent. More disturbing was the fact that Cagney's character, Cody Jarrett, was so full of what appeared to him motiveless malignity. All the brutal violence for which the film remains justifiably famous appears to have been suggested in the original script, which according to Walsh was inspired by the depredations of Ma Barker and her notorious gang, whose top guns were her offspring. But

Cagney wanted some sort of explanation for Cody's behavior, and since the film was to be set contemporaneously, the old excuses, based on iniquitous social conditions, wouldn't do. (Indeed, the picture is an anachronism, the roving mobsters of the Thirties, the Dillingers, the Bonnies and the Clydes, having disappeared.) It was at this point, as he tells it, that Cagney had the idea that permitted him not merely to play the role, but to make it the signature piece for the last years of his career. 'I said, why don't we make him nuts, make him crazy? So that was when we put in the fits.'

Yes. The fits. Which were indicated by a high-pitched, staccato moan, the perfect auditory symbol of what Cody would say the pain felt like, a buzz saw reaming through his skull. This, of course, was accompanied by frenzied writhings capable of bringing him to his knees, hand clawing frantically at his cranium. Some critics have proposed that Cody may have been an epileptic, but whatever is afflicting Cody is unlikely to be found in any physician's handbook. The fits are a symbolic device, a wonderfully vivid way of signalling to the audience that they are in the presence of psychopathy, a condition that certainly manifests itself in mad acts, but generally offers symptoms that can be read only by a specialist, and certainly cannot be seen from the back of the balcony as Cody Jarrett's can be.

From the actor's point of view, this inexplicable illness is very liberating. We are led to believe that it is a condition he was born with, a cruel joke of God or nature, and that implies that he is as much the plaything of blind destiny as his victims are. In other words, he need take no moral responsibility for his character's actions. If anything, Cagney was freer of such obligations in this role than he was in any outlaw role he had ever done. We cannot imagine any fork in the road where Cody might have made a choice between good and evil, thus he cannot be burdened with guilt (and our opprobrium) for making the wrong choice. Nor do we have to stretch toward the existen-

tial explanation, as we do in trying to comprehend Tom Powers. To rationalize his choice of the role all Cagney had to do was say that there are crazy people in the world, some of whom are to be found in the life of crime, and an actor has a perfect right to play one of them if he feels like it and if he does not present such a figure as worthy of emulation. In fact, he could have said that *White Heat* implies that only a 'nut' would become a criminal of this violent type, that it thus warns off normal souls from such behavior.

But that says nothing about the special quality of the furies he has loosed here, the utter singularity of this characterization, which is that it is his greatest comic portrayal. Yes, comic. It states that premise early on, when Cody and his gang are holed up in their mountain hideaway, resting from their last caper, looking forward to the next. That's when Cody suffers the first of his wracking brainstorms, and is led into a bedroom by his mother (well and broadly played by Margaret Wycherly) for

a little tender loving care, and climbs into her lap to facilitate her massage of his bursting temples. It was Cagney's idea, this bit of business, and even bold Raoul Walsh was stunned by it, uncertain that they could get away with such crude Freudianism. But they did, and in the process firmly established the film's lunatic premises. Cagney: 'That was a good thing to do, because people haven't stopped talking about it ever since we did it.'

And there was more to come. Consider the scene where Cody has a prisoner locked in the trunk of a car and the chap complains that he can't breathe in there. 'Oh, stuffy, huh? I'll give you some air.' Whereupon he unlimbers an enormous ·45 and ventilates the trunk with some well-placed shots, killing both the complaints and the complainant. Doubtless the scene was written by scenarist Ivan Goff and Ben Roberts. But they couldn't have written the cheery, helpful tones in which Cagney plays the scene. And one doubts that the script called for him to be off-handedly gnawing a chicken

The best laid plans . . . A train robbery goes awry (below left). And Margaret Wycherley, playing Cody's mother, visits him in the slammer. But you can't keep a bad man down: sprung, Cody goes after a tempting payroll.

leg while he conducts his bloody business. Even the scene that usually draws the sharpest intake of breath in the theater, a scene where Virginia Mayo as Cody's moll is standing on a chair, showing off her new fur coat to her lover (Steve Cochran) and Cody noncommitally tumbles her to the floor with one well-aimed, jealous blow at the back of her knees, is at some dark, strange level funny. Or maybe it is not so strange. His madness permits no mediating reflections on Cody's part. His response to every situation is a pure expression of the id, raging unchecked. Like Tom Powers at the beginning of Cagney's career, he is the natural man, the ignoble savage, and if there is shock in the laughter that greets his deadly antics, that laughter is not without its envying tones.

The film's creators did balance the scales in a rough way. Cagney is at least as often the victim of his own lunacy as everyone else is. In a picture full of unforgettable sequences none is more so than the much anthologized prison cafeteria scene, where Cagney asks a newly jailed prisoner for news of his Mom. The question is whispered down the long tables and the answer is whispered back to him: she is dead. When he hears what he dreads, there is a stunned suspended moment before he starts banging his tin coffee cup on the table. After that he mounts the table and lunges down it, food and dishware scattering in all directions as he screams over and over, 'Let me out of here', alternating the words with his buzz saw whine. Again, a simply-stated idea was improvisationally embroidered on the set. 'That was ad-libbed. It wasn't written. I said put two strong men down at the end of the table and Raoul put two big husky guys there, so that when I climbed up on the thing and stumbled along the table . . . I landed on the both of these fellows and they both landed on the deck. I tumbled them over and I went on going – off my nut.' He knocks out several more guards before he is himself brutally subdued and placed in solitary confinement. Pauline Kael has called this 'perhaps the most daring sequence Cagney ever performed,' and the ironic choreography of the scene is marvelous, with Cody losing whatever was left of his mental rhythms, but with the physical rhythms of

148

Walsh's shots and the blows Cagney gives and takes almost metronomic.

There is more craziness to come. After he is sprung from jail and reunited with his gang, Cagney goes for a little night-time stroll in the country and there encounters Hank Fallon (Edmund O'Brien), a federal agent who has not only infiltrated the gang but has become, since his mother's death, Cody's only confidant. They fall to discussing mother love and when Fallon confesses that his died before he could know her, Cody for the first and only time in the film expresses something like genuine sympathy for another human being. He was himself talking to his departed Mother on his little constitutional, he admits. 'That was a good feeling out there, talking to Ma,' he says. And then a sly, wild grin lights his face. 'Maybe I *am* nuts,' he confides. That grin illuminates Cagney's entire acting strategy for *White Heat*. At that moment one realizes that all along he has pitched his performance just one subtle notch beyond the purely realistic, that he has not merely been playing craziness, but has been parodying it. Or, perhaps it would be more

accurate to say he has been commenting through his work on the pop-Freudian explanations for anti-social behavior that had begun to creep into movies during this period.

Now Cody is rushed to his doom. All along he has had his eye on an oil company payroll and, at the film's end, he and his mob stage their raid on it. But betrayed by Fallon they are thwarted and Cagney is at last cornered atop a huge, globe-shaped oil storage tank, with Fallon ordering him to surrender, to which the gangster's response is cackling astonishment. The G-Man then wounds Cody with a shot, to which he responds by firing his revolver into the tank's piping, setting the oil aflame. 'Made it, Ma! Top of the world!' he famously cries, echoing a promise Ma undoubtedly first crooned to him from cribside. When the tank blows, the smoke billows from it in an unmistakable mushroom cloud, just like the plume that an atomic explosion creates.

The symbolism is unmistakable. Something more than Cody Jarrett's earthly form vanished in that explosion. The cinematic con-

ventions that had sustained the gangster genre for almost two decades went up in that smoke. Beyond that certain broad social assumptions, perhaps unspoken, but nevertheless underlying almost all American movies that had the provision of melodramatic entertainment as their principal business, were also blown away. Until this moment – and perhaps excepting *The Public Enemy* – we assumed that there was an explicable, and therefore curable, cause for bad behavior of every sort. But all the familiar, rational explanations for monstrousness of the kind that Cody Jarrett displays are simply ignored in *White Heat*. In the end the picture leaves us with nothing but the thought that in a chance universe one of the mischances we may well encounter is a gun shoved in our faces by a psychopath, with whom there is no reasoning, for whose behavior there is no ready explanation. Given our history as it has developed in the third of a century since this picture was made, can anyone say they were wrong?

On the other hand, one cannot say that its makers were consciously aware that they were standing athwart one of the great fault lines of our recent social history. They were just movie people, after all, not social philosophers – although the latter were scarcely demonstrating any great prescience about the shape of things to come in 1949. What Cagney and his colleagues were aware of was that the traditional Hollywood ways of doing business were ending. Indeed, when they were in production the witch-hunters from the House Un-American Activities Committee had been at their most menacing, posing their vividly cynical threat to the American social compact and – looking at the committee's work more narrowly – threatening the unspoken, live-and-let-live arrangements that had pertained between political America and show biz America. One must at least speculate that as the makers of *White Heat* went about their movie business as usual, seeking a sensation or two that would bring the folks in, they could not help but reflect some of the anxiety that was in the air

of the moment. Be that as it may, in Hollywood's most dismal decade, the 1950s, this movie about a sport of nature would, itself come to seem a sport of nature – a last feverish burst of energy before the screens widened and jaws slackened at the general sobriety, piety and all-around goopishness of the Hollywood product, though it is only in a still longer perspective that it begins to seem a prescient movie, perhaps even a watershed movie.

Which was exactly what James Cagney did not want it to be. The film was a great hit, the first he had enjoyed since *Yankee Doodle Dandy*. And there was an irony in that – perhaps a bitter irony – which he immediately perceived. He had been at great pains to offer the public a version of his best self – mild, wise, sweet-spirited – and they had stayed away by the millions. Now, pressed to re-establish himself, he had made this 'cheapie', in which he had permitted his old gangster character to turn entirely rancid with age (he was fifty the year *White Heat* was released), and the audience had returned in chortling droves. It was discouraging to the idealist in him, discouraging to the artist in him. And, perhaps, encouraging to whatever in him was cynical and weary.

In any event, it seems that he sensed before anyone else did that Cody Jarrett was as much a trap for him as Tom Powers had been. He would twist and turn and try to escape from the long shadow of that character. But it would point the way inescapably for him for the last decade of his career. He would make fifteen major appearances before his retirement in 1961, but all of his truly memorable roles in this period would be impregnated with Cody's bad seed. And Cagney himself would, more stridently than ever, insist that 'I am not the characters I play', that 'it has been more valuable to me to stand on the sidelines and, with a certain degree of impersonality, register the reactions I have noted', and 'The idea of playing oneself is essentially fallacious' . . . and so on. It is no wonder that, in later years, his

151

The short grey line. Gene Nelson and Gordon MacRae, as cadets, flank a new recruit – Cagney playing a Broadway director brought in to stage the cadets' annual musical in *The West Point Story*. And Cagney taught them how to strut.

memory grew so selective, his sense of pride
his work so dim, his insistence that all he ha
ever done was just a job so stubborn. In the
last years he was, indeed, not much more tha
an honest craftsman. For it must be said tha
he added nothing essential to his basic scree
character after *White Heat* and that most
his attempts to abandon or radically vary tha
character sadly failed.

He went immediately into a gaudy, silly an
rather anachronistic musical, *The West Poi*
Story, playing an out-of-work Broadway dire
tor hired to help the cadets stage their annu
variety show. Cagney blusters about, trying t
whip his cast into shape (and incidentally try
ing to get what he judges to be its most talente
member, played by Gordon MacRae, to resig
from the Academy and seek Broadwa
stardom). He is Chester Kent of *Footligh*
Parade, grown older, less attractive. There
some heat in the musical numbers, but non
of the older film's loopy charm. The idea

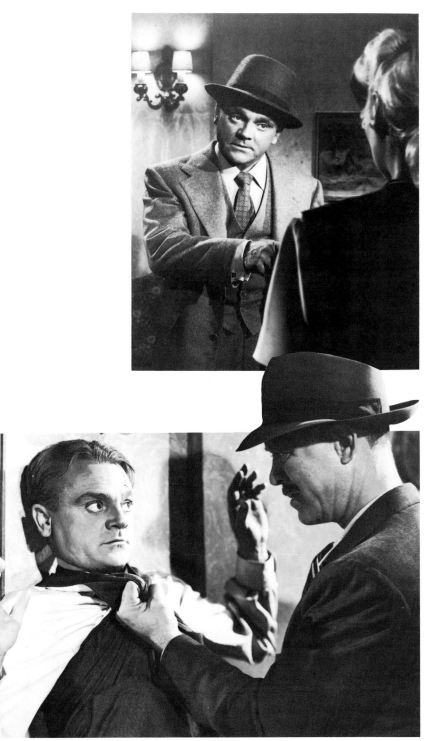

Menaces. Cagney threatens Barbara Payton, Ward Bond threatens Cagney, in *Kiss Tomorrow Goodbye*.

surely, was to return Cagney to lovability after *White Heat*, or anyway to remind people that the tough guy could sing, dance and do comedy. But *West Point Story*, shot in wretched Warnercolor, is a loud, harsh and utterly charmless movie, everything that Cagney's two previous full-scale musicals were not.

If it appeared to be groping for an effective way to employ its star, the film that followed it, *Kiss Tomorrow Goodbye*, represents a more interesting miscalculation of the same problem. Indeed, it is one of the most curious failures in the entire Cagney canon. A Cagney Production of a script based on novelist Horace McCoy's magnum opus, it was a film the actor particularly wanted to do. He felt it offered an opportunity to employ his gangster in a morally edifying way. And, reading the novel, one can see how he reached that conclusion. McCoy, who was discovered by French critics of an existentialist bent long before he was acknowledged by the American literary world as anything but a pulpster, wrote a flat, neo-Hemingway sort of prose, admirably suited to his tales of luckless and marginal figures who discover that the more privileged world to which they aspire is both more corrupt and more corrupting than they imagined. In the end it dispenses with them as casually as it picked them up, without much regret and (most especially) without moral qualms. In McCoy's novel the narrator, Ralph Cotter, is a con who engineers a jail break, goes to ground in a nearby city, takes up with Holiday (Barbara Payton), girl friend of a man he has killed in the escape. Soon enough he discovers that the town's cops and a large segment of its leading citizens are involved in chicanery that makes his own criminal activity look paltry – and unprofitable – by comparison. He also falls in love with an heiress (Helena Carter) who is the daughter of the town's leading, and most honorable, citizen. If he can cleanse himself of his past he can have her – and a life of respectable ease. But Holiday, sensing that she is

153

about to be dispensed with, dispenses with him. 'Kiss tomorrow goodbye' she snarls as he writhes on the floor, expiring from the shots she has pumped into him.

It is not a bad story and coolly told, with a hooded, whispering figure like Robert Mitchum, so cynical that he doesn't know he's cynical, as Cotter, it might have worked on the screen. It might even have worked with Cagney – if Cody Jarrett and the popular success he had enjoyed were not so fresh in mind. But Cagney comes on playing a version of Cody, a cunning psychopath who shoots first and never thinks later. He even has a scene that is the precise equivalent to the one in the earlier film where he cuts down Virginia Mayo. Here he whips Payton with a hot, heavily water-soaked towel – a truly brutal scene, even in the censored version that survived to the final cut. It, like all the unpleasantnesses Cagney visited on women, does not turn us off of him completely precisely because Cagney is, perhaps, the least sexy star in the history of the movies. At his best palship, not passion, seems to be his goal. At his worst – well, a certain amount of rough stuff is the price anyone must pay for being one of the boys. If one had ever understood his brutal behavior to be the visible manifestation of an unseen sadistic sexuality it would have been unbearable. Still, it must be said that *Kiss Tomorrow Goodbye* comes closer to making that implication, in part because of Payton's sluttish, ready-for-anything playing, than any of Cagney's other films.

But that is not what undoes the picture. Its insoluble problem is Cagney's initial psychopathy. This is not a little behavioral quirk; this is a chilling, profound and ineradicable illness. We cannot believe that even enlightened self-interest, let alone the discovery of true love and awakened morality, could cause him to abandon the affectless indifference with which he deals out pain. The irony he originally intended, showing a man coming belatedly to morality yet being punished for past transgressions, simply does not come off. A Cody Jarrett clone just cannot make that point – much as the public enjoyed that figure.

Come Fill the Cup, also a Cagney Brothers project, is also marred by ambivalent aims. Based on a tough-sentimental novel about newspapering by Harlan Ware, adapted by the Goff-Roberts team and directed by quick Gordon Douglas, who had proved in *Kiss Tomorrow Goodbye* that he could achieve a *noir*ish air on a tight schedule, the picture aspires at once to be both a cautionary tale about alcoholism and a crime melodrama. It succeeds moderately well in the first of these aims, though coming six years after *The Lost Weekend* – not to mention several other imitations – it can scarcely be accused of radical originality. It introduces Cagney as Lew Marsh, ace reporter and falling-down drunk, doing a superb impression of the tentative dignity with which an alcoholic holds himself and moves when he is trying to hide his condition. His editor, however, sees through the charade, fires him and we follow Lew down to skid row where, unshaven and wide-eyed, Cagney reprises the pathos of his downfall passages in *The Roaring Twenties*. Befriended by a reformed drunk (crisp, expert, deservedly beloved James Gleason, who becomes his room-mate-guardian-conscience), he battles back to the editorship of the paper that fired him, staffing it with several reporters who, like himself, are fighting to stay off the bottle.

So far, so good. Like the novel on which it is based, the movie up to its midpoint offers a realistic portrayal of life on a metropolitan daily, only slightly and acceptably romanticized (though the movie skips some of the knowing, cynical dialogue that expertly flavors the book). But then Marsh as the resident expert on alcoholism is recruited by his iron-whimmed, Hearst-like publisher (Raymond Massey) to try to dry out his boozed-out, burned-out nephew (well played by Gig Young). The task is freighted with emotional ambiguity because this wastrel has made off with Lew's girl (Phyllis Thaxter) while he was filling and refilling his many cups. Turns out the lad has fallen into bad company – gangsters no less – and before Marsh can straighten him out, he must endure the loss of his friend, Gleason (it almost puts him back on the sauce), and resort to some rather conventionally confrontational heroics with the heavies. In the novel these did not stand out from the rest of its busy life so starkly, but in the movie they play like a standard fast wind-up. Here, perhaps, the Cagneys were bending not so much to their sense of what his public expected of the star, but to the simplifying imperatives of screen narrative. If, however, *Come Fill the Cup* has a slight air of compromise about it, it does represent an intelligent effort to break away from Cagney's psychopathic image.

This is more than can be said for Cagney's next film, which followed a cameo appearance in *Starlift*, a star-studded revue. It was no less than a remake of *What Price Glory?* directed by no less than John Ford, and giving Cagney

the opportunity to play the character Pat O'Brien had so often imitated in their earlier military manoeuvers, Captain Flagg. The result is arguably the worst movie either Ford or Cagney ever made, and unarguably the worst picture Cagney made in this period.

Vulgar is the word for it: glaring Technicolor, loud, obvious jokes, mainly about booze and broads, sound staginess in the realization of World War One France. And since Ford always loved choruses of public domain songs sung by massed soldiery, lots of those, too. The relationship playwrights Maxwell Anderson and Laurence Stallings had so long ago established between Flagg and Quirt (played here by Dan Dailey) depends on the former always playing the stooge, so that he is constantly in a state of belated anger over some victimization or other. But the one thing Cagney never was, never could be, was a dummox. He is too fast on his feet, too articulate, for the role. As a consequence, the movie's central relationship is thrown fatally out of kilter, although in the general hubbub of the picture, one can scarcely discern it anyway. Indeed with his careless, throw-away staging Ford buries the emotional high point of the original play, and of the extraordinarily fine silent movie Raoul Walsh made of it in 1927, the death of a young soldier during his first action, potentially a moment of unbearable irony and pathos.

In a way, however, *What Price Glory?* was a paradigmatic picture, symbolic of the problems Cagney, Ford, everyone who had made their careers in the more stable and confident motion picture industry of the Thirties and Forties faced in the Fifties. Here was a classic property, something people of their generations loved, respected and believed in. Yet, in this puzzling new era they felt they could not trust it, or perhaps more properly, felt they could not trust their suddenly enigmatic audience to appreciate it in its pure form. The result is not an adaptation but an adulteration, and not just of the play they were working on. They adulterated, as well, their own gifts, in the

156

Against type. Cagney played a Huey Long type politician in *A Lion Is In the Streets,* **a western good/bad man in** *Run for Cover* **(below).**

process imparting to their work an air of desperation that is both sad and infuriating to witness.

For Cagney, this period is all groping. And more groping. As witness *A Lion is in the Streets.* The Cagney brothers had acquired the rights to Adrian Locke Langley's novel, which is based on the life of Huey Long, the Louisiana demagogue, shortly after it was published in 1945, but had apparently not been able to attract backing for a movie version. In the intervening years, however, Robert Rossen had made his adaptation of *All the King's Men,* Robert Penn Warren's more distinguished novel on the same subject, and it had won both popular success and the Academy Award for the best picture of 1949. Now, in the immemorial Hollywood tradition, it became possible to sell an imitation. Again, one wonders: is this what the fight for independence was all about?

Not that *A Lion is in the Streets* is a bad picture. To be sure, as the critics of the time pointed out, Cagney's bayou accent had an inescapable admixture of Manhattan, but in a strange way, that works for him. His Hank Martin, hustling his way up from his dinky law practice, putting together his coalition of the disaffected and the disenfranchised, fighting the established political and economic interests that have controlled his state, reminds us of all the marginal, slightly shady, more than slightly charming young men Cagney played in the Thirties, in which period, and earlier, this picture is set. We succumb to his wit and energy as we used to, and so do the characters he encounters in the movie. In fact, his performance is in some respects preferable to that of Broderick Crawford in the Rossen film, for which Crawford won an Oscar. His is a heavy, brooding, shouting piece of work, always shadowing, in the early passages, the evil and corruption that are to come. It is a little difficult to see what roused the rabble to follow him. By contrast, Cagney makes you see the dream he believes in, and makes you want to follow him. And that, in its way, heightens the tragedy of his fall from grace at the end. Moreover, there was, as always, a lightness and ease to Raoul Walsh's direction, a sense of exuberance and even fun, that suggest the circus-like appeal of Hank's early political ventures perhaps more effectively than Rossen's more portentous *mise en scène* does. Technicolor, however, was a mistake; there are moments when one half-expects Hank Martin to lead his crowds in a production number. And, though Cagney is himself compelling when power begins to bend his mind at the end of the film – there is a touch of Cody Jarrett in him, here, too – the film, rather shoddy in its continuity, does not gather the dark resonances that *All the King's Men* does. Despite some intrinsic merits, *Lion* looked like a cheap imitation to most people.

Run for Cover has a similarly imitative air. A Western, it too echoed an earlier hit – *High Noon* – and not merely because at the end, the call of stern moral duty isolates its sheriff-hero (Cagney) from the craven townspeople who will not help him to protect the peace they are so eager to enjoy. Directed by that quintessential Fifties director, Nicholas Ray, whose very next film would be *Rebel Without a Cause*, it was, like so much of his work, shadowed by a debilitating self-consciousness. Here, he was telegraphing the news that he was employing Western conventions metaphorically to convey a contemporary anti-McCarthyite message. Cagney's Matt Dow is introduced as a man who has served a jail term for a crime he did not commit. Heading West to escape that unhappy past, he links up with young Davey Bishop (John Derek), for whom he is a kindly father figure. The pair are, however, almost lynched by a posse who mistake them for members of a bandit gang they are pursuing,

158

and Davey is left with a permanent and embittering limp from a wound they inflict. Both men are thus victims of false accusations, as so many people were in this era. Still, the bourgeois world has need of men with their skills, and they are hired on as lawmen – except that the kid has a debt to settle, and forms a secret alliance with the local brigands, a fact Matt suspects. When, deserted by citizenry, they must track down and face the leader of the gang, both draw simultaneously – Matt killing Davey, even as Davey, recovering his senses and his first loyalty, drills the criminal to protect Matt. Who then weeps, of course, for having misplaced his faith in the lad. If *Run for Cover* plays better than it sounds, that is in large measure because it contains Cagney's sunniest Fifties performance. He's a crusty old guy, to be sure, but basically avuncular, and considering the amount of injustice Matt has absorbed in his life, rather agreeable in manner. Matt relates more to the victim side

Reprise: Cagney played George M. Cohan a second time in a cameo in Bob Hope's biopic, *The Seven Little Foys*. Their tabletop tap dance was the picture's high point.

A title belied. *Tribute to a Bad Man* produced these gentle stills (opposite). The lady being serenaded is co-star Irene Papas.

Renewal: Cagney's portrayal of Ruth Etting's obsessed manager-husband in *Love Me Or Leave Me* brought him his third Oscar nomination. His co-star was Doris Day. The director (below) was Charles Vidor.

of Cagney's screen character than to the aggressive side of it, but with a certain weary self-acceptance in this instance.

Still, *Run for Cover* cannot be judged more than a routine picture and at this midpoint of the Fifties Cagney was living off the capital of his previously acquired good will. Since *White Heat* he had made a tired musical, a dreadful remake, and three films that were essentially imitations of movies that had been done better before to show for his efforts. More than most of his contemporaries, he had held before him a vision of what independence could mean for an actor. Now it had arrived, but at this ungratifying historical moment when movies in general were at their blandest and mo elephantine stage and Cagney himself was, reason of his age, a character actor masquera ing as a star, no longer able to do what he h dreamed of doing as a younger man. His stat was pretty much that which was once describ by a younger rival, Robert Mitchum, w remarked that at a certain stage in his care an actor reaches a point where 'You don't g to do better, just more'.

One gets a sense of him beginning to bail ou emotionally. In 1955, for example, he found y another farm, the one where he still lives Dutchess County, New York. Unlike the pro erty he had so long held on Martha's Vineyar these 711 acres could be worked as a farm the fullest sense of the word, and thus it cou be made to serve his needs for a happy, th is to say active, retirement. In this same yea too, he took the first supporting role he ha played since he was a young contract player Warner Brothers, that of the comically bonke captain in the film adaptation of *Mr Rober* a picture that, of course, belonged to Hen Fonda, who had created the title role on stag and to whoever played the pivotal part Ensign Pulver – Jack Lemmon in the case the picture. But it was apparently a happ occasion for Cagney. The part, of cours suited him admirably. The paranoid office

160

lurking in his cabin, pouncing erratically on his subordinates when something happened to arouse his suspicions of conspiracy, but meantime delighted to let Roberts run his rust-bucket cargo ship, in effect permitted Cagney to play an overtly comic version of the psychopathic creature he had been developing since *White Heat*, and there is a relish in his work that had not been visible for some time. But then, he and Lemmon, who received the supporting actor Academy Award for his performance, and for whom Cagney conceived great professional regard and personal affection during the course of shooting, emerged best from a troubled production, one that never quite achieved the elegiac spirit that had made the Thomas Heggin-Joshua Logan play such a great success.

The picture began under the direction of Fonda's old friend and frequent director, John Ford, but after the first day's shooting – it was on location, on Midway Island in the Pacific – Fonda was miserable. He thought Ford was entirely missing the rhythm of the play, a rhythm that he had established and honed to perfection over the three years he had played the role on stage, and that night he went to the director to complain. Ford was in his cups and took a swing at Fonda, and though they patched up the quarrel, the mood of the picture

was irreversibly altered. Ford continued to sit in the director's chair for the remainder of location shooting on Midway and in Hawaii, but he sulkily looked over to Fonda for approval of every shot, drank up to two cases of beer per day, and, after they took their toll, permitted the leading member of his stock company, Ward Bond, to act as *de facto* director. Eventually, Ford was stricken with a kidney ailment, and had to be hospitalized and operated upon. The remainder of the picture, the studio sequences, were made by Mervyn Leroy, who came in at a day's notice, and did his usual efficient, characterless job. Two important retakes were handled by Logan, who was serving as the film's co-producer. But no one connected with the original theatrical production ever liked the movie, although it was successful at the box office. As for Cagney, he had not been present for the Midway blowup and when he arrived in Honolulu, he found he could pass most of the time relaxing on the beach with his co-star, William Powell, whose role as Doc offered little more screen time than Cagney's did. The shooting he would later, blandly write, 'progressed in good order'.

But yet there was one bit of luck left to him. While he was working on *Mr Roberts*, he was sent the script for *Love Me or Leave Me*, which actually went into release before the Navy film

did. It was a biography of Ruth Etting, the singer, and her relationship with the small-time hood, Martin 'The Gimp' Snyder, who became her husband and manager and whose love for her was both obsessive and brutal. There was a vogue for this sort of thing at the time – stories of tragic show folk, mostly women, who must perform through the tears occasioned by some affliction or other. But this script was stronger, more tough-minded and less sentimental than others in what was not a very distinguished genre, perhaps because its author, along with Isobel Lennart, was Daniel Fuchs, the very fine novelist who somehow fused the American realist tradition with something a little more interesting and exotic – in the symbolist vein in the view of some critics. 'There was nothing to be added, nothing to be taken away', Cagney later wrote of the screenplay. 'It was in fact that extremely rare thing, a perfect script.'

Certainly, it was a gloomy one – maybe even an ugly one in certain respects. But it quickened Cagney's interest as little else did in this period. Indeed, when I talked with him, his memories of this movie were warmer and more detailed than they were of anything from this period save *White Heat*. He was especially proud of his ability to imitate The Gimp's gimpy walk, the result of pre-natal polio, according to Cagney. 'Now, they had all kinds of devices to clamp on my leg to induce a gimp. And when I walked in, I said, "This is what we're going to do here," and I slapped the foot, and they said, "Oh." That's all there was to it.' Cagney became so adept at this pantomine that he could vary it according to his character's mood, his state of exhaustion. Indeed, by the end of the picture, the old dancer was doing this bit of business entirely without thinking. Once, at the end of a take, he apologized to director Charles Vidor for forgetting to limp. But the director said he had indeed done so, and the dailies proved him right.

The role gave Cagney a chance to physicalize emotion as he had not done since *Yankee*

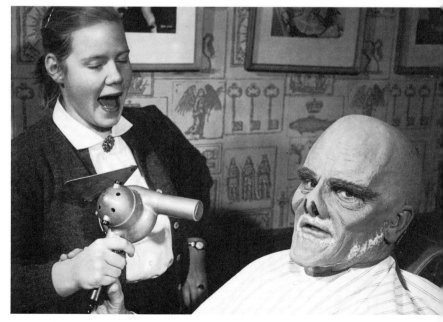

Doodle Dandy and at least partly because of that he gave a stunning performance, as gutty in its way as any he had ever done. There is scarcely a moment after the early, establishing scenes, which he plays with something like his youthful energy and unconscious charm, when his behavior is anything but appalling. Etting, who is well played by Doris Day, is simply overwhelmed by him. (Cagney would say the 'little gal' was 'unshrewd', meaning, it would seem, that she had a natural guilelessness – at least at this stage of her career – that encouraged people to take her to heart.) Led into the marriage almost against her will, she is also driven out of it almost against her will, Cagney's whirlwind characterization forcing her emotions, forcing her actions. Since both were moved by pressures incomprehensible to them this is, in the literary sense of the word,

among the most naturalistic movies he ever made (and surely the same must be said for Day). But it worked. Somehow, this rather unpleasant story of a mean-spirited man's desperate love, destroying himself and the woman to whom he is hopelessly in thrall, reached people, perhaps because each was, in a curious way, an innocent. He did not consciously understand how out of control he was. She did not understand what in her was leading him on, because, really, she didn't mean to do so. It is, perhaps, too much to say that audiences sympathized with both parties, but they were fascinated by the play of emotions they heedlessly set off in one another. If love is just a matter of neurotic chemistry, if it has nothing to do with finer, more poetic emotions, then it could be argued that *Love Me or Leave Me* is among the most honest love stories ever

163

made in Hollywood. In any event, it won
Cagney his third Oscar nomination. He joined
his old pal Spencer Tracy in losing to Ernest
Borgnine for his role in a much more sentimental piece of realism, or, more properly, pseudo-
realism, *Marty*.

Cagney ended his professional activities for
the year by doing a cameo, reprising his Cohan
role, in Bob Hope's biopic, *The Seven Little
Foys*. It was no ordinary guest shot. It was a
full-scale tap duet, with the pair hoofing atop
a long boardroom conference table, and it is
a wonderful number, especially for a pair of
portly gentlemen in their mid-fifties. Its verve
is the more remarkable because in rehearsals
Cagney had strained his knees, and did most
of the routine in intense pain, with the injured
joints swollen to twice their normal size. It was
pretty much of a lark, a favor, but his mood
was suddenly outgoing, energized, at this time.
It was as if a couple of good, solid roles, com-
mercially successful, had revived his spirits.

That year, for example, he made his television
debut, re-enacting a *Mr Roberts* scene with
Fonda and Lemmon on 'The Ed Sullivan
Show' to publicize the film's release, introducing some beauty contest winners on a Bob
Hope program that aided charity. A year later,
he would do another large favor, appearing as
an embittered Army sergeant escorting a
friend's body home in *Soldier from the Wars
Returning* on 'Robert Montgomery Presents'.
His old friend was having ratings troubles with
his series and needed Cagney's name to get the
year's schedule off to a strong start.

But the biggest favor he did in this period
was to replace Spencer Tracy when he quit the
location early in the shooting of a Western,
Tribute to a Bad Man. His obstreperousness
brought an end to his twenty-five-year relationship with MGM, and it is possible that
Cagney's replacing him – along with increasingly divergent political opinions – contributed
to cooling their long friendship. The role

164

Cagney took over was that of Jeremy Rodock, a rancher who has built a livestock empire out of nothing and now, in middle age, takes a peculiar pleasure in defending it against all depredations – emphasis on peculiar. In fact, as it develops he is nothing less than a sadist looking for excuses to punish anyone who even hints at poaching on his range, or for that matter, attempting to thwart his iron whim in less muscular ways. Until he rather unpersuasively learns the lesson of humanity at the end, old Jeremy comes close to being Cody Jarrett in chaps. The piece is briskly directed by Robert Wise, and it features Irene Pappas, fierce and handsome, in her first American role. She was rather an exotic bloom to be found flowering on this prairie, and in fact, *Tribute to a Bad Man* is yet another example of a miscalculated trend of the time, the attempt to blend Freud and the frontier drama. If this film was not as ludicrous as some in this vein it remains awkward and unpersuasive.

Still, it is more entertaining than *Those Wilder Years*, in which Cagney played a wealthy businessman who, in his middle years, decides to search for the illegitimate son he had abandoned as a baby. In this soapy quest, he is abetted by Barbara Stanwyck, playing the head of a foundling home. In the end, he discovers the boy, now grown and happy, in his humble foster home. Cagney pays his debt to propriety by adopting a young woman who has just borne an illegitimate child of her own. He thus becomes a father and a grandfather all at once – and there is a broad hint that he may also marry the Stanwyck character at some later date. It is plain awful, the largest emotion it awakens being regret that this fiery pair had not met at some earlier point in their careers. There is a bite to their scenes together that makes one realize how good they would have been for each other in the days when they rarely found a player of the opposite sex who could balance their strengths.

Man of a Thousand Faces, in 1957, had a more interesting potential, for in it Cagney was asked to play Lon Chaney, the great makeup and mime artist, whose sympathetic portrayals of the psychologically and physically maimed constitute one of the most curious and affecting bodies of work in movie history. But this opportunity was vitiated by a rather lackluster production, directed by a low-budget specialist, Joseph Pevney, whose only major film this was, photographed in particularly gloomy black and white. Chaney was the son of deaf-mutes, whose skill at mime had developed out of need to communicate with them, and whose sympathy for the afflicted developed from the same source. Moreover, his rather isolated nature and his profound desire to hide in plain sight, that is beneath makeup and/or peculiar mannerisms, struck a chord with Cagney. Finally, Chaney's marriage was extremely unhappy, his wife refused to divorce him and Cagney once again had an opportunity to strike a victimized note in his characterization. The fact that Chaney died prematurely, at the age of forty-seven, added to the general lugubriousness of the venture. Cagney is all right in it, but yet, he also seems lost in the darkness of a heavily shadowed film that is always portending tragedy, but never convincingly moves us toward that end.

Cagney was groping again. For his friend, A. C. Lyles, a maker of B pictures in which he was wont to give older actors he had once admired last-chance roles, Cagney tried his hand at directing – a remake of Graham Greene's *This Gun for Hire*, shot on a twenty-day schedule. It was a change of pace for the producer – this time, he was introducing newcomers he thought more 'promising' than the public eventually did – as well as for Cagney, who found he did not enjoy directing. This was a favor for which Cagney received no rewards whatever, since he took no fee and received no plaudits.

At that, it was probably not less gratifying than *Never Steal Anything Small*, an ill-advised musical drama based on a project intended for the stage by Maxwell Anderson and Rouben Mamoulian. Cagney was a more than slightly larcenous longshoreman, supposedly charming in his rough way, making his way upward by crooked means to the presidency of the dock wallopers' union. It wasn't funny, it made no sense as the basis for a musical treatment, and Shirley Jones was a preposterous co-star for Cagney. The picture's obvious cross-references both to Cagney's past and to more recent memories of *On the Waterfront* were also ludicrous.

Shake Hands with the Devil, written by Goff and Roberts, directed by Michael Anderson and with a good cast that co-starred Don Murray, Dana Wynter, Glynis Johns, with the likes of Michael Redgrave, Sybil Thorndyke and Cyril Cusack in support, was infinitely superior. Shot on location in Ireland and set in the time of the troubles, it introduces Cagney as a benign-appearing surgeon who is also a leader of the Irish Republican Army, a task he makes one feel, at first, is a logical extension

One, Two, Three – and out. Cagney retired from the screen for twenty years after completing Billy Wilder's cold war comedy in West Berlin. In the smaller picture the director is visible at left and Cagney is flanked by Pamela Tiffin and Horst Buchholz – the only player he has ever publicly criticized. The charge? Ego-tripping.

of his humanitarian calling – cutting out the cancer in his society and all that. Murray is an American student of Irish descent drawn idealistically to the cause, but unable to keep from falling in love with Wynter's character, the daughter of the English general leading the counter-revolutionary forces, whom the IRA kidnap and threaten to kill unless she is exchanged for captured colleagues. At this juncture, it begins to be apparent that the doctor's revolutionary activities merely provide an idealistic cover for a man who loves violence for its own sake. At the climax, even though a truce has been signed, and an Irish Free State is in the process of forming, he insists that they all must keep fighting. And that they must kill their hostage as planned. It is Murray who must choose between his mentor and his love

– and he chooses her, gunning down Cagney in a handsomely staged confrontation on a sea cliff.

On the whole, the film is tight and tough and, with its use of Irish locations, rather more striking to look at than most of Cagney's pictures. Moreover, it uses Cagney's psychopath for the first time to make a valid, valuable point, which is that terrorism, however idealistic the ideology in which it wraps itself, has its own awful momentum, and is always a sign of the profound derangement that no actor has ever more chillingly or accurately portrayed than Cagney did.

Little noted at the time, *Shake Hands with the Devil* is the one Cagney film of the Fifties that seems to grow rather than shrink in significance with the passage of time. It required

courage to make it on Irish soil, which has never been free of the disease the film condemns. And now, over a quarter of a century later, when men of precisely the type that Cagney played persist in their insane destructiveness, and not only in Ireland, it seems tragically prescient. Indeed, it can fairly be said that no movie, before it or since it, has more instructively taken up this subject.

Still, it was but another signpost on a road increasingly difficult to find and follow. The next year, Cagney and Montgomery combined forces to produce, with the latter directing, *The Gallant Hours*, intended as a tribute to a man they admired, Admiral William F. ('Bull') Halsey, the no-nonsense sailor who was the great American naval commander of World War Two. There are hints that they would also have liked to have made something along the lines of *12 O'Clock High* or *Command Decision*, in which, eventually, leaders are broken by the necessity of sending brave young men to their deaths in battle. But, of course, Halsey never reached that point, and Cagney, whose physical resemblance to the Admiral was strong, must maunder rather inconclusively and undramatically about the military man's central moral dilemma. Mostly, the film is an exercise in talking and walking, with Montgomery pumping choral music in through the sound track to try to impart a little false sentiment to a distant and ultimately stupefying film.

Stupefying is not a word one would apply to *One, Two, Three*. Strident would be more like it. In a sense, Billy Wilder's film can be said to have brought Cagney's career full-circle. If, in critical theory, the gangster represented the American businessman in disguise, then this film could be said to represent the businessman as a gangster in disguise. Cagney's C. P. MacNamera, the Coca-Cola executive in charge of the West Berlin territory, is a man determined to return to the home office in Atlanta, after a lifetime devoted to building the soft drink's empire across the waters, and sink into a warm, safe vice-presidency. He has his German employees whipped into shape and some of Wilder's best comedic shafts in the film are aimed at their heel-clicking devotion to authority. The analogy between the way they treat MacNamera and the way they once responded to Hitler is, putting the point as gently as possible, not something the director wants the audience to miss. But it is not his film's main point. MacNamera is detailed to chaperone the daughter of one of his bosses – she is played by Pamela Tiffin – during a visit to Berlin, and he sees his career threatened with ruin when she falls in love with an ideologically insistent boy from the wrong (Communist) side of The Wall (Horst Buchholz). Most of the picture is really a succession of well-staged chases and less well-handled verbal exchanges done with insistent, and ultimately wearying, loudness and speed .

Some of the dialogue is funny, but one has the impression that Wilder, who co-wrote it with his faithful collaborator, I. A. L. Diamond, did not have much confidence in it, so rapidly does he force his players to hurtle through it. Particularly Cagney, who argued with Wilder to give the picture, and its audience, some breathing space, but obviously lost that good fight. He needed some *lebensraum* himself, for some of his scenes require a complex blend of business and dialogue, both conducted at a literally breathtaking pace, and it is said that Cagney, for the first time in his career, experienced an inability to master a scene in a few takes. This obviously affected his confidence, and he found working with Buchholz highly unpleasant. The kid was a determined and frenetic scene-stealer and he is literally the only professional colleague Cagney disparagingly mentions by name in his autobiography.

Of course, neither problem alone would have been enough to make him retire, if he had been able to find something like consistent rewards in his work in recent years. But he had not, and now this major production, under the guidance of a man who was, by common consent of the moment, the leading comedic director (which says a great deal about the quality of the moment) had become a painful chore.

On the set, the inexperienced Tiffin had found it difficult to maintain eye contact with Cagney, a problem quite common among young performers thrown in among the lions of their craft. Cagney, who clearly liked her, noticed, drew her aside and offered some advice that had been given to him as a young actor. 'You walk in, plant yourself, look the other fella in the eye and tell the truth.' 'Well, that's the essential,' he would say to me, 'To understand what the requirements of the part are and then go at it with everything you have. Don't fool with it – just do it.'

It was his credo. No more than a craftsman's credo, perhaps, but as much as he ever cared to venture in public about how he did what he did. There might have been, must have been, more to it, but it is impossible to doubt that it was the basis of everything he did. And now here he was, over sixty, in a foreign country, working with a director he did not entirely trust, with a co-star he didn't entirely like, and with his confidence in himself not all that it might be. He knew what was missing, knew that in the past he had been able to draw on himself to weather worse problems, worse lunacies, than these. But now that thing which always sustains those of us who pride ourselves on professionalism, who depend on craft, energy and knowledgeability to get through the bad patches, simply failed him. He just wanted to get through it as quickly as possible and get home. You can see it in his performance. He had always known how to suggest, if only for a moment or two, the weakness and vulnerability behind the brashest of his characters, or the maddest of them. Or the worst written and worst directed of them. But not here. Not this time. He is abrasive and coarse as he had never been before, no matter what the provocation.

He has spoken often of the moment it came

to him that he had reached the end. In some accounts, he mentions a letter he had received that day from friends to whom he had lent his yacht. In it was a picture of them, relaxed and sun-drenched, and the contrast between their ease and his tension gutted him. In the very simple way he put it to me, no correspondence is mentioned: 'It was a beautiful day, a perfectly beautiful day, and I was outside, just walking up and down, getting some exercise – just moving – and it hit. Inside, blackness. When they closed the doors (of the sound stage) it was all dark . . . and that was it. I said, "I'm all through" . . . and forgot about it from that point on. Went back to the farm and stayed there for twenty years.'

One believes him. At heart, he was always a simple man. Or, anyway, a man looking for the simplest, most abiding truths in a scene or a character, unwilling to discuss all the nuances and complexities leading up to the discovery and enunciation of whatever essence he finally found. Best let him, the subject, rest there: 'Inside, darkness.' Now, as he saw it, he would have nothing but the light. He had earned it.

SHREWD MEANS...

THERE WAS NO FORMAL ANNOUNCEMENT OF James Cagney's retirement. It was an event that took place only in his own mind, and was communicated at first only to a few intimates. Indeed, at least once he was briefly tempted to take a role again – that of Alfred Doolittle, the dustman, in the movie version of *My Fair Lady*; after all, it contained a couple of nice songs and the chance for a little hoofing. But no, in the end he decided against it. He had gone out with a hit; *One, Two, Three* had been a commercial success and had been fairly well esteemed by the critics.

And, for more than a decade Cagney was more than content. His principle residence was the Dutchess County place, but he kept the Martha's Vineyard property for a time, and he retained his home off of Coldwater Canyon in Los Angeles, spending most winters there, driving cross country or taking the train because, despite the dashing aviators he had portrayed, he was afraid of flying. The life was good. He worked the farm in a gentlemanly way, raising prize cattle and Morgan horses, collecting antique carriages. There was plenty of time for painting, for reading, for the doggerel poetry he had always liked to scribble. Each day, he let it be known, he danced a bit, just for the exercise.

There was plenty of money too, and it continued to be handled cannily, for he was concerned to leave his beloved Bill and their two adopted children, who reached their majority in this period, well fixed. But though he remained out of the public eye he was by no means a recluse. He kept up his old friendships and when he was on the East Coast would often drive in to the Players Club on New York's Gramercy Park for a pipe night, or just to take a meal with friends. His circle was not confined entirely to old acquaintances. Young performers who revered him and wanted to meet him could generally arrange to do so.

Occasionally he would even do some light work in what he regarded as the public interest. In 1962, for example, he narrated *Road to the Wall*, an anti-Communist documentary about the partition of Berlin, which CBS produced for the Department of Defense. Four years later he was recruited to play the cautionary voice of Big Brother in an animated TV show, *Ballad of Smokey the Bear*, which promoted forest conservation. Once or twice in this period he ventured forth to colleges where, in the course of receiving an honorary degree, he would lecture on the need to preserve the land, the one quasi-political topic that could enlist his passion. He even ventured very modestly into commercial show business one last time, contributing the opening voice-over narration to his friend A. C. Lyles' production, *Arizona Bushwackers*. But it was not until 1974 that he stepped fully out of the shadows, albeit briefly, to accept the second annual American Film Institute Life Achievement Award. He grudgingly sat for a few interviews to help publicize the television program that is always made of the presentation banquet. He said he was accepting the award because the TV show raised money for worthy AFI aims, like film preservation and the training of young people in the film arts and crafts. It made sense. What had all those struggles been about all those years ago if not to get Jack Warner and the rest of them to see that film was an art, which history would judge?

The following year he published his autobiography, that rather stiff and reticent volume that his son-in-law and a professional ghost writer helped him complete. That, too, brought him some attention, though mostly in the form of disappointment that he had revealed so little of himself. In subsequent years there was talk of trying to make either a movie or a stage musical of his early life, and conversations were held with sundry producers, writers and performers, but nothing came of them. In these years his health began to decline. By 1984 a published list of his ailments included sciatica, gout, neuritis and a thyroid condition. In addition he suffered several strokes and, later, a heart attack.

Add illness to the firmness with which Cagney had hymned the joys of retirement in his book, and the decision to come back to the screen in *Ragtime* in 1980 could not have been more surprising. Yet the rationale for his return was at least superficially plausible. His physical condition had deepened his sense of isolation to something like the danger point, and if some of his friends and relatives feared his part in the picture would overtax him, others thought it might be an antidote to the depression and lethargy that had seemed to be growing more profound in recent years.

He did not mix much with the *Ragtime* company in London, keeping pretty much to his hotel when he was not required on the set. But the O'Briens were staying there, too, and 'Bill' was, as ever, chirpingly present, and Marge Zimmermann found ways to keep him occupied. Moreover, when he was on the set he seemed happy, joshing pleasantly with make-up people, assistant directors and the rest of the picture's technical functionaries. He had always been the most democratic of stars, and Pat O'Brien was moved to recall how, in the old days, he and Cagney would contrive to forget their lines late in the afternoon, sending the day's work into overtime, which gave them the double pleasure of costing Jack Warner money and putting some additional pay into the extras' pockets.

Most important, Cagney's work in *Ragtime* turned out to be excellent. To be sure, he had to use cue cards because he could not remember lines. But the concentration and the attack were there, the old snarling force. Given the cherubic quality of his countenance in his late years, the hints of cynicism and corruption he suggested in the character of his police commissioner were particularly ironic in their implications.

The film was generally not well received when it was released a year later. It was full of good performances, but – speak of ironies – it seemed somehow less cinematic than E. L. Doctorow's novel, a quick-cut panorama of urban American life at the turn of the century, had been. The movie was cautious where the novel had been full of heedless electricity. Nonetheless, Cagney was welcomed back warmly and a few critics, at least, seemed to feel that in his few scenes he had caught the rhythms of the original work better than anyone.

By the time the picture was finished a year later my little documentary was completed, too, and a couple of nights before *Ragtime*'s première I took it over to the hotel where he was staying in New York doing his bit to publicize the picture, and ran it for Cagney. He seemed to have failed somewhat in the year since I had seen him last, but he was cordial,

172

and watching him watch the film, which contained clips from many films that he had either never seen or had forgotten that he had seen, was a curious experience. At first he was almost impassive, but then he seemed to warm to the recollections it awakened. By the end he was both laughing and crying. But what seemed to amuse him the most were the most dramatic sequences – like his death at the end of *The Roaring Twenties* or the death house sequence in *Angels with Dirty Faces*. What seemed to awaken tenderer sentiments were the comedy bits, especially those where he was working with old comrades he now missed. At the end of the screening he pronounced approval and invited me to join his table at the party after

the première, the high point of which for him was sneaking a few bites of forbidden cheesecake while Marge's back was turned – a wicked little boy indulging himself. Mostly, though, he was content to soak up the atmosphere of the old Luchow's restaurant on 14th St., which had remained as it had been in the days when Rheinlander Waldo may well have eaten there, and which Cagney himself had proposed as the site of the party.

There was talk of new projects, none of which came to fruition, but for the next couple of years Cagney remained quite visible, accepting awards, making appearances for charity – shy and distant in the face of standing ovations. And then, in the fall of 1983, it was announced that he would star in a two-hour television movie, *Terrible Joe Moran*, playing the title character, an old boxer, estranged from his family, his friends mostly dead, living wealthily but bitterly in a Manhattan town house attended only by an old retainer, played by Art Carney. His granddaughter (Ellen Barkin, a fine young actress, who was excellent in the part) penetrates his lair, intent on worming money out of him to support her ne'er do well lover, but then, after several melodramatic contretemps, discovers she really loves him while he discovers in her a reason to live.

The project had originally been developed for Katherine Hepburn who, in the central role, was to have been a former tennis star. But when she refused it sex and occupation changes had made the picture appropriate for Cagney, if unwise for him to do. It was not just that it was terribly ordinary television fare, but that his remaining physical vigor had visibly dwindled. He was never seen outside his wheelchair and, worse, his speech was now slow and slurred. It was clear, when the film was finally broadcast in the spring of 1984, that almost all of his lines had had to be re-voiced by some actor doing a not very successful Cagney imitation.

Worse, from his point of view, his appearance became the occasion for an article in *Life* by a writer named Anthony Cook, which asked, as a subhead in the magazine put it, 'Is the ailing star being helped or used by the mystery woman who dominates his life?' The piece, which was widely quoted in other journals, implied that Marge Zimmermann had, through the years, advanced from unpaid helper, to paid assistant to a point where she was not merely managing Cagney's comeback career, but his finances and his friendships as well. It implied that she had been instrumental in estranging him from his children, from his surviving siblings, William and Jeanne (who has since died), and from all of his friends who refused to pay her proper obeisance. The article suggested she was now personally collecting a

percentage of his fees for this TV work plus a salary as the show's associate producer. It claimed she and her husband had collected substantial gifts of land from Cagney, and that she had now replaced Cagney's daughter as executor of his will, having long since gained power of attorney from him. It was further implied that he could not have obtained medical clearance to do the television show if she had not found a malleable doctor to certify that he was fit to work and unlikely to be damaged by it. At best, according to Cook, both Cagney and his wife 'appeared to be victims of what gerontologists call "learned helplessness". In a curious way, Cagney's public reappearance coincided with a growing personal isolation. The more insulated he and his wife were, the more dependent on Marge they became.'

Both Cagneys immediately rebutted this piece in follow-up stories, insisting that they were in control of their lives, that the Zimmermanns were what they had always been, trusted friends and employees who made no decisions without careful consultation with their employers. And, it must be said, Cook's piece was a tissue of innuendos, deliberately placing the worst possible interpretation on ambiguous facts, quoting from sources who had their own interests to advance. In any event, one can testify, from personal observation, that Marge Zimmermann undertook the process of remobilizing Cagney with the best of intentions, that is, with a desire to prolong her beloved 'Jamsie's' life by giving him something to live for. She may later have found herself in waters unknown to her and tricky to anyone – namely that of deal-making show business. Certainly one must judge *Terrible Joe Moran* a mistake, but one which anyone might honestly have made if, loving Cagney, it was difficult to acknowledge that his physical decline was now such that it rendered all but the simplest professional demands impossible for him to fulfil.

Putting the matter specifically, Cagney's brief role in *Ragtime* had been well within his

physical capabilities. As important, it was a logical extension of his screen personality as everyone had come to understand it. This old man, barking commands at his underlings, bullying the villain of the piece, generally in command of a tense dramatic situation in a conscientiously made movie, was Cagney as we hoped he would be if we chanced to encounter him in his old age. On the other hand Joe Moran, in his wheelchair, whispering his lines at us in a strange voice, dependent on others for his welfare, uncomfortably reminded us of what age all too commonly is for most people. Moreover, he had too much screen time. We had too much time to study him, and it could not help but be borne in even on people who knew nothing of Cagney's status that this character was uncomfortably close to his private reality, that, he was, indeed, 'playing himself'. It was not just a matter of seeing his current physical status all too clearly. It was also that that curious passivity of his, that air of being in some sense fortune's plaything, which had clung to so many of his past roles (and to almost all of the best ones) and which had functioned as a kind of side light, casting a curious shadow on it, was now at the center of his performance. By the end of the program one was averting one's eyes from the screen, convinced this was Cagney's last role and saddened that it should be in this inept and desperate context. It was precisely the way one does not want to see a figure like him go out.

Yet understanding Cagney's temperament it was possible to believe something like *Terrible Joe Moran* was inevitable. We have seen that especially in his later career he would respond to appeals for a favor. The ability to grant them, to do as he pleased when and where the spirit struck him, was one of the reasons he had struggled for independence. To put the matter simply, he could be as whimsical as he pleased – in his acceptances as well as his refusals. Thus he had risked injury doing his cameo for Bob Hope in *The Seven Little Foys*. He had gone into *Tribute to a Bad Man* to help out a desper-

ate producer. He had done Robert Montgomery's television show to help his friend in his fight for ratings and he had worked on A. C. Lyles' B pictures because he, too, was a friend who seemed to need Cagney. Even his appearance in *Ragtime* had been undertaken because Milos Forman had proved to be an attentive acquaintance. If, now, Marge wanted him to do this television thing, and if she stood to make a few dollars from it, it was all right with him. It was yet another way of showing his indifference to being a 'legend', just as once he had enjoyed showing his indifference to being a star.

But, in the largest sense, the fault was not his, or Marge Zimmermann's, or even that of the producers so eager to keep their project alive that they would run the risk of seeming to exploit a beloved legend. There was a larger, unstated issue here, one quite beyond the capacity of vulgar journalism, which must ever seek the easily explained motive in order to offer its hasty readers quick comprehension of the complex world. For it turns out that the unearned, and quite unexpected, increment of movie stardom, particularly at its highest level is, of all belated benisons, a curious form of agelessness, one last fictional convention within which the star is expected by his public to live and which he violates at his peril.

There is a large irony in this, for after a star enters his mid-forties the great and implacable enemy is age, and typically a decade or two is spent fighting it, if not with toupé and corsetry, plastic surgery or diffusion filter, then at least in the ways we have witnessed James Cagney fighting it, by imposing brutal variations on his screen character, or by groping ineffectually for mature pleasantries. Ultimately, of course, this effort is to no avail. And to no point, either. For sometime in the star's sunset years, probably at about the moment that outward appearances cease to mean anything to him, and he can afford to relax gratefully into retirement, it must be borne in upon him that an element of his past – the most important part of it, in fact – is not going to behave like everyone else's, is not going to fade and blur as memory plays its selective tricks on it. He is going to discover that the moving images that were created out of the flesh and blood of heedless youth, in what seemed (for Cagney's generation) a transitory, even contemptible medium, are going to hang about looking as fresh and forceful, as vividly defined, as they did the day they were born on some sound stage or backlot. These images haunt the late-night and mid-afternoon television screens. They lurk in the shadows of the revival theaters and in the dimmed classrooms of the film schools. You can buy or rent them at the corner video salon. They populate the pages of books like this one. To put it simply, they are reborn in media and in venues only dreamed of when they were originally created. And because this is so, older generations are offered that rarest of boons, total and perfect recall of pleasures past. And one almost as pleasant – that of sharing those pleasures with newer generations, who often as not embrace these images with the same giddy innocence that their parents and grandparents did, and with some of the older crowd's proprietary curiosity as well.

In some cases, alas, that curiosity is less warm, more driven than it should be. For at the heart of a truly compelling stardom there is always an enigma that some among us cannot stop worrying. What in these great screen presences is a projection of the unmediated self? What in them is a selected and heightened presentation of elements of that self and what in them is the product of repressions and denials? And what in them is pure fiction, or, perhaps more properly, an accretion of fictions, an anthology of memorable moments invented for the star by shrewd writer or director which he has, in his artfulness, made his own, or anyway passed off as his own? Not that anyone possessed of these questions can ever articulate them so coherently, or at all, so messily do they chase themselves around the unkempt mind of the typical fan.

Even when he is at his peak these are matters the star himself, if he is wise, does not wish to contemplate. It is not merely that they are the source of the endlessly importunate curiosity that his public visits upon him. It is also that self-consciousness, over-intellectualization, are inimical to his art. This being so, imagine how much more annoying these questions are to him later on, when he discovers that his screen personality, his public self, something he has ceased to work on, to care about, continues to exercise a hold on an audience that, defying all logic, not to mention common civility, refuses to disband, even though he has long since ceased putting on shows for it. Indeed, the star discovers at this point that his former screen self, that youthful folly of his, is not merely alive and well, but is actually the controlling reality in almost every encounter he has with strangers.

Amazing! He knows, of course, that whatever he projected in the past was but a version of himself, a fiction made up of materials conveniently to hand and easy to read on the screen. He also knows – and here is where a genuine poignancy enters our accounting – that with the passing years he has moved farther and farther away from that half-fiction of youth, to a point where his estrangement from it is almost total. And yet so powerful is it, so much does it matter in the inner lives of others, he is expected to live within its terms, knows that when he does not, when he cannot make his ageing self fulfill the ancient, accidental bargain he struck with his public, he is bound to spread disappointment, even dismay among its members. The thought may even occur to him that he must not only continue to live in character, but perhaps even die in character. That is to say, provide a final exit that suits the role he had played in our minds – romantic, heroic, whatever.

It is monstrous, this implicit demand. And we are all capable of being monsters, even those of us who pride ourselves on a sophisticated understanding of stardom as an institution, celebrity as a peculiar distortion of the traditional balance between public duty and private life. I realized, watching *Terrible Joe Moran*, that I had myself been making that unreasonable demand on James Cagney when I had spoken with him in London four years earlier – only unconsciously I hope. I had wanted that kindly and obliging old man to be now what he had once seemed to be on screen. I had wanted him to cheat age and its infirmities and imperatives as once he sometimes had on the screen. Or, failing that, I wanted him to embrace it as once he had embraced death on the screen, with knowing gallantry.

This faint and feeble television effort at least showed me how unreasonable I had been, perhaps how unreasonable we all are. Of course I was sorry he had done it. I would have much preferred that his final appearance as an actor had been the one in *Ragtime*, so vivid and forceful, so in character as it were. But there is, perhaps, falsity in this sentiment. In life we do not normally get to choose our deaths. 'The distinguished thing' catches us unaware, unprepared, in disarray. One could argue that it is the final honesty in an honestly drawn fiction like Cagney's screen character, this one last appearance in a foolish, futile and essentially corrupt fiction. Possibly it is more instructive, truer to life, than a nobler curtain call might have been. If James Cagney fully participated in the decision to do so, it might be better to admire the honesty with which he presented this final image of what he had inevitably become than to deplore the circumstances of its presentation. If he did not, if those circumstances were at least partially imposed upon him in his indifference, distance and passivity, we might yet more profitably reflect on the sad, possibly bitter truths about ageing that his appearance in this film offers. There was little, if any, art about it. But there was reality in it.

But enough. About such nice considerations James Cagney has long since ceased to care. When he was nineteen or twenty years old he

wrote two simple lines of verse 'Each man starts with his very first breath / To devise shrewd means of outwitting death.' Reciting those lines to me, he added: 'Don't know why I wrote that.' But, of course, he did – it is no less a truth for being a simple truth – and, of course, he understood that forty or fifty years ago he achieved the aim to which his rhyme alluded. This placed him among the most fortunate of men, and since it is immodest to talk about one's own good luck he has chosen to be silent when possible, evasive when pressed, about the matter. Men of his time and background were taught that any other course was idle and self-serving. If he had ever had any need for that sort of thing it had passed ages ago. Don't ask him when. He couldn't possibly remember.

FILMOGRAPHY

1 Sinner's Holiday
DIRECTOR John G. Adolfi
SCENARIO Harvey Thew, George Rosener, based on the play *Penny Arcade* by Marie Baumer
PHOTOGRAPHY Ira Morgan
EDITOR James Gibbons
CAST Angel Harrison (Grant Withers); Jennie Delano (Evalyn Knapp); Harry Delano (James Cagney); Myrtle (Joan Blondell); Mr Delano (Lucille Laverna); Buck (Noel Madison); George (Otto Hoffman); Mitch McKane (Warren Hymer); Sikes (Purnell B. Pratt); Joe Delano (Ray Gallagher); Happy (Hank Mann)
RUNNING TIME 55 minutes
RELEASE DATE 1930
PRODUCED BY Warner Bros

2 The Doorway to Hell
(GB title: A Handful of Clouds)
DIRECTOR Archie Mayo
SCENARIO George Rosener, based on the story *A Handful of Clouds* by Rowland Brown
PHOTOGRAPHY Barney 'Chick' McGill
EDITOR Robert Crandall
CAST Louis Ricarno (Lewis [Lew] Ayres); Sam Marconi (Charles Judels); Doris (Dorothy Mathews); Jackie Lamar (Leon Janney); Captain O'Grady (Robert Elliott); Steve Mileway (James Cagney); Captain of Military Academy (Kenneth Thomson); Joe (Jerry Mandy); Rocco (Noel Madisono); Bit (Bernard 'Bunny' Granville); Machine Gunner (Fred Argus); Girl (Ruth Hall); Gangsters (Dwight Frye, Tom Wilson, Al Hill)
RUNNING TIME 78 minutes
RELEASE DATE 1930
PRODUCED BY Warner Bros

3 Other Men's Women
(AKA Steel Highway)
DIRECTOR William A. Wellman
SCENARIO William K. Wells, based on the story by Maude Fulton
PHOTOGRAPHY Barney 'Chick' McGill
EDITOR Edward McDermott
CAST Bill (Grant Withers); Lily (Mary Aston); Jack (Regis Toomey); Ed (James Cagney); Marie (Joan Blondell); Haley (Fred Kohler); Pegleg (J. Farrell MacDonald); Waitress (Lillian Worth); Bixby (Walter Long); Railroad Workers (Bob Perry, Lee Morgan, Kewpie Morgan, Pat Hartigan)
RUNNING TIME 70 minutes
RELEASE DATE 1931
PRODUCED BY Warner Bros

4 The Millionaire
DIRECTOR John G. Adolfi
SCENARIO Julian Josephson, Maude T. Powell, based on *Idle Hands* by Earl Derr Biggers, Dialogue by Booth Tarkington
PHOTOGRAPHY James Van Trees
EDITOR Owen Marks
CAST James Alden (George Arliss); Barbara Alden (Evalyn Knapp); Bill Merrick (James Cagney); Carter Andrews (Branwell Fletcher); Mrs Alden (Florence Arliss); Peterson (Noah Beery); Dr Harvey (Ivan Simpson); McCoy (Sam Hardy); Dan Lewis (J. Farrell MacDonald); Briggs (Tully Marshall); Doctor (J. C. Nugent)
RUNNING TIME 82 minutes
RELEASE DATE 1930
PRODUCED BY Warner Bros

5 The Public Enemy
(GB title: Enemies of the Public)
DIRECTOR William A. Wellman
SCENARIO Kubec Glasmon, John Bright. Adaptation and dialogue: Harvey Thew. Based on the original story *Beer and Blood* by John Bright
PHOTOGRAPHY Dev Jennings
EDITOR Ed McCormick
CAST Tom Powers (James Cagney); Gwen Allen (Jean Harlow); Matt Doyle (Edward Woods); Mamie (Joan Blondell); Ma Powers (Beryl Mercer); Mike Powers (Donald Cook); Kitty (Mae Clarke); Jane (Mia Marvin); Nails Nathan (Leslie Fenton); Paddy Ryan (Robert Emmett O'Connor); Putty Nose (Murray Kinnell); Bugs Moran (Ben Hendricks Jr); Molly Doyle (Rita Flynn); Dutch (Clark Burroughs); Hack (Snitz Edwards); Mrs Doyle (Adele Watson); Tommy as a Boy (Frank Coghlan Jr); Matt as a Boy (Frankie Darro); Officer Pat Burke (Robert E. Homans); Nails' Girl (Dorothy Gee); Officer Powers (Purnell Pratt); Steve the Bartender (Lee Phelps); Little Girls (Helen Parrish, Dorothy Gray, Nanci Price); Bugs as a boy (Ben Hendricks III); Machine Gunner (George Daly); Joe the Headwaiter (Sam McDaniel); Pawnbroker (William H. Strauss)
RUNNING TIME 84 minutes
RELEASE DATE 1931
PRODUCED BY Warner Bros

6 Smart Money
DIRECTOR Alfred E. Green
SCENARIO Kubec Glasmon, John Bright. Additional dialogue by Lucien Hubbard, Joseph Jackson. Based on the original story by Lucien Hubbard, Joseph Jackson
PHOTOGRAPHY Robert Kurrle
EDITOR Jack Killifer
CAST Nick Venizelos (Edward G. Robinson); Irene Graham (Evalyn Knapp); Jack (James Cagney); Marie (Noel Francis); District Attorney (Morgan Wallace); Mr Amenoppopolus (Paul Porcasi); Greek Barber (Maurice Black); D. A.'s Girl (Margaret Livingston); Schultz (Clark Burroughs); Salesman (Billy House); Two-Time Phil (Edwin Argus); Sleepy Sam (Ralf Harolde); Sport Williams (Boris Karloff); Small Town Girl (Mae Madison); Dealer Barnes (Walter Percival); Snake Eyes (John Larkin); Lola (Polly Walters); Hickory Short (Ben Taggart); Cigar Stand Clerk (Gladys Lloyd); Matron (Eulalie Jensen); Desk Clerk (Charles Lane); Reporter (Edward Hearn); Tom, a Customer (Eddie Kane); George, the Porter (Clinton Rosemond); Machine Gunner (Charles O'Malley); Joe, Barber Customer (Gus Leonard); Cigar Stand Clerk (Wallace MacDonald); Dwarf on Train (John George); Gambler (Harry Semels); Girl at Gaming Table (Charlotte Merriam); with Larry McGrath, Spencer Bell, Allan Lane
RUNNING TIME 90 minutes
RELEASE DATE 1931
PRODUCED BY Warner Bros

7 Blonde Crazy
(GB title: Larceny Lane)
DIRECTOR Roy Del Ruth
SCENARIO Kubec Glasmon, John Bright, based on an original story by Kubec Glasmon, John Bright
PHOTOGRAPHY Sid Hickox
EDITOR Ralph Dawson
CAST Bert Harris (James Cagney); Ann Roberts (Joan Blondell); Dapper Dan Barker (Louis Calhern); Helen Wilson (Noel Francis); A. Rupert Johnson Jr (Guy Kibbee); Joe Reynolds (Raymond Milland); Peggy (Polly Walters); Four-Eyes, Desk Clerk (Charles [Levinson] Lane); Colonel Bellock (William Burress); Dutch (Peter Erkelenz); Mrs Snyder (Maude Eburne); Lee (Walter Percival); Hank (Nat Pendleton); Jerry (Russell Hopton); Cabbie (Dick Cramer); Detective (Wade Boteler); Bellhops (Ray Cooke, Edward Morgan); Conman (Phil Sleman)
RUNNING TIME 73 minutes
RELEASE DATE 1931
PRODUCED BY Warner Bros

8 Taxi!
DIRECTOR Roy Del Ruth
SCENARIO Kubec Glasmon, John Bright.

Based on the play *The Blind Spot* by
Kenyon Nicholson
PHOTOGRAPHY James Van Trees
EDITOR James Gibbons
CAST Matt Nolan (James Cagney); Sue
Reilly (Loretta Young); Skeets (George E.
Stone); Pop Reilly (Guy Kibbee); Buck
Gerard (David Landau); Danny Nolan
(Ray Cooke); Ruby (Leila Bennett); Marie
Costa (Dorothy Burgess); Joe Silva (Matt
McHugh); Father Nulty (George
MacFarlane); Polly (Polly Walters);
Truckdriver (Nat Pendleton); Mr West
(Berton Churchill); William Kenny (George
Raft); Monument Salesman (Hector V.
Sarno); Cleaning Lady (Aggie Herring);
Onlooker (Lee Phelps); Cabbie (Harry
Tenbrook); Cop with Jewish Man (Robert
Emmett O'Connor); Dance Judges (Eddie
Fetherstone, Russ Powell); Cop (Ben
Taggart); The Cotton Club Orchestra
RUNNING TIME 70 minutes
RELEASE DATE 1932
PRODUCED BY Warner Bros

9 The Crowd Roars
DIRECTOR Howard Hawks
SCENARIO Kubec Glasmon, John Bright,
Niven Busch. Based on a story by Howard
Hawks, Seton I. Miller
PHOTOGRAPHY Sid Hickox, John Stumar
EDITOR Thomas Pratt
CAST Joe Greer (James Cagney); Anne
(Joan Blondell); Lee (Ann Dvorak); Eddie
Greer (Eric Linden); Dad Greer (Guy
Kibbee); Spud Connors (Frank McHugh);
Bill Arnold (William Arnold); Jim (Leo
Nomis); Mrs Spud Connors (Charlotte
Merriam); Dick Willshaw (Regis Toomey);
Auto Drivers (Harry Hartz, Ralph
Hepburn, Fred Guisso, Fred Frame, Phil
Pardee, Spider Matlock, Jack Brisko, Lou
Schneider, Bryan Salspaugh, Stubby
Stubblefield, Shorty Cantlon, Mel Keneally,
Wilbur Shaw); Mechanic (James Burtis);
Ascot Announcer (Sam Hayes); Tom,
Counterman (Robert McWade); Official
(Ralph Dunn); Announcer (John Conte);
Red, Eddie's Pitman (John Harron)
RUNNING TIME 85 minutes
RELEASE DATE 1932
PRODUCED BY Warner Bros

10 Winner Take All
DIRECTOR Roy Del Ruth
SCENARIO Wilson Mizner, Robert Lord.
Based on the magazine story *133 At 3* by
Gerald Beaumont
PHOTOGRAPHY Robert Kurrle
EDITOR Thomas Pratt
CAST Jim Lane (James Cagney); Peggy
Harmon (Marian Nixon); Joan Gibson
(Virginia Bruce); Pop Slavin (Guy Kibbee);
Rosebud, the Trainer (Clarence Muse);
Dickie Harmon (Dickie Moore); Monty
(Allan Lane); Roger Elliott (John Roche);
Legs Davis (Ralf Harolde); Forbes (Alan
Mowbray); Ben Isaacs (Clarence Wilson);
Butler (Charles Coleman); Ann (Esther
Howard); Lois (Renee Whitney); Al West
(Harvey Perry); Pice (Julian Rivero); Ring
Announcer (Selmer Jackson); Manager

(Chris Pin Martin); Interne (George
Hayes); Tijuana Referee (Bob Perry);
Second (Billy West); Reporter (Phil Tead);
Waiter (Rolfe Sedan); Boxing Spectator
(John Kelly); Ring Announcer,
Championship (Lee Phelps); Society Man
(Jay Eaton); Blonde (Charlotte Merriam)
RUNNING TIME 68 minutes
RELEASE DATE 1932
PRODUCED BY Warner Bros

11 Hard to Handle
DIRECTOR Mervyn Le Roy
SCENARIO Wilson Mizner, Robert Lord.
Based on a story by Houston Branch
PHOTOGRAPHY Barney 'Chick' McGill
EDITOR William Holmes
CAST Lefty Merrill (James Cagney); Ruth
Waters (Mary Brian); Lil Walters (Ruth
Donelly); Radio Announcer (Allen
Jenkins); Marlene Reeves (Claire Dodd);
John Hayden (Gavin Gordon); Mrs Hawks,
Landlady (Emma Dunn); Charles Reeves
(Robert McWade); Ed McGrath (John
Sheehan); Joe Goetz (Matt McHugh); Mrs
Weston Parks (Louise Mackintosh);
Antique Dealer (William H. Strauss);
Merrill's Secretary (Bess Flowers); Hash-
slinger (Lew Kelly); Colonel Wells (Berton
Churchill); Colonel's Associate (Harry
Holman); Fat Lady with Vanishing Cream
(Grace Hayle); Dance Judge (George Pat
Collins); District Attorney (Douglass
Dumbrille); Andy (Sterling Holloway);
Jailer (Charles Wilson); with Jack
Crawford, Stanley Smith, Walter Walker,
Mary Doran
RUNNING TIME 81 minutes
RELEASE DATE 1933
PRODUCED BY Warner Bros

12 Picture Snatcher
DIRECTOR Lloyd Bacon
SCENARIO Allen Rivkin, P. J. Wolfson.
Based on a story by Danny Ahern
PHOTOGRAPHY Sol Polito
EDITOR William Holmes
CAST Danny Kean (James Cagney);
McLean (Ralph Bellamy); Patricia Nolan
(Patricia Ellis); Allison (Alice White); Jerry
(Ralf Harolde); Casey Nolan (Robert
Emmett O'Connor); Grover (Robert
Barrat); Hennessy, the Fireman (George
Pat Collins); Leo (Tom Wilson); Olive
(Barbara Rogers); Connie (Renee
Whitney); Colleen (Alice Jans); Speakeasy
Girl (Jill Dennett); Reporter (Billy West);
Machine Gunner (George Daly); Head
Keeper (Arthur Vinton); Prison Guard
(Stanley Blystone); Hood (Don Brodie);
Reporter (George Chandler); Journalism
Student (Sterling Holloway); Mike,
Colleen's Boyfriend (Donald Kerr); Pete, a
Drunken Reporter (Hobart Cavanaugh);
Reporter Strange (Phil Tead); Sick
Reporter (Charles King); Reporter outside
Prison (Milton Kibbee); Editors (Dick
Elliott, Vaughn Taylor); Bartender (Bob
Perry); Barber (Gino Corrado); Speakeasy
Proprietor (Maurice Black); Record Editor
(Selmer Jackson); Police Officer (Jack
Grey); Captain (John Ince); Little Girl

(Cora Sue Collins)
RUNNING TIME 77 minutes
RELEASE DATE 1933
PRODUCED BY Warner Bros

13 The Mayor of Hell
DIRECTOR Archie Mayo
SCENARIO Edward Chodorov, based on a
story by Islin Auster
PHOTOGRAPHY Barney 'Chick' McGill
EDITOR Jack Killifer
CAST Patsy Gargan (James Cagney);
Dorothy Griffith (Madge Evans); Mike
(Allen Jenkins); Mr Thompson (Dudley
Digges); Jimmy Smith (Frankie Darro);
Smoke (Farina); Mrs Smith (Dorothy
Peterson); Hopkins (John Marston); Guard
(Charles Wilson); Tommy's Father (Hobart
Cavanaugh); Johnny Stone (Raymond
Borzage); Mr Smith (Robert Barrat);
Brandon (George Pat Collins); Butch
Kilgore (Mickey Bennett); Judge Gilbert
(Arthur Byron); the Girl (Sheila Terry); Joe
(Harold Huber); Louis Johnston (Edwin
Maxwell); Walters (William V. Mong); Izzy
Horowitz (Sidney Miller); Tony's Father
(George Humbert); Charlie Burns (George
Offerman Jr); Tommy Gorman (Charles
Cane); Johnson's Assistant (Wallace
MacDonald); Car Owner (Adrian Morris);
Hemingway (Snowflake); Guard (Wilfred
Lucas); Collectors (Bob Perry, Charles
Sullivan); Sheriff (Ben Taggart)
RUNNING TIME 90 minutes
RELEASE DATE 1933
PRODUCED BY Warner Bros

14 Footlight Parade
DIRECTOR Lloyd Bacon, Busby Berkeley
SCENARIO Manuel Seff, James Seymour
PHOTOGRAPHY George Barnes
EDITOR George Amy
CAST Chester Kent (James Cagney); Nan
Prescott (Joan Blondell); Bea Thorn (Ruby
Keeler); Scotty Blair (Dick Powell); Silas
Gould (Guy Kibbee); Harriet Bowers
Gould (Ruth Donelly); Vivian Rich (Claire
Dodd); Charlie Bowers (Hugh Herbert);
Francis (Frank McHugh); Al Frazer
(Arthur Hohl); Harry Thompson (Gordon
Westcott); Cynthia Kent (Renee Whitney);
Joe Farrington (Philip Faversham); Miss
Smythe (Juliet Ware); Fralick, the Music
Director (Herman Bing); George
Appolinaris (Paul Porcasi); Doorman
(William Granger); Cop (Charles C.
Wilson); Gracie (Barbara Rogers);
Specialty Dancer (Billy Taft); Chorus Girls
(Marjean Rogers, Pat Wing, Donna Mae
Roberts); Chorus Boy (David O'Brien);
Drugstore Attendant (George Chandler);
Title-Thinker-Upper (Hobart Cavanaugh);
Auditor (William V. Mong); Mac, the
Dance Director (Lee Moran); Mouse in
"Sittin' on a Backyard Fence" Number
(Billy Barty); Desk Clerk in "Honeymoon
Hotel" Number (Harry Seymour); Porter
(Sam McDaniel); Little Boy (Billy Barty);
House Detective (Fred Kelsey); Uncle
(Jimmy Conlin); Sailor-Pal in "Shanghai
Lil" Number (Roger Gray); Sailor Behind
Table (John Garfield); Sailor on Table

(Duke York); Joe, the Assistant Dance Director (Harry Seymour); Chorus Girls (Donna La Barr, Marlo Dwyer)
RUNNING TIME 104 minutes
RELEASE DATE 1933
PRODUCED BY Warner Bros

15 Lady Killer
DIRECTOR Roy Del Ruth
SCENARIO Ben Markson. Based on *The Finger Man* by Rosalind Keating Shaffer, adaptation by Ben Markson, Lillie Hayward
PHOTOGRAPHY Tony Gandio
EDITOR George Amy
CAST Dan Quigley (James Cagney); Myra Gale (Mae Clarke); Duke (Leslie Fenton); Lois Underwood (Margaret Lindsay); Ramick (Henry O'Neill); Conroy (Willard Robertson); Jones (Douglas Cosgrove); Pete (Raymond Hatton); Smiley (Russell Hopton); Williams (William Davidson); Mrs Wilbur Marley (Marjorie Gateson); Brannigan (Robert Elliott); Kendall (John Marston); Spade Maddock (Douglass Dumbrille); Thompson (George Chandler); The Escort (George Blackwood); Oriental (Jack Don Wong); Los Angeles Police Chief (Frank Sheridan); Jeffries, Theater Manager (Edwin Maxwell); Usher Sargeant Seymour (Phil Tead); Movie Fan (Dewey Robinson); Man with Purse (H. C. Bradley); J. B. Roland (Harry Holman); Dr Crane (Harry Beresford); Butler (Olaf Hytten); Ambulance Attendant (Harry Strong); Casino Cashier (Al Hill); Man in Casino (Bud Flanagan [Dennis O'Keefe]); Hand-out (James Burke); Jailer (Robert Homans); Lawyer (Clarence Wilson); Porter (Sam McDaniel); Los Angeles Cop (Spencer Charters); Western Director (Herman Bing); Letter-Handler (Harold Waldridge); Director (Luis Alberni); Property Man (Ray Cooke); Hood (Sam Ash)
RUNNING TIME 76 minutes
RELEASE DATE 1933
PRODUCED BY Warner Bros

16 Jimmy the Gent
DIRECTOR Michael Curtiz
SCENARIO Bertram Milhauser, based on the original story by Laird Doyle and Ray Nazarro
PHOTOGRAPHY Ira Morgan
EDITOR Thomas Richards
CAST Jimmy Corrigan (James Cagney); Joan Martin (Bette Davis); Mabel (Alice White); Louie (Allen Jenkins); Joe Rector [Monty Barton] (Arthur Hohl); James J. Wallingham (Alan Dinehart); Ronnie Gatston (Philip Reed); the Imposter (Hobart Cavanaugh); Gladys Farrell (Mayo Methot); Hendrickson (Ralf Harolde); Mike (Joseph Sawyer); Blair (Philip Faversham); Posy Barton (Nora Lane); Judge (Joseph Crehan); Civil Judge (Robert Warwick); Jitters (Merna Kennedy); Bessie (Renee Whitney); Tea Assistant (Monica Bannister); Man Drinking Tea (Don Douglas); Chester Coote (Bud Flanagan [Dennis O'Keefe]); Man in Flower Shop (Leonard Mudie); Justice of the Peace (Harry Holman); File

Clerk (Camille Rovelle); Pete (Stanley Mack); Grant (Tom Costello); Ferris (Ben Hendricks); Halley (Billy West); Tim (Eddie Shubert); Stew (Lee Moran); Eddie (Harry Wallace); Irish Cop (Robert Homans); Ambulance Driver (Milton Kibbee); Doctor (Howard Hickman); Nurse (Eula Guy); Viola (Juliet Ware); Blonde (Rickey Newell); Brunette (Lorena Layson); Second Young Man (Dick French); Third Young Man (Jay Eaton); Reverend Amiel Bottsford (Harold Entwistle); Bailiff (Charles Hickman); Ticket Clerk, Steamship (Leonard Mudie); Steward (Olaf Hytten); Second Steward (Vesey O'Davoren); Chalmers (Lester Dorr); Secretary (Pat Wing)
RUNNING TIME 67 minutes
RELEASE DATE 1934
PRODUCED BY Warner Bros

17 He Was Her Man
DIRECTOR Lloyd Bacon
SCENARIO Tom Buckingham, Niven Busch, based on a story by Robert Lord
PHOTOGRAPHY George Barnes
EDITOR George Amy
CAST Flicker Hayes (James Cagney); Rose Lawrence (Joan Blondell); Nick Gardella (Victor Jory); Pop Sims (Frank Craven); J. C. Ward (Harold Huber); Monk (Russell Hopton); Red Deering (Ralf Harolde); Mrs Gardella (Sarah Padden); Dutch (J. M. [John] Qualen); Dan Curly (Bradley Page); Gassy (Samuel S. Hinds); Waiter (George Chandler); Whitey (James Eagles); Fisherman (Gino Corrado)
RUNNING TIME 70 minutes
RELEASE DATE 1934
PRODUCED BY Warner Bros

18 Here Comes the Navy
DIRECTOR Lloyd Bacon
SCENARIO Ben Markson, Earl Baldwin, based on the story by Ben Markson
PHOTOGRAPHY Arthur Edeson
EDITOR George Amy
CAST Chesty O'Connor (James Cagney); Biff Martin (Pat O'Brien); Dorothy Martin (Gloria Stuart); Droopy (Frank McHugh); Gladys (Dorothy Tree); Commander Denny (Robert Barrat); Lieutenant Commander (Willard Robertson); Floor Manager (Guinn Williams); Droopy's Ma (Maude Eburne); First Girl (Martha Merrill); Second Girl (Lorena Layson); Aunt (Ida Darling); Riveter (Henry Otho); Hat Check Girl (Pauline True); Porter (Sam McDaniel); Foreman (Frank La Rue); Recruiting Officer (Joseph Crehan); CPO (James Burtis); Supply Sergeant (Edward Chandler); Professor (Leo White); Officer (Niles Welch); Sailor (Fred 'Snowflake' Toone); Skipper (Eddie Shubert); Admiral (George Irving); Captain (Howard Hickman); Navy Chaplain (Edward Earle); Lieutenant (Emmett); Bit (Gordon [Bill] Elliott); Workman (Nick Copeland); Attendant (John Swor); Marine Orderly (Eddie Cuff); Hood at Dance (Chuck Hamilton); Sailor (Eddie Fetherstone)
RUNNING TIME 86 minutes

RELEASE DATE 1934
PRODUCED BY Warner Bros

19 The St Louis Kid
(GB title: A Perfect Weekend)
DIRECTOR Ray Enright
PRODUCER Samuel Bischoff
SCENARIO Warren Duff, Seton I. Miller, based on a story by Frederick Hazlitt Brennan
PHOTOGRAPHY Sid Hickox
EDITOR Clarence Kolster
CAST Eddie Kennedy (James Cagney); Ann Reid (Patricia Ellis); Buck Willetts (Allen Jenkins); Farmer Benson (Robert Barrat); Richardson (Hobart Cavanaugh); Merseldopp (Spencer Charters); Brown (Addison Richards); Gracie (Dorothy Dare); Judge Jones (Arthur Aylesworth); Harris (Charles Wilson); Joe Hunter (William Davidson); Louie (Harry Woods); The Girlfriend (Gertrude Short); Pete (Eddie Shubert); Gorman (Russell Hicks); Sergeant (Guy Usher); Cops (Cliff Saum, Bruce Mitchell); Policeman (Wilfred Lucas); Girl (Rosalie Roy); Office Girl (Mary Russell); Motor Cop (Ben Hendricks); Mike (Harry Tyler); Paymaster (Milton Kibbee); Cook (Tom Wilson); Secretaries (Alice Marr, Victoria Vinton); Farmer (Lee Phelps); Girl in Car (Louise Seidel); Giddy Girl (Mary Treen); First Girl (Nan Grey); Second Girl (Virginia Grey); Third Girl (Martha Merrill); Sherriff (Charles B. Middleton); Prosecutor (Douglas Cosgrove); First Deputy (Monte Vandergrift); Second Deputy (Jack Cheatham); Driver (Stanley Mack); Attendant (Grover Liffen); Broadcast Officer (Frank Bull); Sergeant (Wade Boteler); Policeman (Frank Fanning); Second Policeman (Gene Strong); Flora (Edna Bennett); Man (Clay Clement); Detective (James Burtis) and Eddie Fetherstone, Joan Barclay
RUNNING TIME 67 minutes
RELEASE DATE 1934
PRODUCED BY Warner Bros

20 Devil Dogs of the Air
DIRECTOR Lloyd Bacon
PRODUCER Lou Edelman
SCENARIO Malcolm Stuart Boylan, Earl Baldwin, based on the story *Air Devils* by John Monk Saunders
PHOTOGRAPHY Arthur Edeson
EDITOR William Clemens
CAST Tommy O'Toole (James Cagney); Lieutenant William Brannigan (Pat O'Brien); Betty Roberts (Margaret Lindsay); Crash Kelly (Frank McHugh); Ma Roberts (Helen Lowell); Mac (John Arledge); Commandant (Robert Barrat); Captain (Russell Hicks); Adjutant (William B. Davidson); Senior Instructor (Ward Bond); Fleet Commander (Samuel S. Hinds); Officer (Harry Seymour); Second Officer (Bill Beggs); Mate (Bob Spencer); Officers (Newton House, Ralph Nye); Medical Officer (Selmer Jackson); Student (Bud Flanagan [Dennis O'Keefe]); Instructor (Gordon [Bill] Elliott); First

Student (Don Turner); Second Student (Dick French); Third Student (Charles Sherlock); Messenger (Carlyle Blackwell Jr); Girl (Martha Merrill); Lieutenant Brown (David Newell); Mrs Brown (Olive Jones); Mrs Johnson (Helen Flint); Communications Officer (Joseph Crehan)
RUNNING TIME 86 minutes
RELEASE DATE 1935
PRODUCED BY Cosmopolitan Productions for Warner Bros

21 G-Men
DIRECTOR William Keighley
SCENARIO Seton I. Miller, based on 'Public Enemy No 1' by Gregory Rogers
PHOTOGRAPHY Sol Polito
EDITOR Jack Killifer
CAST James 'Brick' Davis (James Cagney); Jean Morgan (Ann Dvorak); Kay McCord (Margaret Lindsay); Jeff McCord (Robert Armstrong); Brad Collins (Barton MacLane); Hugh Farrell (Lloyd Nolan); McKay (William Harrigan); Danny Leggett (Edward Pawley); Gerard (Russell Hopton); Durfee (Noel Madison); Eddie Buchanan (Regis Toomey); Bruce J. Gregory (Addison Richards); Venke (Harold Huber); The Man (Raymond Hatton); Analyst (Monte Blue); Gregory's Secretary (Mary Treen); Accomplice (Adrian Morris); Joseph Kratz (Edwin Maxwell); Bill, the Ballistics Expert (Emmett Vogan); Agent (James Flavin); Cops (Stanley Blystone, Pat Flaherty); Agent (James T. Mack); Congressman (Jonathan Hale); Bank Cashier (Ed Keane); Short Man (Charles Sherlock); Henchman at Lodge (Wheeler Oakman); Police Broadcaster (Eddie Dunn); Interne (Gordon [Bill] Elliott); Doctor at Store (Perry Ivins); Hood Shot at Lodge (Frank Marlowe); Collins' Moll (Gertrude Short); Gerard's Moll (Marie Astaire); Durfee's Moll (Florence Dudley); Moll (Frances Morris); Hood (Al Hill); Gangster (Huey White); Headwaiter (Glen Cavender); Tony (John Impolito); Sergeant (Bruce Mitchell); Deputy Sheriff (Monte Vandergrift); Chief (Frank Shannon); Announcer (Frank Bull); Nurse (Martha Merrill); Lounger (Gene Morgan); J. E. Glattner, the Florist (Joseph De Stefani); Machine Gunners (George Daly, Ward Bond); Prison Guard (Tom Wilson); Police Driver (Henry Hall); McCord's Aide (Lee Phelps); Hood at Lodge (Marc Lawrence); Man (Brooks Benedict)
RUNNING TIME 85 minutes
RELEASE DATE 1935
PRODUCED BY Warner Bros

22 The Irish in Us
DIRECTOR Lloyd Bacon
PRODUCER Samuel Bischoff
SCENARIO Earl Baldwin, based on a story by Frank Orsati
PHOTOGRAPHY George Barnes
EDITOR James Gibbons
CAST Danny O'Hara (James Cagney); Pat O'Hara (Pat O'Brien); Lucille Jackson (Olivia De Havilland); Mike O'Hara (Frank McHugh); Car-Barn McCarthy (Allen Jenkins); Ma O'Hara (Mary Gordon); Captain Jackson (J. Farrell MacDonald); Doc Mullins (Thomas Jackson); Joe Delancy (Harvey Perry); Lady in Ring (Bess Flowers); Neighbor (Mabel Colcord); Doctor (Edward Keane); Cook (Herb Haywood); Girl (Lucille Collins); Announcer (Harry Seymour); Chick (Sailor Vincent); Referee (Mushy Callahan); Messenger Boy (Jack McHugh); Men (Edward Gargan, Huntly Gordon, Emmett Vogan, Will Stanton)
RUNNING TIME 84 minutes
RELEASE DATE 1935
PRODUCED BY Warner Bros

23 A Midsummer Night's Dream
DIRECTOR Max Reinhardt, William Dieterle
PRODUCER Jack L. Warner
SCENARIO Charles Kenyon, Mary McCall Jr, based on the play by William Shakespeare
PHOTOGRAPHY Hal Mohr
EDITOR Ralph Dawson
CAST Bottom (James Cagney); Lysander (Dick Powell); Flute (Joe E. Brown); Helena (Jean Muir); Snout (Hugh Herbert); Theseus (Ian Hunter); Quince (Frank McHugh); Oberon (Victor Jory); Hermia (Olivia De Havilland); Demetrius (Ross Alexander); Egeus (Grant Mitchell); First Fairy [Prima Ballerina] (Nina Theilade); Hippolyta, Queen of the Amazons (Verree Teasdale); Titania (Anita Louise); Puck (Mickey Rooney); Snug (Dewey Robinson); Philostrate (Hobart Cavanaugh); Starveling (Otis Harlan); Ninny's Tomb (Arthur Treacher); Fairies: Pease-Blossom (Katherine Frey); Cobweb (Helen Westcott); Moth (Fred Sale); Mustard-Seed (Billy Barty)
RUNNING TIME 132 minutes
RELEASE DATE 1935
PRODUCED BY Warner Bros

24 Frisco Kid
DIRECTOR Lloyd Bacon
PRODUCER Samuel Bischoff
SCENARIO Warren Duff, Seton I. Miller, based on an original story by Warren Duff, Seton I. Miller
PHOTOGRAPHY Sol Polito
EDITOR Owen Marks
CAST Bat Morgan (James Cagney); Jean Barrat (Margaret Lindsay); Paul Morra (Ricardo Cortez); Bella Morra (Lily Damita); Charles Ford (Donald Woods); Spider Burke (Barton MacLane); Solly (George E. Stone); William T. Coleman (Addison Richards); James Daley (Joseph King); Judge Crawford (Robert McWade); McClanahan (Joseph Crehan); Graber (Robert Strange); Slugs Crippen (Joseph Sawyer); Shanghai Duck (Fred Kohler); Tupper (Edward McWade); Jumping Whale (Claudia Coleman); The Weasel (John Wray); First Lookout (Ivar McFadden); Second Lookout (Lee Phelps); Evangelist (William Wagner); Drunk (Don Barclay); Captain (Jack Curtis); Miner (Walter Long); Man (James Farley); Shop Man (Milton Kibbee); Salesman (Harry Seymour); Madame (Claire Sinclair); Young Drunk (Alan Davis); Dealer (Karl Hackett); First Policeman (Wilfred Lucas); Second Policeman (John T. [Jack] Dillon); First Man (Edward Mortimer); Second Man (William Holmes); Usher (Don Downen); Mrs Crawford (Mrs Willfred North); Speaker (Charles Middleton); Man (Joe Smith Marba); Doctor (Landers Stevens); Mulligan (Frank Sheridan); Men (J. C. Morton, Harry Tenbrook); Dealer (Lew Harvey); Rat Face (Eddie Sturgis); Captain [Vigilante] (William Desmond); Maid (Jessie Perry); Contractors (Edward Keane, Edward Le Saint); Vigilante Leaders (Robert Dudley, Dick Rush); Doctor (John Elliott) and Helene Chadwick, Bill Dale, Dick Kerr, Alice Lake, Vera Steadman, Jane Tallent
RUNNING TIME 77 minutes
RELEASE DATE 1935
PRODUCED BY Warner Bros

25 Ceiling Zero
DIRECTOR Howard Hawks
PRODUCER Harry Joe Brown
SCENARIO Frank Wead, based on the play *Ceiling Zero* by Frank Wead
PHOTOGRAPHY Arthur Edeson
EDITOR William Holmes
CAST Dizzy Davis (James Cagney); Jack Lee (Pat O'Brien); Tommy Thomas (June Travis); Texas Clark (Stuart Erwin); Tay Lawson (Henry Wadsworth); Lou Clark (Isabel Jewell); Al Stone (Barton MacLane); Mary Lee (Martha Tibbetts); Joe Allen (Craig Reynolds); Buzz Gordon (James H. Bush); Les Bogan (Robert Light); Fred Adams (Addison Richards); Eddie Payson (Carlyle Morre Jr); Smiley Johnson (Richard Purcell); Transportation Agent (Gordon [Bill] Elliott); Baldy Wright (Pat West); Doc Wilson (Edward Gargan); Mike Owens (Garry Owen); Mama Gini (Mathilde Comont); Birdie (Carol Hughes); Stunt Fliers (Frank Tomick, Paul Mantz); Pilots (Jimmy Aye, Howard Allen, Mike Lally, Harold Miller); Mechanic (Jerry Jerome); Hostesses (Helene McAdoo, Gay Sheridan, Mary Lou Dix, Louise Seidel, Helen Erickson); Office Workers (Don Wayson, Dick Cherney, Jimmie Barnes, Frank McDonald); Teletype Operator (J. K. Kane); Tall Girl (Jayne Manners); Girls (Maryon Curtiz, Margaret Perry)
RUNNING TIME 95 minutes
RELEASE DATE 1935
PRODUCED BY Cosmopolitan Productions for Warner Bros

26 Great Guy
(GB title: Pluck of the Irish)
DIRECTOR John G. Blystone
PRODUCER Douglas Maclean
SCENARIO Henry McCarthy, Henry Johnson, James Edward Grant, Harry Rusking, based on *The Johnny Cave Stories* by James Edward Grant
PHOTOGRAPHY Jack McKenzie
EDITOR Russell Schoengarth
CAST Johnny Cave (James Cagney); Janet Henry (Mae Clarke); Pat Haley (James

Burke); Pete Reilly (Edward Brophy); Conning (Henry Kolker); Hazel Scott (Bernadene Hayes); Captain Pat Hanlon (Edward J. McNamara); Cavanaugh (Robert Gleckler); Joe Burton (Joe Sawyer); Al (Ed Gargan); Tim (Matty Fain); Mrs Ogilvie (Mary Gordon); Joel Green (Wallis Clark); The Mayor (Douglas Wood); Clerk (Jeffrey Sayre); Meat Clerk (Eddy Chandler); Store Manager (Henry Roquemore); Client (Murdock MacQuarrie); Woman at Accident (Kate Price); Detective (Frank O'Connor); Furniture Salesman (Arthur Hoyt); Truck Driver (Jack Pennick); Reporter (Lynton Brent); City Editor (John Dilson); Guests (Bud Geary, Dennis O'Keefe); Parker (Robert Lowery); Grocery Clerk (Bobby Barber); Nurse (Gertrude Green); Burton's Girl Friend (Ethelreda Leopold); Cop at Accident (Bruce Mitchell); Party Guests (James Ford, Frank Mills, Ben Hendricks Jr); Deputy (Kernan Cripps); Second Meat Clerk (Bill O'Brien); Chauffeur (Lester Dorr); Receiving Clerk (Harry Tenbrook); Mike the Cop (Lee Shumway) and Gertrude Aston, Vera Steadman, Mildred Harris, Bert Kalmar Jr, Walter D. Clarke Jr
RUNNING TIME 75 minutes
RELEASE DATE 1936
PRODUCED BY Grand National

27 Something to Sing About
DIRECTOR Victor Schertzinger
PRODUCER Zion Myers
SCENARIO Austin Parker, based on a story by Victor Schertzinger
PHOTOGRAPHY John Stumar
EDITOR Gene Milford
CAST Terry Rooney (James Cagney); Rita Wyatt (Evelyn Daw); Hank Meyers (William Frawley); Stephanie Hajos (Mona Barrie); Bennett O'Regan (Gene Lockhart); Orchestra Soloist (James Newhill); Pinky (Harris Barris); Candy (Candy Candido); Soloist (Cully Richards); Cafe Manager (William B. Davidson); Blaine (Richard Tucker); Farney (Marek Windheim); Easton (Dwight Frye); Daviani (John Arthur); Ito (Philip Ahn); Miss Robbins (Kathleen Lockhart); Transportation Manager (Kenneth Harlan); Studio Attorney (Herbert Rawlinson); Edward Burns (Ernest Wood); Man Terry Fights (Chick Collins); Dancers (Harland Dixon, Johnny Boyle, Johnny [Skins] Miller, Pat Moran, Joe Bennett, Buck Mack, Eddie Allen); Singer (Bill Carey); Specialty (The Vagabonds); Girls (Elinore Welz, Eleanor Prentiss); Arthur Nelson's Fighting Cats (Pinkie and Pal); Cabby (Frank Mills); Stuntman (Duke Green); Studio Official (Larry Steers); Sailor in Drag (John [Skins] Miller); S F Theatre Manager (Eddie Kane); Studio Guard (Edward Hearn); Three Shades of Blue (Dottie Messmer, Virginia Lee Irwin, Dolly Waldorf); Ship's Captain (Robert McKenzie); Head Waiter (Alphonse Martel)
RUNNING TIME 80 minutes
RELEASE DATE 1935
PRODUCED BY Warner Bros

28 Boy Meets Girl
DIRECTOR Lloyd Bacon
PRODUCER George Abbott
SCENARIO Bella Spewack, Sam Spewack
PHOTOGRAPHY Sol Polito
EDITOR William Holmes
CAST Robert Law (James Cagney); J. C. Benson (Pat O'Brien); Susie (Marie Wilson); C. Elliott Friday (Ralph Bellamy); Rossetti (Frank McHugh); Larry Toms (Dick Foran); Rodney Bevan (Bruce Lester); Announcer (Ronald Regan); Happy (Paul Clark); Peggy (Penny Singleton); Miss Crews (Dennie Moore); Songwriters (Harry Seymour, Bert Hanlon); Major Thompson (James Stephenson); B. K. (Pierre Watkin); Cutter (John Ridgely); Office Boy (George Hickman); Smitty (Cliff Saum); Commissary Cashier (Carole Landis); Dance Director (Curt Bois); Olaf (Otto Fries); Extra (John Harron); Wardrobe Attendant (Hal K. Dawson); Nurse (Dorothy Vaughan); Director (Bert Howard); Young Man (James Nolan); Bruiser (Bill Telaak); Cleaning Woman (Vera Lewis); Nurses (Jan Holm, Rosella Towne, Loi Cheaney); LA Operator (Janet Shaw); Paris Operator (Nanette Lafayette); NY Operator (Peggy Moran); Jascha (Eddy Conrad); and Sidney Bracy, William Haade, Clem Bevans
RUNNING TIME 80 minutes
RELEASE DATE 1938
PRODUCED BY Warner Bros

29 Angels With Dirty Faces
DIRECTOR Michael Curtiz
PRODUCER Sam Bischoff
SCENARIO John Wexley, Warren Duff, based on an original story by Rowland Brown
PHOTOGRAPHY Sol Polito
EDITOR Owen Marks
CAST Rocky Sullivan (James Cagney); Jerry Connelly (Pat O'Brien); James Frazier (Humphrey Bogart); Laury Martin (Ann Sheridan); MacKeefer (George Bancroft); Soapy (Billy Halop); Swing (Bobby Jordan); Bim (Leo Gorcey); Hunky (Bernard Punsley); Pasty (Gabriel Dell); Crab (Huntz Hall); Rocky [as a Boy] (Frankie Burke); Jerry [as a Boy] (William Tracy); Laury [as a Girl] (Marilyn Knowlden); Steve (Joe Downing); Blackie (Adrian Morris); Guard Kennedy (Oscar O'Shea); Guard Edwards (Edward Pawley); Bugs, the Gunman (William Pawley); Police Captain (John Hamilton); Priest (Earl Dwire); Death Row Guard (Jack Perrin); Mrs Patrick (Mary Gordon); Soapy's Mother (Vera Lewis); Warden (William Worthington); R R Yard Watchman (James Farley); Red (Chuck Stubbs); Maggione Boy (Eddie Syracuse); Policeman (Robert Homans); Basketball Captain (Harris Berger); Pharmacist (Harry Hayden); Gangsters (Dick Rich, Steven Darrell, Joe A. Delvin); Italian Storekeeper (William Edmunds); Buckley (Charles Wilson); Boys in Poolroom (Frank Coghlan Jr, David Durand); Church Basketball Team (Bill Cohee, Lavel Lund,

Norman Wallace, Gary Carthew, Bibby Mayer); Mrs Maggione (Belle Mitchell); Newsboy (Eddie Brian); Janitor (Bill McLain); Croupier (Wilber Mack); Girl at Gaming Table (Poppy Wilde); Adult Boy (George Offerman Jr); Norton J. White (Charles Trowbridge); City Editor, Press (Ralph Sanford); Police Officer (Wilfred Lucas); Guard (Lane Chandler); Cop (Elliott Sullivan) and Lottie Williams, George Mori, Dick Wessel, John Harron, Vince Lombardi, Al Hill, Thomas Jackson, Jeffrey Sayre
RUNNING TIME 97 minutes
RELEASE DATE 1938
PRODUCED BY Warner Bros

30 The Oklahoma Kid
DIRECTOR Lloyd Bacon
ASSOCIATE PRODUCER Samuel Bischoff
SCENARIO Warren Duff, Robert Buckner, Edward E. Paramore, based on an original story by Edward E. Paramore
PHOTOGRAPHY James Wong Howe
EDITOR Owen Marks
CAST Jim Kincaid (James Cagney); Whip McCord (Humphrey Bogart); Jane Hardwick (Rosemary Lane); Hudge Hardwick (Donald Crisp); Ned Kincaid (Harvey Stephens); John Kincaid (Hugh Sothern); Alec Martin (Charles Middleton); Doolin (Edward Pawley); Wes Handley (Ward Bond); Curley (Lew Harvey); Indian Jack Pasco (Trevor Bardette); Ringo (John Miljan); Judge Morgan (Arthur Aylesworth); Hotel Clerk (Irving Bacon); Keely (Joe Delvin); Sheriff Abe Collins (Wade Boteler); Kincaid's Horse (Whizzer); Professor (Ray Mayer); Deputy (Dan Wolheim); Juryman (Bob Kortman); Old Man in Bar (Tex Cooper); Secretary (John Harron); President Cleveland (Stuart Holmes); Times Reporter (Jeffrey Sayre); Land Agent (Frank Mayo); Mail Clerk (Jack Mower); Settler (Al Bridge); Drunk (Don Barclay); Bartenders (Horace Murphy, Robert Homans George Lloyd); Manuelita (Rosina Galli); Pedro (George Regas); Post Man (Clem Bevans); Indian Woman (Soledad Jiminez); Foreman (Ed Brady); Homesteader (Tom Chatterton); Henchman (Elliott Sullivan) and Joe Kirkson, William Worthington, Spencer Charters
RUNNING TIME 85 minutes
RELEASE DATE 1939
PRODUCED BY Warner Bros

31 Each Dawn I Die
DIRECTOR William Keighley
ASSOCIATE PRODUCER David Lewis
SCENARIO Norman Reilly Raine, Warren Duff, Charles Perry, based on the novel by Jerome Odlum
PHOTOGRAPHY Arthur Edeson
EDITOR Thomas Richards
CAST Frank Ross (James Cagney); Hood Stacey (George Raft); Joyce Conover (Jane Bryan); Warden John Armstrong (George Bancroft); Fargo Red (Maxie Rosenbloom); Mueller (Stanley Ridges); Pole Cat Carlisle (Alan Baxter); W. J.

Grayce (Victor Jory); Pete Kassock (John Wray); Dale (Edward Pawley); Lang (Willard Robertson); Mrs Ross (Emma Dunn); Garsky (Paul Hurst); Joe Lassiter (Louis Jean Heydt); Limpy Julien (Joe Downing); D. A. Jesse Hanley (Thurston Hall); Bill Mason (William Davidson); Stacey's Attorney (Clay Clement); Judge (Charles Trowbridge); Temple (Harry Cording); Lew Keller (John Harron); Jerry Poague (John Ridgeley); Patterson (Selmer Jackson); Mac (Robert Homans); Snake Edwards (Abner Biberman); Mose (Napoleon Simpson); Accident Witness (Stuart Holmes); Girl in Car (Maris Wrixon); Men in Car (Garland Smith, Arthur Gardner); Policeman (James Flavin); Gate Guard (Max Hoffman Jr); Turnkey (Walter Miller); Guard in Cell (Fred Graham); Bailiff (Wilfred Lucas); Jury Woman (Vera Lewis); Prosecutor (Emmett Vogan); Judge Crowder (Earl Dwire); Bud (Bob Perry); Johnny, a Hood (Al Hill); Convict (Elliot Sullivan); Court Officer (Chuck Hamilton) and Nat Carr, Wedgewood Nowell, Frank Mayo, Dick Rich, Lee Phelps, Jack Wise, Granville Bates
RUNNING TIME 92 minutes
RELEASE DATE 1939
PRODUCED BY Warner Bros

32 The Roaring Twenties
DIRECTOR Raoul Walsh
PRODUCER Hal B. Wallis
ASSOCIATE PRODUCER Samuel Bischoff
SCENARIO Jerry Wald, Richard Macaulay, Robert Rossen, based on an original story by Mark Hellinger
PHOTOGRAPHY Ernie Haller
EDITOR Jack Killifer
CAST Eddie Barlett (James Cagney); Jean Sherman (Priscilla Lane); George Hally (Humphrey Bogart); Lloyd Hart (Jeffrey Lynn); Panama Smith (Gladys George); Danny Green (Frank McHugh); Nick Brown (Paul Kelly); Mrs Sherman (Elisabeth Risdon); Pete Henderson (Ed Keane); Sergeant Pete Jones (Joseph Sawyer); Lefty (Abner Biberman); Luigi, the Proprieter (George Humbert); Bramfield, the Broker (Clay Clement); Bobby Hart (Don Thaddeus Kerr); Orderly (Ray Cooke); Mrs Gray (Vera Lewis); First Mechanic (Murray Alper); Second Mechanic (Dick Wessel); Fletcher, the Foreman (Joseph Crehan); Bootlegger (Norman Willis); First Officer (Robert Elliott); Second Officer (Eddy Chandler); Judge (John Hamilton); Man in Jail (Elliott Sullivan); Jailer (Pat O'Malley); Proprietor of Still (Arthur Loft); Ex Cons (Al Hill, Raymond Bailey, Lew Harvey); Order-takers (Joe Devlin, Jeffrey Sayre); Mike (Paul Phillips); Masters (George Meeker); Piano Player (Bert Hanlon); Drunk (Jack Norton); Captain (Alan Bridge); Henchman (Fred Graham); Doorman (James Blaine); Couple in Restaurant (Henry C. Bradley, Lottie Williams); Commentator (John Deering); Soldier (John Harron); Bailiff (Lee Phelps); Waiter

(Nat Carr); Policeman (Wade Boteler); Customer (Creighton Hale); Saleswoman (Ann Codee); Cab Drivers (Eddie Acuff, Milton Kibbee, John Ridgely) and James Flavin, Oscar O'Shea, Frank Wilcox, the Jane Jones Trio, Harry Hollingsworth, Frank Mayo, Emory Parnell, Billy Wayne, Philip Morris, Maurice Costello, John St Clair
RUNNING TIME 104 minutes
RELEASE DATE 1939
PRODUCED BY Warner Bros

33 The Fighting 69th
DIRECTOR William Keighley
PRODUCER Jack L. Warner
EXECUTIVE PRODUCER Hal B. Wallis
SCENARIO Norman Reilly Raine, Fred Niblo Jr, Dean Franklin
PHOTOGRAPHY Tony Gandio
EDITOR Owen Marks
CAST Jerry Plunkett (James Cagney); Father Duffy (Pat O'Brien); Wild Bill Donovan (George Brent); Joyce Kilmer (Jeffrey Lynn); Sergeant Big Mike Wynn (Alan Hale); 'Crepe Hanger' Burke (Frank McHugh); Lieutenant Ames (Dennis Morgan); Lieutenant Long John Wynn (Dick Foran); Timmy Wynn (William Lundigan); Paddy Dolan (Guinn 'Big Boy' Williams); the Colonel (Henry O'Neill); Captain Mangan (John Litel); Mike Murphy (Sammy Cohen); Major Anderson (Harvey Stephens); Private Turner (De Wolfe [William] Hopper); Private McManus (Tom Dugan); Jack O'Keefe (George Reeves); Moran (John Ridgely); Chaplain Holmes (Charles Trowbridge); Lieutenant Norman (Frank Wilcox); Casey (Herbert Anderson); Healey (J. Anthony Hughes); Captain Bootz (Frank Mayo); Carroll (John Harron); Ryan (George Kilgen); Tierney (Richard Clayton); Regan (Edward Dew); Doctors (Wilfred Lucas, Emmett Vogan); Sergeant (Frank Sully); Doctor (Joseph Crehan); Supply Sergeant (James Flavin); Jimmy (Frank Goghlan Jr); Eddie (George O'Hanlon); Major (Jack Perrin); Alabama Men (Trevor Bardette, John Arledge, Frank Melton, Edmund Glover); Engineer Officer (Edgar Edwards); Medical Captain (Ralph Dunn); German Officers (Arno Frey, Roland Varno); Hefferman (Robert Layne Ireland); O'Brien (Elmo Murray); Waiter (Jacques Lory); Chuck (Jack Boyle Jr) and Creighton Hale, Benny Rubin, Eddie Acuff, Jack Mower, Nat Carr, Jack Wise
RUNNING TIME 90 minutes
RELEASE DATE 1940
PRODUCED BY Warner Bros

34 Torrid Zone
DIRECTOR William Keighley
PRODUCER Mark Hellinger
SCENARIO Richard Macaulay, Jerry Wald
PHOTOGRAPHY James Wong Howe
EDITOR Jack Killifer
CAST Nick Butler (James Cagney); Steve Case (Pat O'Brien); Lee Donley (Ann Sheridan); Wally Davis (Andy Devine); Gloria Anderson (Helen Vinson); Bob

Anderson (Jerome Cowan); Rosario (George Tobias); (George Reeves); Carlos (Victor Kilian); Rodriquez (Frank Puglia); Gardner (John Ridgely); Sam (Grady Sutton); Garcia Sancho (Paul Porcasi); Lopez (Frank Yaconelli); Hernandez (Dick Boteler); Shaffer (Frank Mayo); McNama (Jack Mower); Daniels (Paul Hurst); Sergeant of Police (George Regas); Rita (Elvira Sanchez); Hotel Manager (George Humbert); First Policeman (Trevor Bardette); Second Policeman (Ernesto Piedra); Chico (Manuel Lopez); Charley (Tony Paton) and Max Blum, Betty Sanko, Don Orlando, Victor Sabuni, Paul Renay, Joe Molina
RUNNING TIME 88 minutes
RELEASE DATE 1940
PRODUCED BY Warner Bros

35 City for Conquest
DIRECTOR/PRODUCER Anatole Litvak
ASSOCIATE PRODUCER William Cagney
SCENARIO John Wexley, based on the novel City for Conquest by Aben Kandel
PHOTOGRAPHY Sol Polito, James Wong Howe
EDITOR William Holmes
CAST Danny Kenny (James Cagney); Peggy Nash (Ann Sheridan); Old Timer (Frank Craven); Scotty McPherson (Donald Crisp); Eddie Kenny (Arthur Kennedy); Mutt (Frank McHugh); Pinky (George Tobias); Dutch (Jerome Cowan); Murray Burns (Anthony Quinn); Gladys (Lee Patrick); Mrs Nash (Blanche Yurka); Goldie (George Lloyd); Lilly (Joyce Compton); Max Leonard (Thurston Hall); Cobb (Ben Welden); Salesman (John Arledge); Gaul (Ed Keane); Doctors (Selmer Jackson, Joseph Crehan); Callahan (Bob Steele); Henchman (Billy Wayne); Floor Guard (Pat Flaherty); MC (Sidney Miller); Dressing Room Blonde (Ethelreda Leopold) and Lee Phelps, Charles Wilson, Ed Gargan, Howard Hickman, Murray Almer, Dick Wessell, Bernice Pilot, Charles Lane, Dana Dale (Margaret Hayes), Ed Pawley, William Newell, Lucia Carroll
RUNNING TIME 101 minutes
RELEASE DATE 1941
PRODUCED BY Warner Bros

36 The Strawberry Blonde
DIRECTOR Raoul Walsh
PRODUCER Jack L. Warner, Hal B. Wallis
ASSOCIATE PRODUCER William Cagney
SCENARIO Julius J. Epstein, Philip C. Epstein, based on the play One Sunday Afternoon by James Hagan
PHOTOGRAPHY James Wong Howe
EDITOR William Holmes
CAST Biff Grimes (James Cagney); Amy Lind (Olivia De Havilland); Virginia Brush (Rita Hayworth); Old Man Grimes (Alan Hale); Nick Pappalas (George Tobias); Hugo Barnstead (Jack Carson); Mrs Mulcahey (Una O'Connor); Harold (George Reeves); Harold's Girl Friend (Lucile Fairbanks); Big Joe (Edward McNamara); Toby (Herbert Heywood); Josephine (Helen Lynd); Bank President

(Roy Gordon); Street Cleaner Foreman (Tim Ryan); Official (Addison Richards); Policeman (Frank Mayo); Bartender (Jack Daley); Girl (Suzanne Carnahan [Susan Peters]); Boy (Herbert Anderson); Baxter (Frank Orth); Inspector (James Flavin); Sailor (George Campeau); Singer (Abe Dinovitch); Guiseppi (George Humbert); Secretary (Creighton Hale); Treadway (Russell Hicks); Warden (Wade Boteler); Young Man (Peter Ashley); Bank President (Roy Gordon); Policemen (Max Hoffman Jr, Pat Flaherty); Girl (Peggy Diggins); Hanger-on (Bob Perry); Woman (Dorothy Vaughan); Dandy (Richard Clayton); Girl (Ann Edmonds); Nurse (Lucia Carroll) and Harrison Green, Eddie Chandler, Carl Harbaugh, Frank Melton, Dick Wessell, Paul Barrett, Nora Gale
RUNNING TIME 97 minutes
RELEASE DATE 1941
PRODUCED BY Warner Bros

37 The Bride Came C.O.D.
DIRECTOR William Keighley
EXECUTIVE PRODUCER Hal B. Wallis
ASSOCIATE PRODUCER William Cagney
SCENARIO Julius J. Epstein, Philip G. Epstein, based on a story by Kenneth Earl, M. M. Musselman
PHOTOGRAPHY Ernest Haller
EDITOR Thomas Richards
CAST Steve Collins (James Cagney); Joan Winfield (Bette Davis); Tommy Keenan (Stuart Erwin); Allen Brice (Jack Carson); Peewee (George Tobias); Lucius K. Winfield (Eugene Pallette); Pop Tolliver (Harry Davenport); Sheriff McGee (William Frawley); Hinkle (Edward Brophy); Judge Sobler (Harry Holman); Reporters (Chick Chandler, Keith Douglas [later Douglas Kennedy], Herbert Anderson); Keenan's Pilot (De Wolfe [William] Hopper); McGee's Pilot (William Newell); Ambulance Driver (Charles Sullivan); Policeman (Eddy Chandler, Tony Hughes, Lee Phelps); Mabel (Jean Ames); Headwaiter (Alphonse Martell); Dance Trio (The Rogers Dancers); First Operator (Peggy Diggins); Second Operator (Mary Brodel); Valet (Olaf Hytten); Detective (James Flavin); Announcer (Sam Hayes); Airline Dispatcher (William Justice [later Richard Travis]); Newsboys (Lester Towne, Richard Clayton, Garland Smith, Claude Wisberg) and Lucia Carroll, Peter Ashley, John Ridgely, Saul Gorss, Jack Mower, Creighton Hale, Garrett Craig
RUNNING TIME 92 minutes
RELEASE DATE 1941
PRODUCED BY Warner Bros

38 Captains of the Clouds
DIRECTOR Michael Curtiz
PRODUCER Hal B. Wallis
ASSOCIATE PRODUCER William Cagney
SCENARIO Arthur T. Horman, Richard Macaulay, Norman Reilly Raine, based on a story by Arthur T. Horman, Roland Gillett
PHOTOGRAPHY Sol Polito, Wilfred M. Cline
AERIAL PHOTOGRAPHY Elmer Dyer, Charles Marshall, Winton C. Hoch

EDITOR George Amy
CAST Brian MacLean (James Cagney); Johnny Dutton (Dennis Morgan); Emily Foster (Brenda Marshall); Tiny Murphy (Alan Hale); Blimp Lebec (George Tobias); Scrounger Harris (Reginald Gardiner); Air Marshal W. A. Bishop (Himself); Commanding Officer (Reginald Denny); Prentiss (Russell Arms); Group Captain (Paul Cavanagh); Store-Teeth Morrison (Clem Bevans); Foster (J. M. Kerrigan); Doctor Neville (J. Farrell MacDonald); Fyffo (Patrick O'Moore); Carmichael (Morton Lowry); Chief Instructor (Frederic Worlock); Officer (Roland Drew); Blonde (Lucia Carroll); Playboy (George Meeker); Popcorn Kearns (Benny Baker); Kingsley (Hardie Albright); Mason (Roy Walker); Nolan (Charles H. Alton); Provost Marshall (Louis Jean Heydt); Student Pilots (Byron Barr [Gig Young], Michael Ames [Tod Andrews]); Willie (Willie Fung); Blake (Carl Harbord); Indians (James Stevens, Bill Wilkerson, Frank Lackteen); Dog Man (Edward McNamara); Bellboy (Charles Smith); Clerk (Emmett Vogan); Woman (Winifred Harris); Churchill's Voice (Miles Mander); Drill Sergeant (Pat Flaherty); Bartender (Tom Dugan); Mechanic (George Offerman Jr); Orderly (Gavin Muir); Duty Officer (Larry Williams) and John Hartley, John Kellogg, Charles Irwin, Billy Wayne, Rafael Storm, John Gallaudet, Barry Bernard, George Ovey, Walter Brooks, Ray Montgomery, Herbert Gunn, Donald Dillaway, James Bush
RUNNING TIME 113 minutes
RELEASE DATE 1942
PRODUCED BY Warner Bros

39 Yankee Doodle Dandy
DIRECTOR Michael Curtiz
PRODUCER Jack L. Warner
EXECUTIVE PRODUCER Hal B. Wallis
ASSOCIATE PRODUCER William Cagney
SCENARIO Robert Buckner, Edmund Joseph, based on an original story by Robert Buckner
PHOTOGRAPHY James Wong Howe
EDITOR George Amy
CAST George M. Cohan (James Cagney); Mary (Joan Leslie); Jerry Cohan (Walter Huston); Sam Harris (Richard Whorf); Dietz (George Tobias); Fay Templeton (Irene Manning); Nellie Cohan (Rosemary De Camp); Josie Cohan (Jeanne Cagney); Schwab (S. Z. Sakall); Erlanger (George Barbier); Manager (Walter Catlett); Nora Bayes (Frances Langford); Ed Albee (Minor Watson); Eddie Foy (Eddie Foy Jr); Harold Goff (Chester Clute); George M. Cohan [Age 13] (Douglas Croft); Josie [Age 12] (Patsy Lee Parsons); Franklin D. Roosevelt (Captain Jack Young); Receptionist (Audrey Long); Madame Bartholdi (Odette Myrtil); White House Butler (Clinton Rosemond); Stage Manager in Providence (Spencer Charters); Sister Act (Dorothy Kelly, Marijo James); George M. Cohan [Age 7] (Henry Blair); Josie Cohan [Age 6] (Jo Ann Marlow); Stage Manager

(Thomas Jackson); Fanny (Phyllis Kennedy); White House Guard (Pat Flaherty); Magician (Leon Belasco); Star Boarder (Syd Saylor); Stage Manager N.Y. (William B. Davidson); Dr Lewellyn (Harry Hayden); Dr Anderson (Francis Pierlot); Teenagers (Charles Smith, Joyce Reynolds, Dick Chandlee, Joyce Horne); Sergeant (Frank Faylen); Theodore Roosevelt (Wallis Clark); Betsy Ross (Georgia Carroll); Sally (Joan Winfield); Union Army Veterans (Dick Wessel, James Flavin); Schultz in "Peck's Bad Boy" (Sailor Vincent); Irish Cop in "Peck's Bad Boy" (Fred Kelsey); Hotel Clerks (George Meeker, Frank Mayo); Actor, Railroad Station (Tom Dugan); Telegraph Operator (Creighton Hale); Wise Guy (Murray Alper); Army Clerk (Garry Owen); Nurse (Ruth Robinson); Reporters (Eddie Acuff, Walter Brooke, Bill Edwards, William Hopper); First Critic (William Forrest); Second Critic (Ed Keane); Girl (Dolores Moran); Chorus Girls, "Little Johnny Jones" (Poppy Wilde, Lorraine Gettman [Leslie Brooks])
RUNNING TIME 126 minutes
RELEASE DATE 1942
PRODUCED BY Warner Bros

40 Johnny Come Lately
(GB title: Johnny Vagabond)
DIRECTOR William K. Howard
PRODUCER William Cagney
SCENARIO John Van Druten, based on the novel McLeod's Folly by Louis Bromfield
PHOTOGRAPHY Theodore Sparkuhl
EDITOR George Arthur
CAST Tom Richards (James Cagney); Vinnie McLeod (Grace George); Gashouse Mary (Marjorie Main); Jane (Marjorie Lord); Aida (Hattie McDaniel); W. W. Dougherty (Edward McNamara); Pete Dougherty (Bill Henry); Bill Swain (Robert Barrat); Willie Ferguson (George Cleveland); Myrtle Ferguson (Margaret Hamilton); Dudley Hirsh (Norman Willis); Blaker (Lucien Littlefield); Winterbottom (Edwin Stanley); Chief of Police (Irving Bacon); First Cop (Tom Dugan); Second Cop (Charles Irwin); Third Cop (John Sheehan); Butler (Clarence Muse); First Tramp (John Miller); Second Tramp Arthur Hunnicutt); Tramp in Box Car (Victor Kilian); Bouncer (Wee Willie Davis); Old Timer (Henry Hall)
RUNNING TIME 97 minutes
RELEASE DATE 1943
PRODUCED BY William Cagney Productions for United Artists

41 Blood on the Sun
DIRECTOR Frank Lloyd
PRODUCER William Cagney
SCENARIO Lester Cole, based on a story by Garrett Fort, additional scenes by Nathaniel Curtis
PHOTOGRAPHY Theodore Sparkuhl
EDITOR Truman K. Wood, Walter Hanneman
CAST Nick Condon (James Cagney); Iris Hilliard (Sylvia Sidney); Ollie Miller (Wallace Ford); Edith Miller (Rosemary De

Camp); Colonel Tojo (Robert Armstrong); Premiere Tanaka (John Emery); Hijikata (Leonard Strong); Prince Tatsugi (Frank Puglia); Captain Oshima (Jack Holloran); Kajioka (Hugh Ho); Yomamoto (Philip Ahn); Hayoshi (Joseph Kim); Yamada (Marvin Miller); Joseph Cassell (Rhys Williams); Arthur Bickett (Porter Hall); Charley Sprague (James Bell); Amah (Grace Lem); Chinese Servant (Oy Chan); Hotel Manager (George Paris); Johnny Clarke (Hugh Beaumont); American Newspapermen in Tokyo (Gregory Gay, Arthur Loft, Emmett Vogan, Charlie Wayne)
RUNNING TIME 98 minutes
RELEASE DATE 1945
PRODUCED BY William Cagney Productions for United Artists

42 13 Rue Madeleine
DIRECTOR Henry Hathaway
PRODUCER Louis De Rochemont
SCENARIO John Monks Jr, Sy Bartlett
PHOTOGRAPHY Norbert Brodine
EDITOR Harmon Jones
CAST Bob Sharkey (James Cagney); Suzanne De Bouchard (Annabella); Bill O'Connell (Richard Conte); Jeff Lassiter (Frank Latimore); Charles Gibson (Walter Abel); Pappy Simpson (Melville Cooper); Mayor Galimard (Sam Jaffe); Duclois (Marcel Rousseau); Psychiatrist (Richard Gordon); Emile (Everett G. Marshall); Madame Thillot (Blanche Yurka); Karl (Peter Von Zerneck); Hans Feinkl (Alfred Linder); Hotel Clerk (Ben Low); RAF Officer (James Craven); Joseph (Roland Belanger); Burglary Instructor (Horace MacMahon); Briefing Officer (Alexander Kirkland); La Roche (Donald Randolph); Peasant Lady (Judith Lowry); Dispatcher (Red Buttons); German Staff Officer (Otto Simanek); Psychiatrist (Walter Greaza); Van Duyval (Roland Winters); Tailor (Harold Young); Chief Operator (Sally McMarrow); Flyers (Coby Neal, Karl Malden); French Peasant (Jean Del Val); Narrator (Reed Hadley)
RUNNING TIME 95 minutes
RELEASE DATE 1946
PRODUCED BY Twentieth Century Fox

43 The Time of Your Life
DIRECTOR H. C. Potter
PRODUCER William Cagney
SCENARIO Nathaniel Curtis, based on the play by William Saroyan
PHOTOGRAPHY James Wong Howe
EDITOR Walter Hannemann, Truman K. Wood
CAST Joe (James Cagney); Nick (William Bendix); Tom (Wayne Morris); Kitty Duval (Jeanne Cagney); Policeman (Broderick Crawford); McCarthy (Ward Bond); Kit Carson (James Barton); Harry (Paul Draper); Mary L. (Gale Page); Dudley James Lydon); Willie (Richard Erdman); Arab (Pedro De Cordoba); Wesley (Reginald Beane); Blick (Tom Powers); a Drunk (John 'Skins' Miller); Society Lady (Natalie Schafer); Society

Gentleman (Howard Freeman); Blind Date (Renie Riano); Newsboy (Lanny Rees); Girl in Love (Nanette Parks); Nick's Mother (Grazia Marciso); 'Killer' (Claire Carleton); Sidekick (Gladys Blake); Nick's Daughter (Marlene Aames); Cook (Moy Ming); Bookie (Donald Kerr); B. Girl (Ann Cameron); Sailor (Floyd Walters); Salvation Army Man (Eddie Borden); Salvation Army Woman (Rena Case)
RUNNING TIME 109 minutes
RELEASE DATE 1948
PRODUCED BY William Cagney Pictures for United Artists

44 White Heat
DIRECTOR Raoul Walsh
PRODUCER Louis F. Edelman
SCENARIO Ivan Goff, Ben Roberts, based on a story by Virginia Kellogg
PHOTOGRAPHY Sid Hickok
EDITOR Owen Marks
CAST Cody Jarrett (James Cagney); Verna Jarrett (Virginia Mayo); Hank Fallon (Edmond O'Brien); Ma Jarrett (Margaret Wycherly); 'Big Ed' Somers (Steve Cochran); Philip Evans (John Archer); Cotton Valetti (Wally Cassell); Het Kohler (Mickey Knox); The Trader (Fred Clark); The Reader (G. Pat Collins); Roy Parker (Paul Guilfoyle); Happy Taylor (Fred Coby); Zuckie Hommell (Ford Rainey); Tommy Ryley (Robert Osterloh); Bo Creel (Ian MacDonald); Chief of Police (Marshall Bradford); Ernie Trent (Ray Montgomery); Police Surgeon (George Taylor); Willie Rolf (Milton Parsons); Cashier (Claudia Barrett); Popcorn Vendor (Buddy Gorman); Jim Donovan (De Forrest Lawrence); Ted Clark (Garrett Craig); Judge (George Spaulding); Clerk (Sherry Hall); Guards (Harry Strang, Jack Worth); Russell Hughes (Sid Melton); Margaret Baxter (Fern Eggen); Nat Lefeld (Eddie Foster); Tower Guard (Lee Phelps)
RUNNING TIME 114 minutes
RELEASE DATE 1949
PRODUCED BY Warner Bros

45 The West Point Story
(GB title: Fine and Dandy)
DIRECTOR Roy Del Ruth
PRODUCER Louis F. Edelman
SCENARIO John Monks Jr, Charles Hoffman, Irving Wallace, based on a story by Irving Wallace
PHOTOGRAPHY Sid Hickox
EDITOR Owen Marks
CAST Elwin Bixby (James Cagney); Eve Dillon (Virginia Mayo); Jan Wilson (Doris Day); Tom Fletcher (Gordon MacRae); Hal Courtland (Gene Nelson); Bull Gilbert (Alan Hale Jr); Harry Eberhart (Roland Winters); Bixby's "Wife" (Raymond Roe); Lieutenant Colonel Martin (Wilton Graff); Jocelyn (Jerome Cowan); Commandant (Frank Ferguson); Acrobat (Russ Saunders); Officer-in-Charge (Jack Kelly); Hoofer (Glen Turnbull); Piano Player (Walter Ruick); Senator (Lute Crockett); Cadets (James Dobson, Joel Marston, Bob Hayden, De Wit Bishop)

RUNNING TIME 107 minutes
RELEASE DATE 1950
PRODUCED BY Warner Bros

46 Kiss Tomorrow Goodbye
DIRECTOR Gordon Douglas
PRODUCER William Cagney
SCENARIO Harry Brown, based on the novel Kiss Tomorrow Goodbye by Horace McCoy
PHOTOGRAPHY Peverell Marley
EDITOR Truman K. Wood, Walter Hannemann
CAST Ralph Cotter (James Cagney); Holiday (Barbara Payton); Inspector Weber (Ward Bond); Mandon (Luther Adler); Margaret Dobson (Helena Carter); Jinx (Steve Brodie); Vic Mason (Rhys Williams); Reece (Barton MacLane); Ezra Dobson (Herbert Heyes); Doc Green (Frank Reicher); Tolgate (John Litel); District Attorney (Dan Riss); Cobbett (John Halloran); Byers (William Frawley); Detective Gray (Robert Karnes); Detective Fowler (Kenneth Tobey); Carleton (Neville Brand); Ralph's Brother (William Cagney); Judge (George Spaulding); Bailiff (Mark Strong); Satterfield (Matt McHugh); Julia (Georgia Caine); Driver (King Donovan); Doctor (Frank Wilcox); Butler (Gordon Richards)
RUNNING TIME 102 minutes
RELEASE DATE 1950
PRODUCED BY William Cagney Productions for Warner Bros

47 Come Fill the Cup
DIRECTOR Gordon Douglas
PRODUCER Henry Blanke
SCENARIO Ivan Goff, Ben Roberts, based on a novel by Harlan Ware
PHOTOGRAPHY Robert Burks
EDITOR Alan Crosland Jr
CAST Lew Marsh (James Cagney); Paula Copeland (Phyllis Thaxter); John Ives (Raymond Massey); Charley Dolan (James Gleason); Boyd Copeland (Gig Young); Dolly Copeland (Selena Royle); Julian Cuscaden (Larry Keating); Maria Diego (Charlita); Lennie Carr (Sheldon Leonard); Ike Bashaw (Douglas Spencer); Don Bell (John Kellogg); Hal Ortman (William Bakewell); Travis Asbourne II (John Alvin); Kip Zunches (King Donovan); Homicide Captain (James Flavin); Welder (Torben Meyer); Ora (Norma Jean Macias); Lila (Elizabeth Flournoy); Bobby (Henry Blair)
RUNNING TIME 113 minutes
RELEASE DATE 1951
PRODUCED BY Warner Bros

48 Starlift
DIRECTOR Roy Del Ruth
PRODUCER Robert Arthur
SCENARIO John Klorer, Karl Kamb, based on a story by John Klorer
PHOTOGRAPHY Ted McCord
EDITOR William Ziegler
CAST Themselves (Doris Day, Gordon MacRea, Virginia Mayo, Gene Nelson, Ruth Roman); Nell Wayne (Janice Rule); Sergeant Mike Nolan (Dick Wesson);

Corporal Rick Williams (Ron Hagerthy); Colonel Callan (Richard Webb); Chaplain (Hayden Rorke); Steve Rogers (Howard St John); Mrs Callan (Ann Doran); Turner (Tommy Farrell); George Norris (John Maxwell); Bob Wayne (Don Beddoe); Sue Wayne (Mary Adams); Dr Williams (Bigelowe Sayre); Mrs Williams (Eleanor Audley); Theatre Manager (Pat Henry); Chief Usher (Gordon Polk); Piano Player (Robert Hammack); Captain Nelson (Ray Montgomery); Co-Pilot (Bill Neff); Ground Officer (Stan Holbrook); Flight Nurse (Jill Richards); Litter Case (Joe Turkel); Virginia Boy (Rush Williams); Pete (Brian McKay); Will (Jack Larson); Nebraska Boy (Lyle Clark); Nurses (Dorothy Kennedy, Jean Dean, Dolores Castle); Boy with Cane (William Hunt); Army Nurse (Elizabeth Flournoy); Driver (Walter Brennan Jr); Lieutenants (Robert Karnes, John Hedloe); Boy with Camera (Steve Gregory); Morgan (Richard Monohan); Soldiers in Bed (Joe Recht, Herb Latimer); Doctor (Dick Ryan); Crew Chief (Bill Hudson); Miss Parson's Assistant (Sarah Spencer); Non-Com (James Brown); Waitress (Ezelle Poule); and the following guest stars: James Cagney, Gary Cooper, Virginia Gibson, Phil Harris, Frank Lovejoy, Lucille Norman, Louella Parsons, Randolph Scott, Jane Wyman, Patrice Wymore
RUNNING TIME 103 minutes
RELEASE DATE 1951
PRODUCED BY Warner Bros

49 What Price Glory
DIRECTOR John Ford
PRODUCER Sol C. Siegel
SCENARIO Phoebe Ephron, Henry Ephron, based on the play by Maxwell Anderson, Laurence Stallings
PHOTOGRAPHY Joseph MacDonald
EDITOR Dorothy Spencer
CAST Captain Flagg (James Cagney); Charmaine (Corinne Calvet); Sergeant Quirt (Dan Dailey); Corporal Kiper (William Demarest); Lieutenant Aldrich (Craig Hill); Lewisohn (Robert Wagner); Nicole Bouchard (Marisa Pavan); Lieutenant Moore (Casey Adams); General Cokely (James Gleason); Lipinsky (Wally Vernon); Cognac Pete (Henry Letondal); Lieutenant Schmidt (Fred Libby); Mulcahy (Ray Hyke); Gowdy (Paul Fix); Young Soldier (James Lilburn); Morgan (Henry Morgan); Gilbert (Dan Brozage); Holsen (Bill Henry); Company Cook (Henry 'Bomber' Kulkovich); Ferguson (Jack Pennick); Nun (Ann Codee); Lieutenant Cunningham (Stanley Johnson); Captain Davis (Tom Tyler); Sister Clotilde (Olga Andre); Priest (Barry Norton); The Great Uncle (Luis Alberni); Mayor (Torben Meyer); English Colonel (Alfred Zeisler); English Lieutenant (George Bruggeman); Lieutenant Bennett (Scott Forbes); Lieutenant Austin (Sean McClory); Captain Wickham (Charles Fitzsimmons); Bouchard (Louis Mercier); MP (Mickey Simpson)

RUNNING TIME 111 minutes
RELEASE DATE 1952
PRODUCED BY Twentieth Century Fox; Technicolor

50 A Lion in the Streets
DIRECTOR Raoul Walsh
PRODUCER William Cagney
SCENARIO Luther Davis, based on the novel by Adria Locke Langley
PHOTOGRAPHY Harry Stradling
EDITOR George Amy
CAST Hank Martin (James Cagney); Verity Wade (Barbara Hale); Flamingo (Anne Francis); Jules Bolduc (Warner Anderson); Jeb Brown (John McIntyre); Jennie Brown (Jeanne Cagney); Spurge (Lon Chaney Jr); Rector (Frank McHugh); Robert J. Castelberry (Larry Keating); Guy Polli (Onslow Stevens); Mr Beach (James Millican); Tim Beck (Mickey Simpson); Lula May (Sara Haden); Singing Woman (Ellen Corby); Prosecutor (Roland Winters); Smith (Burt Mustin); Sophy (Irene Tedrow); Townswoman (Sarah Selby)
RUNNING TIME 88 minutes
RELEASE DATE 1953
PRODUCED BY William Cagney Productions for Warner Bros; Technicolor

51 Run for Cover
DIRECTOR Nicholas Ray
PRODUCER William H. Pine
SCENARIO William C. Thomas, based on a story by Harriet Frank Jr, Irving Ravetch
PHOTOGRAPHY Daniel Fapp
EDITOR Howard Smith
CAST Mat Dow (James Cagney); Helga Swenson (Viveca Lindfors); Davey Bishop (John Derek); Mr Swenson (Jean Hersholt); Gentry (Grant Withers); Larsen (Jack Lambert); Morgan (Ernest Borgnine); Sheriff (Ray Teal); Scotty (Irving Bacon); Paulsen (Trevor Bardette); Mayor Walsh (John Miljan); Doc Ridgeway (Guy Schilling); Bank Manager (Emerson Treacy); Harvey (Denver Pyle); Townsman (Henry Wills)
RUNNING TIME 92 minutes
RELEASE DATE 1953
PRODUCED BY Pine-Thomas/Paramount; Technicolor and Vistavision

52 Love Me or Leave Me
DIRECTOR Charles Vidor
PRODUCER Joe Pasternak
SCENARIO Daniel Fuchs, Isobel Lennart, based on original story by Daniel Fuchs
PHOTOGRAPHY Arthur E. Arling
EDITOR Ralph E. Winters
CAST Ruth Etting (Doris Day); Martin 'The Gimp' Snyder (James Cagney); Johnny Alderman (Cameron Mitchell); Bernard V. Loomis (Robert Keith); Frobisher (Tom Tully); Georgie (Harry Bellaver); Paul Hunter (Richard Gaines); Fred Taylor (Peter Leeds); Eddie Fulton (Claude Stroud); Jingle Girl (Audrey Young); Greg Trent (John Harding); Dancer (Dorothy Abbott); Bouncer (Phil Schumacher); Second Bouncer (Otto Teichow); Bouncer

(Henry Kulky); Orry (Jay Adler); Irate Customer (Mauritz Hugo); Hostess (Veda Ann Borg); Claire (Claire Carleton); Stage Manager (Benny Burt); Mr Brelston, Radio Station Manager (Robert B. Carson); Assistant Director (James Drury); Dance Director (Richard Simmons); Assistant Director (Michael Kostrick); First Reporter (Roy Engel); Second Reporter (John Damler); Woman (Genevieve Aumont); Propman (Roy Engel); Stagehands (Dale Van Sickel, Johnny Day); Chorus Girls (Larri Thomas, Patti Nestor, Winona Smith, Shirley Wilson); Doorman (Robert Malcolm); Waiter (Robert Stephenson); Drapery Man (Paul McGuire); Guard (Barry Regan); Photographers (Jimmy Cross, Henry Randolph); Chauffeur (Chet Brandenberg)
RUNNING TIME 122 minutes
RELEASE DATE 1955
PRODUCED BY MGM, Cinemascope and Eastman Color

53 Mister Roberts
DIRECTOR John Ford, Mervyn Leroy
PRODUCER Leland Hayward
SCENARIO Frank Nugent, Joshua Logan, from the play by Joshua Logan, Thomas Heggen, based on the novel by Thomas Heggen
PHOTOGRAPHY Winton C. Hoch
EDITOR Jack Murray
CAST Lieutenant (J. G.) Roberts (Henry Fonda); Captain (James Cagney); Ensign Frank Thurlowe Pulver (Jack Lemmon); Doc (William Powell); CPO Dowdy (Ward Bond); Lieutenant Ann Girard (Betsy Palmer); Mannion (Phil Carey); Reber (Nick Adams); Stefanowski (Harry Carey Jr); Dolan (Ken Curtis); Gerhart (Frank Aletter); Lidstrom (Fritz Ford); Mason (Buck Kartalian); Lieutenant Billings (William Henry); Olson (William Hudson); Schlemmer (Stubby Kruger); Cookie (Harry Tenbrook); Rodrigues (Perry Lopez); Insignia (Robert Roark); Bookser (Pat Wayne); Wiley (Tige Andrews); Kennedy (Jim Moloney); Gilbert (Denny Niles); Johnson (Francis Conner); Cochran (Shug Fisher); Jonesy (Danny Borzage); Taylor (Jim Murphy); Nurses (Kathleen O'Malley, Maura Murphy, Mimi Doyle, Jeanne Murray-Vanderbilt, Lonnie Pierce); Shore Patrol Officer (Martin Milner); Shore Patrolman (Gregory Walcott); MP (James Flavin); Marine Sergeant (Jack Pennick); Native Chief (Duke Kahanamoku); Chinese Girl who Kisses Bookser (Carolyn Tong); French Colonial Officer (George Brangier); Naval Officer (Clarence E. Frank)
RUNNING TIME 123 minutes
RELEASE DATE 1955
PRODUCED BY Orange Productions for Warner Bros; Cinemascope and Warnercolor

54 The Seven Little Foys
DIRECTOR Melville Shavelson
PRODUCER Jack Rose
SCENARIO Melville Shavelson, Jack Rose

PHOTOGRAPHY John F. Warren
EDITOR Ellsworth Hoagland
CAST Eddie Foy (Bob Hope); Madeleine Morando (Milly Vitale); Barney Green (George Tobias); Clara (Angela Clarke); Judge (Herbert Heyes); Stage Manager (Richard Shannon); Brynie (Billy Gray); Charley (Lee Erickson); Richard Foy (Paul De Rolf); Mary Foy (Lydia Reed); Madeleine Foy (Linda Bennett); Eddie Jr (Jimmy Baird); George M. Cohan (James Cagney); Irving (Tommy Duran); Father O'Casey (Lester Matthews); Elephant Act (Joe Evans, George Boyce); Santa Claus (Oliver Blake); Driscoll (Milton Frome); Harrison (King Donovan); Stage Doorman (Jimmy Conlin); Soubrette (Marian Carr); Stage Doorman at Iroquois (Harry Cheshire); Italian Ballerina Mistress (Renata Vanni); Dance Specialty Double (Betty Uitti); Priest (Noel Drayton); Theatre Manager (Jack Pepper); Tutor (Dabbs Greer); Customs Inspector (Billy Nelson); Second Priest (Joe Flynn); Brynie [5 Years] (Jerry Mathers); Presbyterian Minister (Lewis Martin)
RUNNING TIME 93 minutes
RELEASE DATE 1955
PRODUCED BY Paramount; Vistavision and Technicolor

55 Tribute to a Bad Man
DIRECTOR Robert Wise
PRODUCER Sam Zimbalist
SCENARIO Michael Blankfort, based on a short story by Jack Schaefer
PHOTOGRAPHY Robert Surtees
EDITOR Ralph E. Winters
CAST Jeremy Rodock (James Cagney); Steve Miller (Don Dubbins); McNulty (Stephen McNally); Jocasta Constantine (Irene Papas); Lars Peterson (Vic Morrow); Barjak (James Griffith); Hearn (Onslow Stevens); L. A. Peterson (James Bell); Mrs L. A. Peterson (Jeanette Nolan); Baldy (Chubby Johnson); Abe (Royal Dano); Fat Jones (Lee Van Cleef); Cooky (Peter Chong); Shorty (James McCallion); Red (Clint Sharp); Tom (Carl Pitti); First Buyer (Tony Hughes); Second Buyer (Roy Engel); Cowboys (Bud Osborne, John Halloran, Tom London, Dennis Moore, Buddy Roosevelt, Billy Dix)
RUNNING TIME 95 minutes
RELEASE DATE 1956
PRODUCED BY MGM, Cinemascope and Eastman Color

56 These Wilder Years
DIRECTOR Roy Rowland
PRODUCER Jules Schermer
SCENARIO Frank Fenton, based on a story by Ralph Wheelwright
PHOTOGRAPHY George J. Folsey
EDITOR Ben Lewis
CAST Steve Bradford (James Cagney); Ann Dempster (Barbara Stanwyck); James Rayburn (Walter Pidgeon); Suzie Keller (Betty Lou Keim); Mark (Don Dubbins); Mr Spottsford (Edward Andrews); Judge (Basil Ruysdael); Roy Oliphant (Grandon Rhodes); Old Cab Driver (Will Wright); Dr

Miller (Lewis Martin); Aunt Martha (Dorothy Adams); Hardware Clerk (Dean Jones); Traffic Cop (Herb Vigran); Miss Finch (Ruth Lee); Gateman (Matt Moore); Chauffeur (Jack Kenny); Doorman (Harry Tyler); Stenographer (Luana Lee); Board of Directors (William Forrest, John Maxwell, Emmett Vogan, Charles Evans); Football Player (Tom Laughlin); Bellhop (Bob Alden); Boy in Pool Room (Michael Landon); Ad Lib Boy (Jimmy Ogg); Spottsford's Secretary (Elizabeth Flournoy); Farmer (Russell Simpson); Prim Lady (Kathleen Mulqueen); Hotel Clerk (Russ Whitney); Proprietress (Lillian Powell)
RUNNING TIME 91 minutes
RELEASE DATE 1956
PRODUCED BY MGM

57 Man of a Thousand Faces
DIRECTOR Joseph Pevney
PRODUCER Robert Arthur
SCENARIO R. Wright Campbell, Ivan Goff, Ben Roberts, based on a story by Ralph Wheelwright
PHOTOGRAPHY Russell Metty
EDITOR Ted J. Kent
CAST Lon Chaney (James Cagney); Cleva Creighton Chaney (Dorothy Malone); Hazel Bennett (Jane Greer); Gert (Marjorie Rambeau); Clarence Locan (Jim Backus); Irving Thalberg (Robert J. Evans); Mrs Chaney (Celia Lovsky); Carrie Chaney (Jeanne Cagney); Dr J. Wilson Shields (Jack Albertson); Pa Chaney (Nolan Leary); Creighton Chaney [At 21] (Roger Smith); Creighton Chaney [At 13] (Robert Lyden); Creighton Chaney [At 8] (Rickie Sorenson); Creighton Chaney [At 4] (Dennis Rush); Carl Hastings (Simon Scott); Clarence Kolb (Himself); Max Dill (Danny Beck); George Loane Tucker (Phil Van Zandt); Comedy Waiters (Hank Mann, Snub Pollard)
RUNNING TIME 87 minutes
RELEASE DATE 1957
PRODUCED BY Universal International; Cinemascope

58 Short Cut to Hell
DIRECTOR James Cagney
PRODUCER A. C. Lyles
SCENARIO Ted Berkman, Raphael Blau, based on a screenplay by W. R. Burnett, from the novel *This Gun for Hire* by Graham Greene
PHOTOGRAPHY Haskell Boggs
EDITOR Tom McAdoo
CAST Kyle (Robert Ivers); Glory Hamilton (Georgann Johnson); Stan (William Bishop); Bahrwell (Jacques Aubuchon); Adams (Peter Baldwin); Daisy (Yvette Vickers); Nichols (Murvyn Vye); Los Angeles Police Captain (Milton Frome); Waitress (Jacqueline Beer); Girl (Gail Land); Los Angeles Policeman (Dennis McMullen); Hotel Manager (William Newell); Adam's Secretary (Sarah Selby); Inspector Ross (Mike Ross); Conductor (Douglas Spencer); Piano Player (Danny Lewis); A. T. (Richard Hale); Mr Henry

(Douglas Evans); Patrolman (Hugh Lawrence); Patrolman (Joe Bassett); Used Car-Lot Manager (William Pullen); Trainman (Russell Trent); Ticket Seller (Joe Forte); Ext Road Driver (Roscoe Ates); Guard (John Halloran); James Cagney appears in a brief prologue to the film
RUNNING TIME 87 minutes
RELEASE DATE 1957
PRODUCED BY Paramount

59 Never Steal Anything Small
DIRECTOR Charles Lederer
PRODUCER Aaron Rosenberg
SCENARIO Charles Lederer, based on the play *Devil's Hornpipe* by Maxwell Anderson, Rouben Mamoulian
PHOTOGRAPHY Harold Lipstein
EDITOR Russ Schoengarth
CAST Jack MacIllaney (James Cagney); Linda Cabot (Shirley Jones); Dan Cabot (Roger Smith); Winnipeg (Cara Williams); Pinelli (Nehemiah Persoff); Words Cannon (Royal Dano); Lieutenant Tevis (Anthony Caruso); O. K. Merritt (Horace MacMahon); Ginger (Virginia Vincent); Sleep-Out Charlie (Jack Albertson); Lennie (Robert J. Wilke); Hymie (Herbie Faye); Ed (Billy M. Greene); Ward (John Duke); Osborne (Jack Orrison); Doctor (Roland Winters); Model (Ingrid Goude); Fats Ranney (Sanford Seegar); Thomas (Ed [Skipper] McNally); Deputy Warden (Greg Barton); Policeman (Edwin Parker); Judge (Jay Jostyn); First Detective (John Halloran); Second Detective (Harvey Perry); Waitress (Phyllis Kennedy); Coffee Vendor (Rebbecca Sand)
RUNNING TIME 94 minutes
RELEASE DATE 1958
PRODUCED BY Universal-International; Cinemascope and Eastman Color

60 Shake Hands with the Devil
DIRECTOR Michael Anderson
PRODUCER Michael Anderson
EXECUTIVE PRODUCER George Glass, Walter Seltzer
SCENARIO Ivan Goff, Ben Roberts, adapted by Marian Thompson, based on the novel by Reardon Conner
PHOTOGRAPHY Erwin Hillier
EDITOR Gordon Pilkington
CAST Sean Lenihan (James Cagney); Kerry O'Shea (Don Murray); Jennifer Curtis (Dana Wynter); Kitty (Glynis Johns); General (Michael Redgrave); Lady Fitzhugh (Sybil Thorndike); Chris (Cyril Cusack); McGrath (John Breslin); Cassidy (Harry Brogan); Sergeant (Robert Brown); Mary Madigan (Marianne Benet); The Judge (Lewis Carson); Mike O'Callaghan (John Cairney); Clancy (Harry Corbett); Mrs Madigan (Eileen Crowe); Captain [Black & Tans] (Alan Cuthbertson); Willie Cafferty (Donal Donnelly); Tommy Connor (Wilfred Dawning); Eileen O'Leary (Eithne Dunne); Doyle (Paul Farrell); Terence O'Brien (Richard Harris); Sergeant Jenkins (William Hartnell); British General (John Le Mesurier); Michael O'Leary (Niall MacGinnis); Donovan (Patrick

McAlinney); Paddy Nolan (Ray McNally); Sir Arnold Fielding (Clive Morton); Liam O'Sullivan (Noel Purcell); Captain [Black & Tans] (Peter Reynolds); Colonel Smithson (Christopher Rhodes); Sergeant [Black & Tans] (Ronald Walsh); Captain Fleming (Alan White)

RUNNING TIME 110 minutes
RELEASE DATE 1959
PRODUCED BY Pennebaker Productions for United Artists

61 The Gallant Hours
DIRECTOR Robert Montgomery
PRODUCER Robert Montgomery
SCENARIO Beirne Lay Jr, Frank D. Gilroy
PHOTOGRAPHY Joe MacDonald
EDITOR Frederick Y. Smith
CAST Fleet Admiral William F. Halsey Jr (James Cagney); Lieutenant Commander Andy Lowe (Dennis Weaver); Captain Harry Black (Ward Costello); Lieutenant Commander Roy Webb (Richard Jaeckel); Captain Frank Enright (Les Tremayne); Major General Roy Geiger (Robert Burton); Major General Archie Vandergrift (Raymond Bailey); Vice Admiral Robert Ghormley (Carl Benton Reid); Captain Horace Keys (Walter Sande); Captain Bill Bailey (Karl Swenson); Commander Mike Pulaski (Vaughan Taylor); Captain Joe Foss (Harry Landers); Father Gehring (Richard Carlyle); Manuel (Leon Lontoc); Admiral Isoroku Hamamoto (James T. Goto); Rear Admiral Jiro Kobe (James Yagi); Lieutenant Harrison Ludlum (John McKee); Major General Harmon (John Zaremba); Colonel Evans Carlson (Carleton Young); Captain Tom Lamphier (William Schallert); Admiral Callaghan (Nelson Leigh); Admiral Scott (Sydney Smith); Admiral Murray (Herbert Lytton); Admiral Chester Nimitz (Selmer Jackson); Admiral Ernest J. King (Tyler McVey); Red Cross Girl (Maggie Magennio); with James Cagney Jr, Robert Montgomery Jr
RUNNING TIME 115 minutes
RELEASE DATE 1960
PRODUCED BY Cagney-Montgomery Productions for United Artists

62 One, Two, Three
DIRECTOR Billy Wilder
PRODUCER Billy Wilder
ASSOCIATE PRODUCER I. A. L. Diamond, Doane Harrison
SCENARIO Billy Wilder, I. A. L. Diamond, based on a one-act play by Ferenc Molnar
PHOTOGRAPHY Daniel Fapp
EDITOR Daniel Mandell
CAST C. P. MacNamara (James Cagney); Otto Ludwig Piffl (Horst Buchholz); Scarlett (Pamela Tiffin); Mrs MacNamara (Arlene Francis); Ingeborg (Lilo Pulver); Hazeltine (Howard St John); Schlemmer (Hanns Lothar); Peripetchikoff (Leon Askin); Mishkin (Peter Capell); Borodenko (Ralf Wolter); Fritz (Karl Lieffen); Dr Bauer (Henning Schluter); Count Von Droste-Schattenburg (Hubert Von Meyerinck); Mrs Hazeltine (Lois Bolton); Newspaperman (Tile Kiwe); Zeidlitz (Karl

Ludwig Lindt); Military Police Sergeant (Red Buttons); Tommy MacNamara (John Allen); Cindy MacNamara (Christine Allen); Bertha (Rose Renee Roth); Military Police Corporal (Ivan Arnold); East German Police Corporal (Helmud Schmid); East German Interrogator (Otto Friebel); East German Police Sergeant (Werner Buttler); Second Policeman (Klaus Becker); Third Policeman (Siegfried Dornbusch); Krause (Paul Bos); Tailor (Max Buschbaum); Haberdasher (Jaspar Von Oertzen); Stewardess (Inga De Toro); Pierre (Jacques Chevalier); Shoeman (Werner Hassenland)
RUNNING TIME 108 minutes
RELEASE DATE 1961
PRODUCED BY Mirisch Company/Pyramid Productions for United Artists; Panavision

63 Arizona Bushwackers
DIRECTOR Lesley Selander
PRODUCER A. C. Lyles
SCENARIO Steve Fisher, based on a story by Steve Fisher and Andrew Craddock
PHOTOGRAPHY Lester Shorr
EDITOR John F. Schreyer
CAST Lee Travis (Howard Keel); Jilly Wyler (Yvonne De Carlo); Dan Shelby (John Ireland); Molly (Marilyn Maxwell); Tom Rile (Scott Brady); Mayor Joe Smith (Brian Donlevy); Sheriff Lloyd Grover (Barton MacLane); Ike Clanton (James Craig); Roy (Roy Rogers Jr); Curly (Reg Parton); Stage Driver (Montie Montana); Bushwacker (Eric Cody). Cagney narrated the opening of the film
RUNNING TIME 87 minutes
RELEASE DATE 1968
PRODUCED BY A. C. Lyles for Paramount

64 Ragtime
DIRECTOR Milos Forman
PRODUCER Dino De Laurentiis
SCENARIO Michael Weller, based on the novel by E. L. Doctorow
PHOTOGRAPHY Miroslav Ondricek
EDITOR Anne V. Coates (UK), Antony Gibbs, Stanley Warnow
CAST Rheinlander Waldo (James Cagney); Younger Brother (Brad Dourif); Booker T. Washington (Moses Gunn); Evelyn Nesbit (Elizabeth McGovern); Willie Conklin (Kenneth McMillan); Delmas (Pat O'Brien); Evelyn's Dance Instructor (Donald O'Connor); Father (James Olson); Tateh (Mandy Patinkin); Coalhouse Walker Jr (Howard E. Rollins); Mother (Mary Steenburgen); Sarah (Debbie Allen); Houdini (Jeff DeMunn); Harry K. Thaw (Robert Joy); Stanford White (Norman Mailer); Jerome (Bruce Boa)
RUNNING TIME 155 minutes
RELEASE DATE 1981
PRODUCED BY Sunley Productions for Paramount; Todd-AO and Technicolor

STAGE WORK

Pitter Patter
Longacre Theatre 29 September 1920
BOOK BY Will M. Hough

LYRICS AND MUSIC BY William B. Friedlander
Adapted from *Caught in the Rain* by William Collier and Grant Stewart
Dances and Ensembles staged by David Bennett
CAST Bob Livingston (John Price Jones); Bryce Forrester (George Edward Reed); Violet Mason (Mildred Keats); Mrs George Meriden (Virginia Cleary); James Maxwell (Frederick Hall); Muriel Mason (Jane Richardson); 'Dick Crawford' (William Kent, replaced by Ernest Truex); George Thompson (Charles Leroy); Howard Mason (Hugh Chilvers); Proprietor of Candy Shop (George Spelvin); Butler (Arthur Greeter); the Girls (Dawn Renard, Anne Fosse, Billie Vernon, Rae Fields, Hazel Rix, Aileen Grenier, Florence Davis, Mabel Benelisha, Katherine Powers, Sunny Harrison, Estelle Callen, Mildred Morgan, Florence Carroll, Pearl Crossman, Violet Hazel, Grace Lee, Agnes Walsh, Marie Boerl); the Boys (Messrs Fields, Cagney, Le Voy, Grager, Maclyn, Smith, Jackson, Jenkins and Mayo)

Outside Looking In
Greenwich Village Playhouse Inc
8 September 1925
Moved to the 39th Street Theatre by December 1925 (113 performances)
by Maxwell Anderson
DIRECTED BY Augustin Duncan
SETTINGS DESIGNED BY Cleon Throckmorton
CAST Shelly (Wallace House); Bill (Raphael Byrnes); Rubin (Slim Martin); Mose (Harry Blakemore); Little Red (James Cagney); Edna (Blyth Daly); Baldy (Reginald Barlow); Hopper (Barry Macollum); Arkansas Snake (David A. Leonard); Oklahoma Red (Charles A. Bickford); Deputy (G. O. Taylor); Chief of Police (Walter Downing); Railroad Detective (Morris Armor); Ukie (Sydney Machat); Blind Sims (Richard Sullivan); Brakeman (George Westlake); Another Deputy (Frederick C. Packard Jr); Sheriff (John C. Hickey)

Broadway
Broadhurst Theatre, New York City 1926–7
by Philip Dunning and George Abbott
STAGED BY The Authors
SETTINGS DESIGNED BY Arthur P. Segal
PRODUCED BY Jed Harris
CAST Nick Verdis (Paul Porcasi); Roy Lane (Lee Tracy [understudy: James Cagney]); Lil Rice (Clare Woodbury); Katie (Elizabeth North); Joe (Joseph Spurin Calleia); Mazie Smith (Mildred Wall); Ruby (Edith Van Cleve); Pearl (Eloise Stream); Grace (Molly Richardel); Ann (Constance Brown); 'Billie' Moore (Elizabeth Allen); Steve Crandall (Robert Gleckler); Dolph (Henry Sherwood); 'Porky' Thompson (William Foran); 'Scar' Edwards (Arthur Vees); Dan McCorn (Thomas Jackson); Benny (Frank Verigun); Larry (Millard Mitchell); Mike (Roy R. Lloyd [replaced by James Cagney in mid-1927])

Women Go On Forever
Forrest Theatre, New York City
7 September 1927 (117 performances)
by Daniel N. Rubin
STAGED BY John Cromwell
SETTINGS DESIGNED BY Louis Kennel
PRODUCED BY William A. Brady Jr and
Dwight Deere Wiman (in association with
John Cromwell)
CAST Minnie (Elizabeth Taylor); Mary
(Edna Thrower); Billy (Sam Wren); Pearl
(Constance McKay); Mrs Daisy Bowman
(Mary Boland); Mr Givner (Francis
Pierlot); Dr Bevin (Willard Foster); Jake
(Morgan Wallace); Pete (Osgood Perkins);
Harry (Douglass Montgomery); Louie
(Edwin Kasper); Daly (David Landau);
Hulbert (Myron Paulson); Mabel (Mary
Law); Eddie (James Cagney); Sven (Hans
Sandquist)

The Grand Street Follies of 1928
A topical review of the season Booth
Theatre 29 May 1928 (144 performances)
BOOK AND LYRICS BY Agnes Morgan, Marc
Loebell and Max Ewing
MUSIC BY Max Ewing, Lily Hyland and
Serge Walter
ENTIRE PRODUCTION DIRECTED BY Agnes
Morgan
DANCES BY James Cagney and Michel
Fokine
MUSIC DIRECTED BY Fred Fleming
SETTINGS AND COSTUMES DESIGNED BY Aline
Bernstein
PRODUCED BY The Actor-Managers Inc
CAST Dorothy Sands, Albert Carroll, Marc
Loebell, Paula Trueman, George Bratt,
James Cagney, Hal Brogan, Vera Allen,
Otto Hulett, Lily Lubell, Ruth McCoonkle,
Mae Nobel, Frances Cowles, Jean
Crittenden, Robert White, Dela Frankau,
Michael McCormack, Robert Gorham,
Blake Scott, Sophia Delza, Harold Minjir,
Richard Ford, Mary Williams, George Elias
Hoag, Laura Edmond, Joanna Roos,
George Hoag, George Heller, Milton Le
Roy, Harold Hecht and John Rynne

The Grand Street Follies of 1929
Booth Theatre, New York 1 May 1929 (53
performances)
BOOKS AND LYRICS BY Agnes Morgan
MUSIC BY Arthur Schwartz and Max Ewing
ADDITIONAL NUMBERS BY William Irwin and
Serge Walter
PRODUCED BY The Actor-Managers Inc (in
association with Paul Moss)
STAGED BY Agnes Morgan
DANCES BY Dave Gould
CAST Albert Carroll, Otto Hulett, Marc
Loebell, Dorothy Sands, Paula Trueman,
Dela Frankau, James Cagney, Junius
Matthews, Hal Brogan, Blaine Cordner,
Geordge Heller, Mary Williams, Mae
Nobel, Kathleen Kidd, Katherine Gauthier

Maggie the Magnificent
Cort Theatre, New York City 21 October
1929 (32 performances) by George Kelly
STAGED BY Mr Kelly
SETTINGS BY Livingston Platt

PRESENTED BY Lauren and Rivers Inc
CAST Katie Giles (Mary Frey); Etta (Joan
Blondell); Margaret (Shirley Warde); Mrs
Reed (Marion S. Barney); Mrs Buchanan
(Mary Cecil); Ward (Frank Rowan);
Elwood (James Cagney); Mrs Groves
(Doris Dagmar); House Boy (Rankin
Mansfield); Burnley (J. P. Wilson); Stella
(Frances Woodbury); Mrs Winters (Ellen
Mortimer)

Penny Arcade
Fulton Theatre, New York City 11 March
1930 (24 performances) by Marie Baumer
DIRECTED BY William Keighley
SETTINGS BY Cleon Throckmorton
PRODUCED BY Mr Keighley and W. P.
Tanner
CAST Bum Rogers (Ackland Powell);
George (Don Beddoe); Mrs Delano (Valerie
Bergere); Angel (Eric Dressler); Happy
(Millard F. Mitchell); Joe Delano (Paul
Guilfoyle); Mitch McKane (Frank
Rowan); Sikes (George Barbier); Myrtle
(Joan Blondell); Harry Delano (James
Cagney); Jenny Delano (Lenita Lane);
Nolan (Martin Malloy); Dugan (Ben
Probst); Dick (Harry Gresham); Mabel
(Desiree Harris); Fred (Jules Cern); Vivian
(Annie-Laurie Jaques); Mr James (Edmund
Norris); Rose (Lucille Gillespie); Jim (John
J. Cameron); Anna (Eleanor Andrus); Bob
(Marshall Hale); Jack (William Whithead);
Johnson (Harry Balcom)

SHORTS

1931 Practice Shots
No 11 of Bobby Jones' *How I Play Golf
Series*
DIRECTOR George Marshall
With James Cagney, Anthony Bushell,
Donald Cook, Louise Fazenda

1933 Hollywood on Parade ♯ 8
With James Cagney, Frankie Darro, Joe E.
Brown

1933 Intimate Interview
Talking Picture Epics
DIRECTOR Grace Elliott

1934 Screen Snapshots ♯11
With Boris Karloff, Bela Lugosi, Genevieve
Tobin, Pat O'Brien, James Cagney,
Maureen O'Sullivan, Eddie Cantor
Columbia

1934 The Hollywood Gad-About
With Gary Cooper, Eddie Cantor, Mary
Astor, Shirley Temple, Alice White, James
Cagney, Chester Morris
PRESENTED BY E. W. Hammons
An Educational Film Corporation of
America Treasure Chest Short
PRODUCED BY Louis Lewyn for Skibo
Productions Inc

1935 A Trip Through a Hollywood Studio
With Dolores Del Rio, Ann Dvorak, Hugh

Herbert, Wini Shaw, Rudy Vallee, Pat
O'Brien, Busby Berkeley, James Cagney
PRODUCED BY Warner Bros

1935 Hollywood Star Hobbies
With James Cagney and All-star Baseball
Team
PRODUCED BY Metro-Goldwyn-Mayer

1938 For Auld Lang Syne
With Paul Muni, James Cagney, Dick
Powell and his Cowboy Octette, Benny
Goodman and his Band, Rudy Vallee,
Bonita Granville, Pat O'Brien, Johnny
Davis, Allen Jenkins, Marie Wilson, Mabel
Todd, Hugh Herbert, Frank McHugh, and
the Schnikkelfritz Band
DIRECTED BY George Bilson, assisted by
Marshall Hageman
PRODUCED BY Warner Bros
SPONSORED BY The Motion Picture Industry
for the Will Rogers Memorial Commission

1943 Show Business at War (Issue ♯10;
Volume IX of *The March of Time*)
With Bette Davis, Humphrey Bogart,
Ginger Rogers, James Cagney, Myrna Loy,
Rita Hayworth, Kay Francis, Frank
Sinatra, Alexis Smith, Gertrude Lawrence,
The Mills Brothers, Jack Benny, Bob Hope,
Fred MacMurray, Ginny Simms
PRODUCED BY 20th Century Fox

1943 You, John Jones
With James Cagney, Ann Sothern,
Margaret O'Brien
DIRECTED BY Mervyn Leroy
PRODUCED BY Metro-Goldwyn-Mayer

1944 Battle Stations
NARRATED BY James Cagney and Ginger
Rogers
PRODUCED BY 20th Century Fox

1962 Road to the Wall
NARRATED BY James Cagney
PRODUCED BY CBS for the Department of
Defense

1966 Ballad of Smokey the Bear
PRODUCED BY General Electric Theatre in
cooperation with the U.S. Dept. of
Agriculture
Cagney as the voice of Big Brother

TELEVISION

The Ed Sullivan Show
20 June 1955
Enactment of scene from *Mister Roberts*
with Henry Fonda and Jack Lemmon

Robert Montgomery Presents
Soldier from the War Returning
10 September 1956
DIRECTED BY Peter Lafferty
NBC

Terrible Joe Moran (UK Video release title:
One Blow Too Many)
27 March 1984, CBS
DIRECTOR Joseph Sargent
PRODUCED BY Robert Halmi Productions